FIX YOUR CLIMATE

A PRACTICAL GUIDE TO REDUCING MICROAGGRESSIONS, MICROBULLYING, AND BULLYING IN THE ACADEMIC WORKPLACE

MYRON R. ANDERSON
KATHRYN S. YOUNG

ACADEMIC IMPRESSIONS | 2020
DENVER, CO

Myron R. Anderson and Kathryn S. Young

Published by Academic Impressions.

CR Mrig Company. 5299 DTC Blvd., Ste. 1400. Greenwood Village, CO 80111.

For reproduction, distribution, or copy permissions, or to order additional copies, please contact the Academic Impressions office at 720.488.6800 or visit:

www.academicimpressions.com

Academic Impressions

ISBN 978-1-948658-16-4

Printed in the United States of America.

ANOTHER BOOK
YOU MAY ENJOY

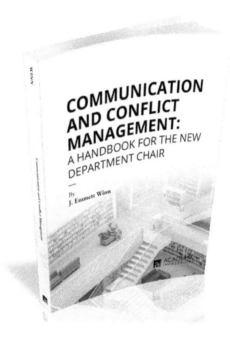

Effective communication will make or break a depart-ment chair. Get a primer on the essential communication and conflict management skills that every department chair needs.

Explore the book at:
https://www.academicimpressions.com/product/
communication-conflict-management-handbook-new-
department-chair/

MYRON R. ANDERSON AND KATHRYN S. YOUNG

CONTENTS

Myron R. Anderson and Kathryn S. Young

FOREWORD

As the world becomes more connected and organizations become more diverse, we must begin to understand the intersection of our internal and external identities to foster the collaborations needed to thrive in the 21st century college or university. It is very important that the organizational climate within your institution is as strong as possible.

In our years of experiences working, consulting, and engaging with many people within many different organizations, we have observed that the top core element to strong organizational functioning (if they can be ranked) is the strength of the human capital within the institution.

Microaggressions have taken place for many years, but it's only recently that the research has reached a wide audience and started to infuse into institutions. Our research draws on existing microaggression research and extends it to the particular variation found within institutions of higher education, *hierarchical microaggressions*. We then also make a connection between microaggressions and bullying and posit that a new concept in the literature, microbullying, links these two experiences. Microaggressions, micro-bullying, and bullying can be the "silent destroyers" of an institution's climate. Similar to high blood pressure, they are difficult to detect on the surface. If undetected and untreated, they can destroy relationships and morale, as well as lead to reduced collaboration, productivity, and sense of belonging, ultimately leading to a toxic environment. A toxic environment destroys the overall climate health of the department, school, college, or university. Simply put, microaggressions and microbullying actions slowly destroy your space and destroy the overall human capital. If left untreated, they can lead to a unit's demise.

Reducing microaggression, microbullying, and bullying actions has an instant positive individual effect on a department, unit, or school, which then leads to systemic, positive organizational effects that create a welcoming climate for everyone within the institution.

Luckily, there is much you can do at the individual and systemic levels to reduce microaggressions, microbullying, and bullying. Committed people are the first line of defense against these behaviors. Leaders are in positions to model expected behavior and to take bad behavior seriously. You can reduce microaggressions so that they do not turn into microbullying or bullying. You can let others know of the department or school's norms and be the first to require all adhere to these norms. You can work to create practices and policies that support a welcoming institution. You can work to create practices and policies to let people know what happens if they cross that line. You can drive these changes to improve campus climate one interaction at a time.

Key Terms

Ally - people who stand up and take on the problems borne of oppression as their own, even if they cannot fully understand what it's like to be oppressed.

Bullying - unwanted repeated, aggressive behavior that involves a real or perceived power imbalance; behavior that manifests as verbal abuse; conduct which is threatening, humiliating, intimidating; or sabotage that interferes with work thus creating a hostile, offensive, and toxic workplace.

Bystander Intervention - anyone in a larger peer culture, whether or not they are present at the time of a specific incident, who can step in and say something about the incident.

Campus Climate - this is a measure of the real or perceived quality of interpersonal, academic, and professional interactions on a campus and consists of "the current attitudes, behaviors, and standards of faculty, staff, administrators, and students concerning the level of respect for individual needs, abilities, and potential" (Hurtado, 1992).

Diversity - the mix of differences that may make a difference in an interaction, always depending on the context such as the ability to meet individual or group goals, the ability to effectively meet intercultural challenges, safety, cost, and legality.

Dominant Identity - an identity that is systematically advantaged by the society.

Equity - providing varying levels of support based on need, context, or ability.

Hierarchical Microaggressions - represent the everyday slights found in higher education that communicate systemic valuing (or devaluing) of a person because of the institutional role held by that person in the institution.

Implicit Bias - the biases that impact us even when we do not really know they are impacting us; often the little voice in our heads that say things related to stereotypes about people.

Inclusion - using differences in a way that increases contributions and opportunities for everyone; often happens when people work together effectively, and their cultural experiences and differences are valued.

Marginalized Identity - an identity that is systematically disadvantaged by the society.

Microaffirmation - tiny acts of opening doors to opportunity, gestures of inclusion and caring, and graceful acts of listening.

Microaggression - a comment or action that subtly and often unconsciously or unintentionally expresses a prejudiced or stereotyping attitude toward a member of a marginalized group.

Microbullying - when the intentional or unintentional microaggressions become repetitive from one individual to another.

Micro-Resistance - when you proactively work, every chance you have, to create an inclusive environment around you.

Mobbing - when more and more people are involved in the bullying of one individual or a small group of individuals.

Positive Inquiry - an approach to organizational change that focuses on strengths of the organization and people in it, rather than on their weaknesses.

Privilege - unearned advantage or entitlement that benefits oneself or harms others; often, if you benefit from privilege you are unaware you have; you might feel like your life is "normal."

Restorative Justice - a space where people (often when there is a power imbalance but not always) can come together with a facilitator to ensure that people are recognizing when they're doing something wrong and finding a way to make it right.

Trigger - a strong emotional/physical response to a person or an event.

A Roadmap for This Book

Each chapter in this book will include:

- A conceptual framework

- Practical scenarios

- Worksheets and items to take for action

Each chapter will close with a list of questions for reflection, a challenge to take on, and a list of resources for learning more.

Chapter 1 of this book is a quick primer on the history and development of microaggression research. We provide definitions of microaggressions, microbullying, and bullying. The chapter explains the difference between a microaggression and an ordinary insult. It goes on to explain how to prevent, identify, reduce, and remove microaggressions and what to do if you did not intend to microaggress against someone. The chapter provides lists of do's and don'ts to help make your campus a more inclusive and welcoming place, thus allowing faculty, staff, and students to thrive. It then explains how to identify and prevent bullying and offers lists of personal and institutional changes to reduce bullying at your institution. Peppered throughout the chapter are reflective and pragmatic tools to use at your own institution.

Chapter 2 details the relationship between micro-aggressions, bullying, and campus climate. It introduces a useful conceptual tool called the 4-Way Implementation Model that campuses can use to examine their own policies and programs in the name of improving campus climate. This chapter explains how to think about institutional policies and programs through four interrelated lenses: systemic, individual, proactive, and reactive. This tool can also be used for short- and long-term planning of new policies and programs. This chapter shares examples of institutional policies and programs that address each of the four areas. The end of the chapter has a series of worksheets that any institution can use to map its own policies and processes using the 4-Way Implementation Model.

Chapters 3 and 4 put these ideas into practice by providing stories of microaggressions that happen in higher education. Each story explains why something is a microaggression, details what the intent and impact of the action might be, and then provides steps to address the microaggression. Chapter 3 shares examples of how deans, vice presidents, and others in senior leadership can address microaggressions at an institution. Chapter 4 focuses on the role of the chair and departmental influencers in responding to microaggressions at the departmental level. Following each story and solution is a reflective tool to use in your own practice. At the end of these chapters, you will be able to create your own stories and put them through the same process.

Chapter 5 moves the conversation from microaggression identification and removal to understanding the relationship between microaggressions, microbullying, and bullying and how one can morph into the next if nothing is done to remove and reduce the negative behaviors. This chapter specifically focuses on the role of microbullying and what units and departments can do to address this problematic behavior.

Chapter 6 explains how institutions often foster bullying through socialization and institutional processes and offers ways to combat bullying throughout departments, units, and the institution.

Chapter 7 offers a case study of how one university developed a bullying policy - the steps taken and the challenges faced in this endeavor. The chapter provides a template of a bullying policy and flow charts of the process from complaint to resolution for different constituent groups.

Chapter 8 provides extra worksheets and scenarios to use in your own unit or department.

How to Use This Book

This book can be used in many ways to improve your institution's climate.

1. As an individual, you might read the book and share or recommend the book to a friend or colleague. This is an organic way to start a discussion and provide a resource that can influence change in your environment. We are believers that, in general, people at their core are good and want to do the right thing as they engage

with colleagues. However, sometimes they do not know or are unaware of the adverse effect of their actions, even though their intent is positive. As discussed in this book, oftentimes micro-aggressions are unintentional while the impact is still harmful. Increased awareness and under-standing will provide a greater opportunity for reduction. Microbullying is a new term. We have found that having a definition helps people feel like they finally have a way to talk about actions that have been harming them but for which they didn't have a name. Naming the actions provides an opportunity to reduce and remove such actions from the community. Without a way to talk about these behaviors, institutions have little chance to take them seriously and correct them before they escalate further and damage the institutional climate.

2. The book can be used as awareness piece and, if read by your workforce, will provide an education platform for your members to check themselves and begin to remove microaggressions, micro-bullying, and bullying actions from the environ-ment. Once aware, you may use this text to review the many scenarios related to microaggressions and microbullying. You have an opportunity to take a deeper educational dive on situations that might be relevant to your environment. This book is packed with many scenarios that involve faculty, staff, and administrators. However, even if the scenario is not exactly titled to your work classification, the spirit of each scenario can be applied throughout many job categories thus providing you with examples and recommendations to reduce microaggressions and microbullying in your institution.

3. You can ask your staff or department to read this book and work through the worksheets, independently or in professional development groups, to increase the shared language about these issues which can magnify the entire organization's work toward improving the climate. Having one or two people read the book within a department or organization is helpful; it is an individual approach. However, if everyone understands these principles then you are more likely to have a significant and systemic impact on daily interactions and practices throughout your institution. This improves your changes of moving the entire institution down a path of creating a more welcoming and inclusive climate.

4. Another strategy may be to use this book as a reminder and a workbook for your institution. This book will provide you with theory and policy examples, will allow you to pull information from scenarios, and will provide "tools for action" for different situations that might relate to your organization. You could encounter an issue similar to a scenario in the book, adopt the "tools for action" examples, and have a resolution you can apply right away. You have instant access to tools for reducing microaggressions and microbullying. In essence, this can serve as your "welcoming and inclusive climate workbook" that deans, chairs, department heads, committee chairs, or anyone who leads an area, department, committee, or group within your college can incorporate as "just-in-time" learning strategies. You can use the information from this book to improve the climate that you lead.

The more people who use this book as an awareness and education tool or a workbook to incorporate "just-in-time" learning strategies to reduce microaggressions and micro-bullying, the greater chance for a behavioral shift, organizational buy-in, and a systemic movement toward creating a welcoming and inclusive climate.

CHAPTER 1: RESEARCH AND DEFINITIONS

SUMMARY

The first chapter of this book is a quick primer on the history and development of microaggression research. We provide definitions of microaggressions, microbullying, and bullying. This chapter explains the difference between a microaggression and an ordinary insult. It goes on to explain how to prevent, identify, reduce, and remove microaggressions as well as what to do if you did not intend to microaggress against someone. This chapter provides lists of do's and don'ts to help make your campus a more inclusive and welcoming place, thus allowing faculty, staff, and students to thrive. It then explains how to identify and prevent bullying and offers lists of personal and institutional changes to reduce bullying at your institution. Peppered throughout the chapter are reflective and pragmatic tools to use at your own institution.

Introduction

Microaggressions feel like a slap in the face. Micro-aggressions hurt both physically and psychologically. If we are not OK with physical violence at colleges and universities, we should not be OK with psychological violence either. Being a good person is not enough to ensure that you will not inadvertently microaggress against someone else.

Read the following excerpt of a new faculty member's experience trying to navigate her way through her new job.

SCENARIO

Maria and two other assistant professors were recently hired. The department they joined is tight on space. The other two junior faculty received an office of their own. Maria was given the office of someone on sabbatical while the department sorted out "what to do with her." She was also told that "she should just be thankful that she did not have to share an office." No one mentioned that the other two new faculty did not have to share their offices nor did they have to squat in someone else's space.

Her new chair, one of the people who interviewed her, helped get her keys and supplies, and was charged with facilitating the onboarding process for the department, would see Maria in the hallway and ask her if she was a new student and needed anything. This happened on and off for over a month.

Finally, Maria thought things were going better, and the chair was beginning to see her as a competent, new faculty member. Then, when discussing something else, the chair mentioned that Maria had been hired through a "Special Hires" program designed to diversify the faculty. Maria was

---

FIX YOUR CLIMATE

stunned. She reminded the chair that she had not been hired through the "Special Hires" program. She had been hired through the traditional institutional hiring process similar to her other two newly hired colleagues. The chair then said, "Oh, yeah," and moved on with the conversation.

Let's unpack

First a little context. In this excerpt, Maria is a newly hired faculty woman of color. The other two newly hired faculty are white women. The department chair is a white woman and has been the chair of the department for many years. This context is important as it establishes race, role, and hierarchy.

You might read this excerpt and assume that the new chair probably thought all the new hires were students. No. Maria asked the others. They were never assumed to be students. You might assume, of course, space is tight, and someone had to squat. You would be right. But did the chair even think of the implications of asking the one faculty of color to squat but not the two white colleagues. You might assume it is an honest mistake for a chair to think a person of color was hired through a special hiring program. You would almost be right. As special hiring programs are becoming more popular, the majority of faculty hirings still take place through traditional hiring processes and making an alternative assumption links to implicit bias when hiring faculty of color. It seems like honest mistake, at least from the chair's position.

Here are the problems with these assumptions. For the chair, a white woman, thinking Maria was a student was

13

funny and highlighted Maria's youthful air. However, this was received as a slight to Maria's accomplishments and ability to perform her faculty duties. For the chair, explaining the hiring process wrong was just a quick mistake. For Maria, this "mistake" placed a label on how she earned her position and implied that she was not hired on her skills and abilities but because of her race or gender. The chair did not even think through the implications of office assignment. Why does the person of color not receive the same office opportunities as her newly hired white colleagues?

For Maria, this was not just one slight, one time. These were several small slights that Maria kept experiencing from her chair, slights that might have related to her age, her role, and/or her ethnicity—Maria did not know what was provoking the chair into interacting with her in these negative ways. All she knew was that she was feeling unwelcome, devalued, not treated like a colleague or even an adult, and that her chair had the impression that she got the job by being "less than" her peers. For Maria, these small experiences were microaggressions. Even though the chair might not have meant anything by what she said or the decisions she made, Maria received the messages loud and clear—messages that were hurtful to her sense of self, personally and professionally.

The experience of these sorts of messages stay with people who experience them forever. Several years later, when Maria shared her stories, she told them with the same emotional pain as if they'd happened yesterday. That is what microaggressions sound like. That is what microaggressions feel like.

Where did the term "microaggression" come from?

The term racial microaggression was coined in the 1970s by Dr. Chester Pierce and his colleagues. They sought to explain experiences African Americans were having that caused physical and psychological pain—experiences that did not look the same or sound the same as pre-Civil Rights forms of discrimination. These microaggressions were experienced as brief and commonplace indignities, whether intentional or unintentional, that communicated hostility or negative slights that potentially had harmful or unpleasant psychological impact. The harm might be expressed as anger, shame, annoyance, pity, or even resignation. Although that should be enough to explain the trouble with microaggressions and why institutions of higher education should reduce them, a compounding problem is that these comments and actions reinforce stereotypes or prejudices about a social group – which makes them not only a slap in the face, but a slap in the collective face of an identity group.

In 2007, a seminal article emerged from Dr. Derald Sue and colleagues titled Racial microaggressions in everyday life: Implications for clinical practice. It led to an explosion of articles, social media sites, and news features related to racial microaggressions in workplaces and in everyday life. This article also led researchers to examine what other social identities might experience microaggressions, beyond the social category of race. Researchers found similar microaggressive experiences related to people's gender, sexuality, age, etc. Across research studies, issues related to people feeling second-class, put down, and less-than appeared again and again across contexts—all related to outward-facing identity characteristics, not personality or internal characteristics.

Ways to experience microaggressions

Microaggressions can be verbal, non-verbal, electronic, environmental, and/or organizational.

- **Verbal microaggressions** are spoken statements or questions that can harm through the actual words, or the tone of the words. An example might be when a new faculty is hired and someone says, "Are you sure you have a PhD?" sending an implication of disbelief for many reasons (e.g., youth, intellect, etc.) and implying lack of trust in your credentials, skills, and abilities.

- **Nonverbal microaggressions** are any sort of body language that sends the message that the receiver of the microaggression is not a person of worth. For example, someone might only greet the dean and ignore anyone of a lower rank who is standing beside the dean.

- **Electronic microaggressions** are sent over email or on social media, such as copying people who are not directly involved in an email chain repeatedly to "out" someone else's ideas or opinions.

- **Environmental microaggressions** are those that are institutionalized into the environment of an institution. An example might be when a person who uses a motorized wheelchair is forced to use the industrial elevator, often located near trash bins, since the regular elevator does not go to the needed floor.

- **Organizational microaggressions** are systemic and are part of the fabric of the policies and programs within an institution. For instance, an institution might only have time off slated for Christian holidays, and you must ask for time off if you practice a different religion than Christianity.

Hierarchical microaggressions

This initial research paved the way for us to examine hierarchical microaggressions—those that happen due to the role or position someone holds at an institution of higher education. Hierarchical microaggressions represent the everyday slights found in higher education that communicate systemic valuing (or devaluing) of a person because of the role held by that person in the institution. These happen in a variety of ways, but most happen by (slightly adapted from Young, Anderson and Stuart, 2016):

1. **Valuing/devaluing someone based on their role/credential:** For example, a department head makes a decision that increases the workload for staff and does not consult with the department staff prior to making that decision. Department staff feel they have no voice and are undervalued. They feel that if they held more high-status positions, their input would be requested.

2. **Changing accepted behavior based on role:** For instance, a senior faculty member comes into the front office of a department and shouts at the front desk staff for forgetting to note down the change in meeting location. The front desk staff gently tells the senior faculty member that the chair of the department is the one who changed the meeting at the last minute; thus, the staff had no role in noting the change in venue. A few minutes later, the same staff person hears the senior faculty member joking about the change in venue with the chair, acting like the lack of notification was no big deal. The staff notices that the senior faculty member feels free to treat a subordinate without respect, but because of the higher status of the chair, will not treat her in a similar manner.

3. **Actions (ignoring/excluding/surprise/interrupting) related to role:** There is a new staff member who is responsible for keeping track of faculty appointments. One faculty member comes in and asks about his appointments for the day. The staff member rattles off the list of appointments without looking at the online schedule. The faculty asks, "Are you sure?" The staff member says, "Yes, I have a good memory." The faculty then says, with surprise, "I didn't know staff could learn things so quickly!" and walks away. The staff member is extremely frustrated by the faculty member's assumption of his lack of memory.

4. **Terminology related to work position:** A student who helps at the front desk at an office within the institution regularly hears, "Oh, you're a just a work-study." They feel that it devalues the work they do and indicates to others their lack of finances, which embarrasses them. They would

prefer to be called a part-time worker, which they are, and not have to endure the connotation of being an under-skilled "charity case."

Climate, productivity, and the presence of microaggressions go hand-in-hand. It is important for institutional leaders to be able to identify microaggressions as a primary step in improving organizational climate. Everyone wants to work where they are valued for who they are, for the work they accomplish. It is important for institutional leaders to be able to identify microaggressions, as a primary step in improving organizational climate. (See the chart on the following pages.)

How to identify microaggressions

Microaggressions hurt, but because of their fleeting nature, one of the ways of recognizing something as a micro-aggression is to note the second guessing you do when you experience one (Did that really happen? Did he really say that? Did I hear it wrong?). Microaggressions attack not just you but an aspect of your identity that you cannot easily change (i.e., race, class, gender, ability, gender identity, age, role, etc.). Microaggressions are defined by the person who experiences them, not the person who says or does them, and are often related to people's non-privileged identities (take this BuzzFeed Quiz to "check" your level of privilege here: *https://www.buzzfeed.com/regajha/how-privileged-are-you?bfsource=bfocompareon*). People in higher education often experience microaggressions that harm several aspects of their identity at once—and that adds to the confusion (Did that happen because I am a woman? Because I am a lesbian? Because I am a student worker?).

HIERARCHICAL MICROAGGRESSIONS
Everyday slights found in higher education that communicate systemic valuing (or devaluing) of a person because of the role held by that person in the university

MICROINSULT
(Often Unconscious)
Behavioral/verbal remarks or comments that convey rudeness or insensitivity and demean a person's racial heritage or identity

MICROINVALIDATION
(Often Unconscious)
Verbal comment or behaviors that exclude, negate, or nullify the psychological thoughts, feelings, or experiential reality of a person of color

ACTIONS RELATED TO ROLE
Interrupting, excluding, ignoring, surprise

CHANGE ACCEPTED BEHAVIOR
A change in a person's behavior based on a person's role, and/or credentials

TERMINOLOGY RELATED TO WORK POSITION
Words used to describe various employment options in an organization

VALUING/DEVALUING OPINION
The valuing or devaluing of an opinion based on the credentials and/or role within a department

Isms Enacted - prejudice or discrimination against (insert a recognized social group here)

Age: Prejudice or discrimination against a particular age-group

Disability: Prejudice or discrimination against a person's physical or mental abilities

Gender: Prejudice or discrimination against the state of being any gender (typically used with reference to social and cultural differences rather than biological ones)

Language: Prejudice or discrimination against someone because of how they speak the dominant language

Race: Prejudice or discrimination against a person's skin color

Role: Prejudice or discrimination against someone for the position s/he holds in an organization

Sexuality: Prejudice or discrimination against a person for their attraction to a specific gender or genders

Other: Includes additional "isms" (including: appearance, culture, general, geographic, income, informality, military, politics, etc.)

(This chart is adapted from Young, Anderson, and Stuart, 2016)

MYRON R. ANDERSON AND KATHRYN S. YOUNG

What is the difference between a common insult and a microaggression?

Social science research shows that one of the major differences between common insults and microaggressions is that microaggressions have been found to affect people long after the actual experience. Insults hurt, but the pain goes away relatively quickly. Microaggressions are cumulative. They happen over and over and are related to someone's social identity characteristics (i.e., race, class, gender, sexuality, disability status, age, role/ position, religion, etc.) and possibly to their role or hierarchy within an organization (e.g., work study, classified staff, affiliate professor, assistant professor, associate professor, dean, administrator, etc.).

Microaggressions often feel like they have to be deciphered. The person is left wondering: did she really say that, or did he really act that way towards me? Insults might also have this component, but since the questions are not related to parts of you that you cannot change, the wondering is not tied to identity.

Microaggressions are reminders of a person's second-class status in society or in their organization. They symbolize historical and organizational injustices like how groups from marginalized backgrounds receive lower pay, are hired at lower rates, recover from recessions more slowly, have worse health and educational outcomes, own houses that appreciate slower, etc. Common insults, on the other hand, do not generate these humiliating associations with the person's identity group.

Microaggressions are like repeated toe stubs. The pain of them builds and grows with each subsequent hit. Imagine if you hit your toe first thing in the morning. It hurts, but you move on. Then you bang your toe nine more times during the day. Finally, while you are grocery shopping, someone accidentally steps on your toe. You cry out, "*Ouch!*" Why did this tiny mishap make you shout so loud? All that happened was that someone accidently slightly stepped on your toe. Your toe has been hurt a little bit so many times in one day, that when it is hurt one more time, the multiplier effect takes place and produces so much pain that you are overwhelmed, and you shout. This last stub, although the same as the first, is worse than the others because of the cumulative harm your foot has experienced throughout the day. The pain from microaggressions grows similarly. Maya Angelou calls this "death by 1,000 cuts."

How do you know if a slight is a microaggression?

Did the slight hurt the person's feelings?

NO	YES

This could be a microaggression, but the person did not notice or did not care about it.	This could just be an insensitive slight.	Does the person feel like the slight is or could be related to the person's social identity?	Does the person feel like the slight is or could be related to the person's professional identity?

	NO	YES	YES

It is probably a microaggression.

Follow the flowchart on the preceding page as a first step to decide if an insult is actually a microaggression.

TAKE FOR ACTION

How not to commit a microaggression
Think before you make a reference, a joke, or tell a story about an identity or cultural group (often one that is not yours) in a professional setting, such as in a class you teach, in a departmental meeting, or elsewhere on campus.

Ask yourself:
Am I making fun of someone's race, ethnicity, cultural traditions, gender, sex, and/or sexual orientation? *If so, don't say it.*

Would I make the same comment about a different identity or cultural group of which I know a lot about their cultural norms? *If not, don't say it.* (**Note:** *If it is not your group, no matter how well you know members from another group, best to not say it.*)

Would a person, their living descendants, or their parents possibly take offense at how I am describing them? *If so, don't say it.*

Were my ancestors (not you personally) responsible for the death or oppression of people from their identity or cultural group? *If so, don't say it.*

If none of the above a true, go ahead and share your reference, joke, or story. It probably is not going to be a microaggression.

What about the First Amendment?

Institutions struggle to balance what Freedom of Speech means in our specific contexts. Does it mean all speech is OK? Does it mean harmful speech (often known as Hate Speech) is OK? Does it mean people should be "policed" for their speech? Does it mean that we must protect one person's speech even if it silences everyone else? Often when institutions send out guides to staff and faculty about better words to use than others so that more people will feel freer to speak on campus, these guides will be later reframed in some circles to say that the institutions are denying others free speech or forcing political-correctness. A great book that takes on this debate is: *What Snowflakes Get Right: Free Speech, Truth, and Equality on Campus* by Ulrich Baer (2019).

We want to encourage you to look back at your institution's mission and vision and think through what sorts of speech will help you achieve your goals. Many institutions want to practice inclusive language so that as many students as possible (as well as staff, faculty, and administrators) feel welcomed, respected, and valued. This book is written with the hope that you find the right balance at your school, the balance that opens dialog for many people while harming few, if any. Thinking through the impact of your words and actions is one way to create brave spaces for people to bring their whole selves to their work and to their learning in higher education.

Your turn

Read these scenarios and see if you would classify them as microaggressions.

Try 1-A

A white, male assistant professor says, "Someone mistook me for a security guard." I ask, "How did that make you feel?" He responds, "Fine, it was funny."

IS THIS A MICROAGGRESSION?

Probably not. His feelings weren't hurt. The incident did not relate to an aspect of his identity. No microaggression.

Try 1-B

If you change the race of the individual, it might change the outcome of deciding if something is a microaggression.

An African-American, male, assistant professor says, "Someone mistook me for a security guard." I ask, "How did that make you feel?" He responds, "I am so sick of it. No one ever sees me, or people who look like me, as a professional with a degree."

IS THIS A MICROAGGRESSION?

Yes. His feelings were hurt. And he felt like the slight was related to his social identity and professional identity—the combination of them together. Also, this action may be a part of an accumulation effect of receiving this, or a similar misunderstanding, multiple times.

And, although the only difference in this scenario is race, this is how microaggressions relate to organizational climate and, more broadly, to societal climate.

WHY IT'S A MICROAGGRESSION:

In Try 1-A, the assistant professor is from a dominant group in society (i.e., white males), so the comment can be considered a one off; the comment can be funny, because it does not happen to him very often.

In Try 1-B, the assistant professor is from a marginalized group in society (i.e., African-American males), so the comment is indicative of so many other comments he has already received related to his perceived intellect linked to his race and his perceived possible professional roles linked to his race; this comment is not funny. It is a microaggression.

Try 2-A

Students and fellow faculty refuse to refer to a female professor of color as Dr. C even when they refer to other professors using "Dr." This professor is often called "Miss C" or just "C," even after the professor corrects them multiple times.

IS THIS A MICROAGGRESSION?

Yes. Her feelings were hurt. She feels like the slight is related to her social and professional identities.

WHY IT'S A MICROAGGRESSION:

Students and other faculty do not "see" her as a faculty member, so they do not use the terms associated with her being a faculty member, even when corrected.

Try 2-B

Students and fellow faculty refuse to refer to a white, female professor as Dr. C even when they refer to other professors using "Dr." This professor is often called "Miss C" or just "C" even after the professor corrects them multiple times.

IS THIS A MICROAGGRESSION?

Yes. Her feelings were hurt. She feels like the slight is related to her professional identity. Students and other faculty do not "see" her as a faculty member, so they do not use the terms associated with her being a faculty member, even when corrected.

WHY IT'S A MICROAGGRESSION:

In both cases, the faculty are trying to remind people that they deserve the same accolades as male professors. If you are going to call male professors doctor and female professors by their name (or by Miss, Ms., or Mrs.), you are not giving the same level of respect to both, despite the fact that both have earned a Ph.D. or an Ed.D. that qualifies a doctoral title.

If individual professors choose not to use the doctoral title, that choice is up to them. It's not for others to make the choice for them.

To recap, when is something a microaggression? The most basic answer is: when the person experiencing it feels like it is one. Following is a list of signs to help you identify microaggressions.

Nuance Alert

If, after reading these early examples, you wonder, "But what about..." or "It could be...," We welcome those inquiries. We know that the stories in this book might seem a little too simple. They are. For the purpose of pointing out microaggressions, microbullying, and bullying, we need stories that show a clear picture. Without a doubt, your stories will be infinitely more complex. The context and history in your location matter; these affect how each event unfolds, whether or not it's problematic, and who each event might impact. You can use conversations in your units and departments to "fill in the gray" in the stories so that they more perfectly suit your experiences.

SIGNS OF MICROAGGRESSIONS

Someone feels hurt (e.g., angry, shocked, shamed, resigned, etc.).

They think about the experience for a long time after it happened.

They are unsure if they are making too much of the experience.

They are unsure if they should bring it up.

They are pretty sure the person making the slight would not have said/done the same thing to someone perceived as having societal or professional power over them or their identity group.

Who decides if a microaggression just took place?

This is a question that comes up often. The person receiving the microaggression makes the final call whether or not they have been "microaggressed." As indicated earlier, there can be a power dynamic in the delivery and reception of microaggressions. However, that power dynamic is not in play when it comes to identifying and confirming if you have been microaggressed. Moreover, if the microaggressee brings to the attention of the microaggressor that they received a microaggression from them, and the microaggressor indicates that it was not a microaggression, that just makes things worse. Oftentimes, this denial comes with a statement like: "You are just being too sensitive," or "You are overreacting." This actually serves as a second microaggression as this action dismisses the micro-aggressee's feelings and devalues their claim that they have been hurt. The person who received the microaggression has the final say.

One of the questions that we recommend you ask yourself if you believe that you may have received a microaggression is, "How did that statement or action make me feel?" This question gets to the interpersonal essence of receiving a microaggression and will allow you a basis to develop your strategy for prevention, reduction, and removal.

What if you really disagree that you committed a microaggression?

What if you really think it was a miscommunication and if they heard you out they would understand? In these instances, it is a good idea to take a breath and listen to their pain, even if you disagree with it. After they have let you know about their experience, and if you see they would be amenable, ask if you can ask clarifying questions or if they would like to hear how you see things. If they say no, leave it for now. The point is not to dispute over is this a microaggression or not; the point is to hear that someone was hurt but what you did or said - even if you did not intend it that way. See more about intent vs. impact on p. XX. Microaggressors often have a different lens than the person experiencing them so even if you explain yourself the person who feels pain might still have that pain because their history and context are different than yours. Your need to explain yourself privileges your pain over theirs and they were the one who were hurt by you, so you should be privileging their pain.

TAKE FOR ACTION

Write about it

Think about a recent microaggressive experience. If someone indicated to you that they had received or witnessed a microaggressions, what did you do?

What did you say?

Whose pain did you prioritize: the person who was harmed or the person who did the harm?

What was your reasoning?

What does it say if you prioritized the harmer, and they are from a dominant social or professional group? What message is sent to your sphere of influence?

What might you do differently next time?

Terminology

We would be remiss without addressing the word *microaggression*, along with the verbs and adjectives related to it. If you do a microaggression, it is called "committing a microaggression." Yes, it sounds like "committing a crime," and that sounds harsh. But to the person experiencing the verbal or non-verbal exchange, it feels like physical harm. It feels like a mini-assault. Imagine if you get slapped or punched. It takes your breath away. That's what microaggressions feel like.

> If you commit a microaggression, you are the microaggressor.

> The person who experiences it is the microaggressee.

Some people are moving away from the term due to the hype in some press circles and are moving towards using "microinequities" or "microinsults." In this book, we use the term *microaggression*, as it is still the term predominately used in the research literature. Plus, painful terms help people understand that these are painful experiences.

Context matters

We have already shared how microaggressions often happen by well-intentioned people who do not always realize the harm they are causing. Microaggressions also depend on context. The same comment said between close friends, or sometimes family members, as said in a professional meeting might not come off as hurtful. The same comment said between people of the same race or gender might not come off as hurtful. Something that is OK to say about a colleague in the department might not be OK to say in front of the president of the institution.

Context matters. This is so important in understanding microaggressions and the harm they cause. It is also the very thing that makes them so hard to pin down and eradicate. Each time people move into a different space with each other, the context changes. Imagine a cup of coffee. You add the right amount of milk. You get it just right. You know exactly what it will taste like. Then someone refills your cup when it is only half empty. Suddenly, the coffee to milk ratio is off, and the coffee is not what you expected to taste. The context has changed. You have to rework it to get the ratios right again.

When different people inhabit different spaces, the context changes. The rules of interaction change as well, because the power dynamics in the space have changed. This does not mean some spaces are primed for microaggressions and some are not. It means everyone in the space, especially the leaders (e.g., chairs, deans, directors, etc.) in that space, need to be mindful of the change in power and relational dynamics. Leaders must work to make the new space inclusive to the new people in that space. When leaders do not work to make space inclusive and welcoming, that is when the specific context can work against them and set the stage for possible microaggressions.

What if you did not mean to microaggress against someone?

Sometimes when a person is accused of a microaggression, their response is, "That is not what I meant," or "That is not what I was trying to say." This makes sense as the person really might not have intended a microaggression. This does not deny the fact that one was committed. Intent does not equal impact.

Someone can mean not to harm, and yet, still harm through their words and actions. In regard to microaggression, this is a moot point. The impact is the pain. Oftentimes, intent or lack of intent is used to justify the action in hopes of reducing the pain of the impact. However, the receiver of the microaggression feels the same - like quick, yet stinging, humiliation. You can't take back that initial feeling.

If you address the microaggression in a diplomatic way, it can serve as an apology, compassion, or understanding of sorts that may lessen the long-term sting of the microaggression after it has happened and improve the interactions between you and the other person—as well as make strides to improving campus climate.

SOMETHING YOU CAN SAY

I'm sorry that I caused you pain. Thank you for telling me about your feelings and this experience. Please tell me more about the impact this had on you. I want to further understand, so I may prevent this from happening in the future.

MYRON R. ANDERSON AND KATHRYN S. YOUNG

Why institutions should care about microaggressions

We have already drawn a link between organizational climate and microaggressions. There are many studies that show a correlation between a toxic climate and reduced productivity. The converse is true as well. A welcoming climate increases productivity, retention, and sense of belonging.

Nine things that increase when institutions **reduce** micro-aggressions:

1. Productivity

2. Quality of work

3. Faculty, staff, and student self-esteem

4. Institutional loyalty

5. Campus and classroom satisfaction between faculty, staff, and students

6. Positive internal relationships between faculty, staff, and students

7. Innovation and learning

8. Faculty, staff, and student sense of belonging

9. A welcoming and inclusive environment for faculty, staff, and students

Nine things that increase when institutions **do not reduce** microaggressions:

1. Depression

2. Anxiety

3. Discouragement

4. Poor physical health

5. Absenteeism

6. Employee and student turnover

7. Faculty, staff, and student complaints

8. Vengeful activities

9. Toxic environments throughout the institution

As you can see, there are many adverse effects that microaggressions have on an institution that affect faculty, staff, students, and the overall campus climate. A negative campus climate has a systemic negative effect on faculty, staff, and students who will feel a lack of sense of belonging at the institution. Poor sense of belonging can be linked to low retention for faculty and staff as well as reduced persistence for students. With student success at the core of an institution's mission, developing strategies to reduce and possibly remove microaggressions throughout your institution will produce many positive outcomes that align with your institution's mission and values.

The role of leadership in reducing microaggressions

Research shows that culture reflects leadership. This means, how you act and talk matters immeasurably for the overall culture of the institution. You need to model what you want from others at all times. How you treat people when you think no one is watching sends a message—because, really, everyone is watching all the time. To be a leader who is mindful of microaggressions and bullying, it means you need to know how others perceive you. Following is a tool to help you see if you are self-focused or focus on how others see you.

TAKE FOR ACTION

Self-Reflection Activity

Write a capital E on your forehead with your finger. What does the E look like in the mirror to someone who would be facing you? Will it look like an E or a backwards E? If it is a backwards E, this means you think about how you would see the E meaning you are self-focused, if it looks correct in the mirror, or to others, it means you are thinking about how others would see the E.

(From *Friend and Foe* by Galinsky and Schweitzer, 2015)

You need to be a leader who writes the E so that others can see it. Powerful people have been found to be overconfident in the support they have from others, often because they are self-focused and think everyone sees them the way they see themselves.

Leaders also need to communicate well to keep the climate warm and welcoming

Research shows that most bullying (and many microaggressions) comes from people in leadership. Sometimes this might be accidental on the part of the leader, but it still might come across to others as aggressive. And if people see their leader as aggressive, the climate will not feel welcoming and productivity will reduce. So, make sure that you are mindful of your words and actions at work.

- When there is no communication from leaders, people will imagine the worst-case scenario while they wait for information.

- When you do communicate, know that people put meaning into your words that you might not intend. Be sure of what you are saying. Avoid sarcasm.

- For example, if you ask someone *below you* at the institution to meet later in the day, know that they may worry all day about the purpose of the meeting, even if you know that you just want to ask the person to read over a document for you. Instead say, "Can we meet later in the day to discuss reading a document for me?" Or at least say, "Don't worry, it is nothing bad," so the person knows not to worry.

- Leaders often intimidate accidentally.

- Leaders with big voices sometimes forget the power of their voice. Keep it in check, or at least know why you are raising it when you are raising it.

- Leaders with big gestures can forget the power of their gestures. Keep your body in check, or at least know why you are moving it around when you are moving it around.

- Focus your energy on team goals rather than on individual goals. It will increase your department's or unit's ability to share information and hear each other's perspectives.

Microaggressions often come from implicit biases

These are biases that impact us, even when we don't know they are impacting us. They are often the little voice in our heads that says things related to stereotypes about people. More dangerous is that our biases affect many things in educational settings. They affect:

- **Our Perception** – how we see people and perceive reality.

- **Our Attitude** – how we react towards certain people.

- **Our Behaviors** – how receptive/friendly we are towards certain people.

- **Our Attention** – which aspects of a person we pay most attention to.

- **Our Listening Skills** – how much we actively listen to what certain people say.

- **Our Microaffirmations** – how much or how little we comfort certain people in certain situations.

How do you prevent microaggressions?

Preventing microaggressions has individual and systemic components.

As an individual, there are things you can do to try to make sure that you are not microaggressing. People commit fewer microaggressions when they are aware of how they interact with others and how others might interact with them. They commit fewer microaggressions when they know about their own identities, how others might perceive them, and how to bridge the distance between the two. People also commit fewer microaggressions when they reflect on interactions they have—when the interactions go well and when they do not go well. Reflection helps us know what we are doing right and what we can do better.

TAKE FOR ACTION

Reflect and Educate

You can reduce microaggressions by educating yourself. Gaining additional knowledge and experiences will allow you to have a more robust identity lens when you engage with others in all aspects of your life.

Of course, you can undertake educating yourself on your own.

You can also learn through some "tests" to help you gain more understanding about your own biases and intercultural competence.

Think about taking some of the implicit bias tests at **Project Implicit** developed by Harvard University. Their website is: https://implicit.harvard.edu/implicit/takeatest.html

Think about having someone administer **the Intercultural Developmental Inventory (IDI)** to help you learn more about the difference between your perceived intercultural competence and your developmental intercultural competence. Their website is: https://idiinventory.com/

Here are some specific ways to increase your awareness so that you are less likely to be a microaggressor.

1. Learn about cultures and social identities on your own and from sources within the group.

It is your responsibility to learn about people you deem "different" from yourself, whatever that may mean to you.

As you read the following list, think about how each of the ideas on the left can be supported through your role as a faculty member, chair, or administrator and how each of the ideas on the right can be reduced.

DO	DON'T
Read books by authors with different identities than yours.	Ask strangers to explain their culture to you, even if you ask nicely.
Go to movies that present perspectives that you are not used to.	Interrupt others during conversation.
Ask a trusted friend about their marginalized experiences.	Interject during pauses when someone else is collecting their thoughts.
Ask how communities refers to themselves as a group of people (e.g., Tribal name, group name, etc.). Double check if you are supposed to use the same naming or something different.	Impose your personal values, morals, or belief on others.
Be honest and clear about your role and expectations and be willing to adapt to meet the needs of the community.	Make insensitive jokes or comments.
	Ask intrusive questions early in the conversation.

2. Surround yourself with diverse people.

One great thing about just being around people that you deem "different" than yourself is that you will naturally start to see people in more nuanced ways.

The more time you spend with people, the more you see their strengths and struggles. You will see these things as coming from an individual, rather than that individual being only a representation of their social identity group.

As you read the following list, think about how each of the ideas on the left can be supported because of your role as a faculty member, chair, or administrator and how each of the ideas on the right can be reduced.

DO	DON'T
Really engage genuinely with diverse perspectives.	Just collect some "trans friends."
Show respect by being open to other ways of thinking and behaving.	Call on your "black friend" to bail you out when you have been racially insensitive.
Create space for casual conversation to establish rapport, so be genuine and use appropriate self-disclosure (e.g., where you are from, work-appropriate personal interests, etc.).	Drop names of people of color as evidence of your good, non-racist intention when you get called on a microaggression.

DO	DON'T
Seek to educate yourself about groups you do not know much about.	Tell stories of "people like them" as an attempt to establish rapport.
Model how to become knowledgeable about the backgrounds of others.	Make a comment about a person of color being hired to meet a "quota."
Build understanding of people from other backgrounds and cultures.	Make a comment about someone "playing the race card."
Admit limited knowledge of cultures.	Tell a woman she is being "overly sensitive" or "overreacting."
Say, "I want to be able to say your name well. I know you and your family can say it well. I will work on it."	Question the ability of a person with a disability.

3. Learn from constant vigilance of that quiet voice in your head.

We are all subject to implicit bias—the quiet voice that is surprised when a person of color is in leadership, the voice that is surprised when a junior faculty has a good idea, and the voice that wonders if the woman was chosen as dean to show that there are no gender problems in the college. When you hear that voice, you actually can train yourself to question the voice's assumptions and even to tell it that it's wrong. The more often you do, the more your brain will listen and make fewer assumptions based on social identity categories. We all fall into single system thinking, where we think our cultural values, morals, and beliefs are the only correct ones. We cannot see our own culture and its relationship to existing policies and practices at the institution. We must work actively and explicitly to be more flexible in our thinking so that we better understand the values, morals, and beliefs of people we work with and people we teach. This step will help reduce implicit biases and the microaggressions that follow.

As you read the following list, think about how each of the ideas on the left can be increased because of your role as a faculty member, chair or administrator and how each of the ideas on the right can be reduced through your role as well.

DO	DON'T
Be open to critique when employees bring up perceived microaggressions or unfair treatment.	Write vague job descriptions.
Develop self-awareness about your own possible role in microaggressing on others.	Give in to your biases.
Notice when your responses, decisions, or behaviors might have been caused by bias or stereotypes. Make a plan to think positive thoughts when encountering members of stigmatized groups in the future.	Listen to your "gut feelings" as the main decider in interviews.

DO	DON'T
Remember, in detail, people who violate expected stereotypes in a positive way and practice thinking about these positive examples.	Believe "fit" is the most important aspect when hiring someone for the department.
Make an effort to evaluate and think about members of stereotyped groups as individuals.	Assume a student with a Spanish-looking last name can speak Spanish.
Give job applicants greater anonymity so that you can see their work product better.	Question a person's gender or sexuality.
Make sure evaluations are conducted in a structured fashion.	Assume women will leave the workforce after having a baby.
Have a stated commitment to diversity and inclusion in decision-making, planning, evaluation, and leadership.	Base future performance of an individual from a stereotyped group on past performance of someone else from that group.

4. Learn by being committed to personal action against racism, sexism, ableism, heterosexism, and other injustices.

It is important to not only learn about histories and cultures, you must also act on your learning. This does not require that you engage in protests and marches (although, feel free to do so if that is how you feel moved to engage with injustice). It means thinking about all the small ways you can fight injustice at your institution. You can speak up and ask for clarification in a meeting where someone is making assumptions about a group of people. You can greet everyone you meet, even with a nod of your head, to make sure they know that you see and value them. You can be quiet in a meeting to make room for others to speak if they come from experiences that wait to talk, rather than being comfortable talking over people. All of these small steps are part of fighting injustice on a personal level.

As you read the following list, think about how each of the ideas on the left can be supported because of your role as a faculty member, chair, or administrator and how each of the ideas on the right can be reduced.

DO	DON'T
Talk with employees if a disparaging comment is made about a colleague or student.	Stereotype based on looks, language, dress, and other outward appearances.
Welcome people's questions and concerns about cultural competence, diversity, and inclusive excellence.	Make excuses for your own or someone else's racist/sexist/etc. behavior.
Understand there might be mistrust toward people in positions of authority.	Downplay a situation by saying, "Oh, he is just like that."

DO	DON'T
Listen actively to the microaggressee because the person is looking for someone to give meaning to their experiences.	Expect thanks for being an ally.
Call attention to institutional talk that puts down certain roles and people in their roles.	Use language like "lame," "crazy," "gay," or "guys," or use "girls" to refer to women.
Create new narratives within the institution that tell a story of valuing employees.	Doubt someone's story related to identity.
Use the pronouns people ask for.	
Apologize when needed.	
Act, not just talk, about inclusion and equity.	

The preceding list includes things anyone can do—chairs, deans, anyone. There are other things individuals can do to change systems and environments because of their leadership role in an institution.

Reducing microaggressions

Reducing microaggressions has great impact at the systemic level. Research shows that creating opportunities for behavioral change through policy, practice, and program changes are more effective than mandatory one-time diversity trainings or worse, diversity trainings as "punishment" when someone has transgressed institutional boundaries.

To reduce microaggressions at the individual level:

When you see or hear a microaggression and want to intervene, you need to sound genuine. If you sound like you are putting someone down, they might take offense and not stay in the conversation, losing the opportunity to figure out how to do better next time. (The tips below are adapted from the *Teaching Tolerance Speak Up Guide*.)

Question

Ask someone to repeat or explain what they said.

Example: "Could you say that again? I'm not sure I heard you right the first time."

Echo

When someone else speaks up, say something, too.

Example: "I agree. Don't say racist jokes around me either."

Interrupt

Say something to stop the microaggression.

Example: "That is not OK to say around here."

Educate

Oftentimes microaggressions come from ignorance, the ignorance of not knowing. These are opportunities, especially in educational settings like higher education, to explain why something is not acceptable.

Example: "You might not know this but using the word 'lame' like that puts down people with disabilities."

To reduce microaggressions at the departmental level:

- Provide chairs with meaningful training (before they assume their role as chair) on how to be leaders of the institution. Include anti-bias instruction as part of this training.

- Ask chairs to become diversity champions, who you can look to for ideas about how to improve departmental and campus climate.

To reduce microaggressions at the school or college level:

- Provide deans and associate deans with meaningful training on how to be leaders of the institution. Include anti-bias instruction as part of this training.

- Create purposeful mentoring programs for every new faculty hired.

- Talk to faculty about being diversity champions when they are hiring for new faculty.

- Develop a Diversity Task Force to look at data and offer solutions.

To reduce microaggressions at the organizational unit level:

- Provide Directors and Assistant Directors with meaningful training on how to be leaders of the institution. Include anti-bias instruction as part of this training.

- Create purposeful mentoring programs for every new staff member hired.

- Rotate (assistant) directors through different units to let them see the interconnectedness of the institution.

- Base promotions on someone's objectively measured performance.

To reduce microaggressions at the institutional level:

- Use a campus climate survey, and develop policy based on the findings.

- Create an idea-catcher where constituents can share ideas for improvement online. Make sure to check for these ideas frequently and respond to people with the ideas if they share their contact information.

- Create self-managed teams, which allow people in different roles and functions to work together on projects as equals. This creates more contacts between "unlike" groups.

- Use the right data to answer the questions being asked. Wrong data leads to wrong conclusions.

- Make transparent accountability where leaders have to explain their decision-making process and the final decision to others.

- Institute a Diversity Office with adequate staff, resources, and space. Put this office in close proximity to The Office of the President.

This short list is just to get you started. Chapter 2 goes into more depth about how to think about systemic change for a more positive campus climate through using our four-way implementation model to list and to evaluate institutional policies, programs, and practices.

Next in this chapter, we explain the evolution from microaggressions to bullying in higher education. ***Note:*** Many acts of bullying start as microaggressions, so learning about microaggressions and how to address them is the first step in addressing bullying. Try hard not to ignore or minimize problematic behavior that might worsen with time.

MYRON R. ANDERSON AND KATHRYN S. YOUNG

How do microaggressions evolve into bullying?

We like to think microaggressions are one-time gaffes by well-intentioned people. And that is true, most of the time. You can reduce and remove future microaggressions through the individual and systemic changes offered in this chapter and throughout this book. Reducing and removing future microaggressions has an impact on campus climate. If you address and reduce microaggressions, you keep them from moving into the category of bullying.

Microaggressions grow when unaddressed, as the microaggressor learns that their way of behaving or acting towards a colleague or staff member is tacitly accepted through the silence of others. These microaggressions are different than other ones—they are the fodder for microbullying, which, in turn, can lead to bullying.

The path from microaggressions to bullying

If unchecked and unmanaged by departmental or unit leadership, microaggressions are likely to evolve into microbullying. Microbullying is when the intentional or unintentional microaggressions become repetitive from one individual to another. The microaggressor engages in repetitive behaviors (intentionally or unintentionally) that make the other person feel bad about themselves. The microaggressor might not yet realize the powerful effect their comments and actions are having on the receiver, or perhaps the microaggressor is not yet engaging with the purpose of control.

If microbullying continues (intentionally or unintentionally), the damage to the person receiving the microbullying actions is extremely painful. Moreover, because the microbullying act is often felt, but is still difficult to name in observable characteristics by the person receiving it or by a bystander, there are no policies developed to provide institutional enforcement to lessen these behaviors. Chapter 5 deals directly with microbullying, its impact on climate, and individual and systemic suggestions to address microbullying.

There is a progression that occurs when these issues are ignored or when a department is not educated about the potential for them to worsen over time. People in leadership, like chairs and deans, need to learn how to stop microbullying and its progression to bullying before it starts.

The preceding chart indicates the progression from microaggressions to microbullying to bullying with organizational climate in the middle. These issues are surrounding the climate; thus, they have an effect on the overall climate.

The slight spacing shows opportunity for stopping microaggressions, microbullying, or bullying, and if not stopped, the severity can move on to the next level of toxic institutional behaviors.

What is bullying?

A main sign of microaggressions is that the aggression happens quickly and is not often repeated by the same person. The aggression is often unintended. Bullying is different. The aggression is often intentional and is related to power and control over another. Research shows that:

- 19% of Americans are bullied.
- Another 19% witness it.
- 61% of Americans are aware of abusive conduct in the workplace.
- 61% of bullies are bosses.
- The majority (63%) operate alone.
- 40% of bullied targets are believed to suffer adverse health effects.
- 29% of targets remain silent about their experiences.
- 71% of employer reactions are harmful to targets.
- 60% of coworker reactions are harmful to targets.

(Work Place Bullying Institute, 2017)

Bullying is unwanted, repeated, aggressive behavior that involves a real or perceived power imbalance, that manifests as verbal abuse; conduct which is threatening, humiliating, intimidating; or sabotage that interferes with work thus creating a hostile, offensive and toxic workplace. Although people in leadership have institutional power, there are other forms of power that matter just as much in a work environment. Social power, seniority, academic degrees, and job knowledge matter deeply at colleges and universities. People also gain power through gossip, lies, and keeping or telling secrets. People who bully usually have assumed, perceived, or real authority in relation to the person they are bullying.

Bullying behavior includes:

- Threatening gestures and/or physical abuse.

- Unwarranted (or undeserved) punishment.

- Criticizing a person persistently or constantly.

- Personal attacks (angry outbursts, profanity, name calling).

- Spreading malicious rumors, gossip, or innuendo.

- Encouragement of others to turn against the targeted employee.

- Undermining or deliberately impeding a person's work.

- Conduct that a reasonable person would find hostile, offensive, unacceptable, and unrelated to the employer's legitimate business interests.

MYRON R. ANDERSON AND KATHRYN S. YOUNG

How do we prevent bullying?

Much as preventing microaggressions is about creating an institutional culture where people feel like they can thrive, institutions can establish and support a strong and consistent culture that stops the desire to bully before bullying begins. Preventing bullying must come from senior leadership, associate chairs, chairs, associate deans, deans, and directors throughout the institution through policies that will address bullying through a reporting structure, through providing professional development so the whole campus community knows what bullying is and how to address it, and through implementing clear and sound processes designed to take action on removing bullying actions from the institution. Faculty and staff must be empowered to report and to be able to do so without retribution.

WHAT EVERYONE CAN DO TO PREVENT BULLYING AT COLLEGES AND UNIVERSITIES:

- Think about how you treat others. How do people react to your interactions with them? How do you act online and in person? Could you accomplish the same goals by interacting in kinder ways to others?
- Think about how others treat you. Are you being treated differently than others? If so, can you pinpoint the reasons for the treatment like changes in schedule, chairs/ supervisors, or assignments?
- If you think you are being treated disrespectfully, have you brought it to the other person's attention and asked them to stop - if it's safe for you to talk with the person? If not, have you brought it up with someone "above" you? (For faculty, chairs count as above you.)

- If you see something, say something to someone in leadership (e.g., chairs, deans, directors, etc.). While you may not be the target of a bully, if you are there when bullying behavior happens, say something either to the person who is acting in a bullying manner (if it's safe) or to your/their chair or supervisor, or even to Human Resources.

- Attend awareness and prevention professional development related to bullying. It is important to know what counts and does not count as bullying at an institution, what to do about it and how to prevent it.

IF YOU ARE IN A POSITION OF LEADERSHIP LIKE BEING A VICE PRESIDENT, CHAIR, DIRECTOR, OR DEAN, YOU CAN:

- Review policies and procedures to assure there is language about respect at the institution and expectations for working with others.

- Make sure everyone knows how to report bullying behavior and ensure there will be no retribution. Anonymous hotlines and climate surveys help do this work at the institutional level.

- Investigate complaints fairly by using a standard policy for investigating them.

- Implement training for everyone about what counts as respectful communication and the consequences of not following institutional code of conduct and other policies.

- Listen to concerns both formally and informally so that you learn what is happening when you are not around.

- Be aware of sudden changes in behavior. This is often a sign something is going awry.

- Address concerns meaningfully either through a documented conversation or enacting the bullying policy procedure.

- Treat co-workers as well as you would treat the president of the institution—respectfully regardless of their institutional position.

- Encourage, and remind others of, respectful interactions from others, even through email and social media.

This is just the beginning of addressing bullying at an institution of higher education. Chapter 6 goes in-depth about bullying behavior and how to address it individually and systemically. It offers stories of bullying on college and university campuses and institutional solutions to those stories as a way to visualize what you can do to reduce and possibly remove bullying from campus. Chapter 7 provides templates for an anti-bullying policy and for bullying reporting structures for staff, faculty, and administrators.

Conclusion

Microaggressions and bullying occur at institutions of higher education. They happen because of an array of interpersonal and institutional factors that make the conditions acceptable for people to harm each other. The factors include: people's personalities, implicit biases, negative hierarchy socialized into institutional roles, the lack of institutional structures to promote an inclusive institution, long-standing policies with racist, classist, sexist, and ableist assumptions embedded into them. Even the history of who was allowed to work in and attend higher education and who was barred from working in and attending institutions of higher education impacts policies to this day.

Given this backdrop, it is imperative that institutions work at every level to create conditions where microaggressions and bullying are the exception, not the norm, at the institution. Institutions must also create formal and informal mechanisms to address microaggressions and bullying. We must teach all those who lead how to not microaggress or bully their colleagues, even inadvertently. And we must know how to deeply engage with others who have experienced microaggressions and bullying so that we do not harm them further through our actions and words.

When you work in leadership, trying to keep everybody happy or to not rock the boat is not enough. You must work to create an organizational climate for you and others to professionally thrive. This means continuing to work on learning about yourself and others. It means increasing your adaptive skills to be able to work with a wide variety of people and it means asking the same of your colleagues. It means examining your policies, processes, and programs to ensure that they are flexible and welcoming. It is everyone's responsibility to make a more welcoming campus climate. It can begin with you.

Think about it – Talk about it

This is an opportunity to think about and discuss some of the concepts in this chapter. On your own, with a few colleagues, or in a departmental or unit meeting, discuss one or more of the questions below.

- Go back to Maria's story on page 12. Imagine she was hired at your institution. Reimagine an onboarding process where she would feel like this is the best place to work. List specific strategies to increase her sense of belonging.

- Have you heard about microaggressions in your sphere of influence (your department, your school, college, or unit)? If so, think of one example. What happened? How was it addressed? Did you agree with the handling? How could it have been done better?

- Look back at pages 42-49. Add three Do's and Don'ts to each way to reduce microaggressions.

- Talk about some common microaggressions you have heard or experienced. Use the tools on pages 50-51 (Question, Echo, Interrupt, Educate) to write down and/or practice your response so that you are ready the next time one happens to or around you.

- Reread the institutional ways to reduce microaggressions on pages 52-53. Come up with one more way to reduce microaggressions at each level at your institution.

- What does bullying look like in your sphere of influence? How similar or different is that from the list on page 57?

- What would it take to reduce bullying in your sphere of influence? At the individual level? At the systemic level?

Cultural Shift Challenge

This is an opportunity to do something! On your own, with a few colleagues, or in a departmental or unit meeting, discuss one or more of the steps below that you (individually and/or collectively) can take to start to improve the culture in your sphere of influence.

1. On a scale of 1-10, how welcoming is the climate in your sphere of influence? Now go ask five other people who you think will be truthful with you who are in the same sphere of influence (your department, your school, college, or unit). Ask one person you consider to be "above" you, one person "below" you, one person who you consider a "peer," and ask two students. Ask each person to suggest one "low hanging fruit" way to improve climate.

2. Challenge yourself in the hallway or on your way across campus. Make eye contact, nod your head, and/ or greet anyone you pass for a day or a week.

3. Look at pages 42-49. Choose one DO to reduce microaggressions in your sphere of influence and try to DO it this week. Next week try another one.

4. Reread the institutional ways to reduce microaggressions on pages 52-53. Email your dean, director, provost, or president and professionally suggest the implementation of one of these strategies.

5. Choose one bullet from the ways to prevent bullying on pages 58-60. Implement it in the next week or two.

Food for Thought

We work at colleges and universities, places of learning. Reducing and removing microaggressions and bullying is first and foremost an educational practice. Removing these actions from our organizations promotes a welcoming and inclusive climate thus allowing faculty, staff, and students to thrive. Below is a list of readings to continue your learning in these areas.

Harvard Business Review articles related to workplace culture and diversity programs:

Beshears, John, and Francesca Gino. "Leaders as Decision Architects." *Harvard Business Review,* May 2015, pp. 2-12.

Bohnet, Iris and Gardiner Morse. "Designing a bias-free organization: It's easier to change your processes than your people. An interview with Iris Bohnet." *Harvard Business Review,* July-August 2016, pp. 63-67.

Dobbin. Frank, and Alexandra Kalev. "Why diversity programs fail and what works better." *Harvard Business Review,* July-August 2016, pp. 52-60.

Dr. Derald Sue, et. al.—key books about micro-aggressions:

Sue, D. W., et al. "Racial microaggressions in everyday life: Implications for clinical practice." *American Psychologist, 62,* 2007, pp. 271-286. DOI: 10. 1037/0003-066X.62.4.271

Sue, D. W. *Microaggressions in everyday life: Race, Gender, and Sexual orientation.* Hoboken, NJ: Wiley, 2010.

Torino, G. C. (Ed), et al. *Microaggression theory: Influence and implications.* Hoboken, NJ: Wiley, 2018.

Drs. Gary and Ruth Namie—key books on workplace bullying:

Namie, G, and R. Namie. *The Bully-Free Workplace: Stop Jerks, Weasels, and Snakes from Killing Your Organization.* Hoboken, NJ : Wiley, 2011.

Namie, G, and R. Namie. *Bullyproof yourself at work! Personal strategies to stop the hurt from harassment.* Work Doctor, 1999.

MYRON R. ANDERSON AND KATHRYN S. YOUNG

CHAPTER 2: THE 4-WAY IMPLEMENTATION MODEL

SUMMARY

Chapter 2 details the relationship between micro-aggressions, bullying, and campus climate. It introduces a useful conceptual tool called the 4-Way Implementation Model that campuses can use to examine their own policies and programs in the name of improving campus climate. This chapter explains how to think about an institution's policies and programs through four interrelated lenses: systemic, individual, proactive, and reactive. The tool can be used for short-term and long-term planning of new policies and programs as well. This chapter shares examples of institutional policies and programs that address each of the four areas. The end of the chapter has a series of worksheets that an institution can use to map its own policies and processes using the 4-Way Implementation Model.

Introduction

Microaggressions and bullying in higher education can be reduced through understanding, examining, and then developing proactive and reactive campus climate policies and programs. This chapter details the 4-Way Implementation Model, a multifaceted guide that allows for a college or university to take a comprehensive look at their policies and programs in order to align and maximize effectiveness toward improved campus climate. Improved campus climate involves a reduction in microaggressions and in bullying.

The **4-Way Implementation Model** is a framework to inventory your institution's program activity to ensure that you are covering the systemic, proactive, individual, and reactive landscape of your institution. It is our experience that an institution should have a ratio of 60% systemic and proactive to 40% individual and reactive program activity to move the needle for improving campus climate. Most institutions have this in reverse, and some have 70% of their programming individual and reactive and 30% systemic and proactive. It is easy to fall into this inverted percentage, because it is easier to see the individual and reactive programs and the initial impact of them.

However, a greater implementation of systemic and proactive policies and programs will have greater impact, because they can be repeated over a longer period, and because they can be implemented through personnel and organizational priorities that take place at colleges and universities.

The Model

The model on the next page indicates a relationship between each of the components as well as across components.

This chapter explains each of the terms, provides examples, and shows how an individual program or policy can often be proactive *and* reactive, and they can be focused on individuals *or* systems, depending on the situation.

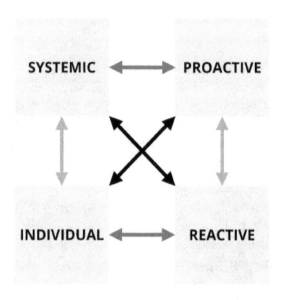

The 4-Way Implementation Model allows institutions to examine current policies and programs to identify which systemic programs and policies focus on improving campus climate. These proactive policies and programs are designed to identify issues before they occur, or in their infancy, to allow time to create resolutions that will prevent irreparable harm. These policies and programs are often indirectly related to reducing microaggressions and bullying on campus. Reactive policies and programs are designed to react to an issue already taking place with the goal to reduce harm. These policies and programs directly relate to the reduction and/or removal of microaggressions and bullying at an institution.

The 4-Way Implementation Model can be used to monitor the percentages of systemic, individual, reactive, and proactive policies and programs, and it can be used to identify gaps so that institutions can create new, effective programs and policies that move the climate improvement needle. Institutions can also use the 4-Way Implementation Model to measure the comprehensiveness and effectiveness of long-term and short-term policies and programs that are meant to combat microaggressions and bullying on campus.

Definitions

Diversity means the mix of identity-based differences that may impact an interaction, always depending on the context. The interactions of these differences in an institution impact the ability to meet individual or group goals, the ability to effectively meet intercultural challenges, safety, cost, legality, etc.

What differences matter in the institutional context?

- Those that impact a group's or an individual's sense of psychological and physical safety.

- Those that impact a group's or an individual's ability to solve problems, learn, and lead.

- Those that impact a group's or an individual's ability to strive for their personal best, to attain a leadership position, or to work well in a group.

Inclusion means highlighting differences in a way that increases contributions and opportunities for everyone. It happens when people work together effectively, and their cultural experiences and differences are valued.

As you seek to inventory what programs and policies you have that support diversity, equity, and inclusion (DEI), as well as what gaps you have in DEI, take a minute to take stock of your institution:

What are some differences that might impact (positively, negatively, or both) your sphere of influence (i.e., department, unit, school, college)?

How does your institution work to make those differences thrive in your context (inclusion)?

Systemic means primarily programs and policies, but it also includes processes, practices, and procedures that are embedded into the workings of an institution. When you look at these elements with a systemic lens, they are oftentimes offices, departments, or permanently funded positions that align with the core values and responsibilities of the institution. These elements have become so much a part of the institution's culture that they become a system within themselves. When a new office receives permanent funding and the productivity of that office is measured by outcomes related to the university's mission, you can say it has become a systemic part of improving campus climate. For example, a university creates a new Multicultural Center. At first, this center might be in response to a need, but when it is given permanent funding and a permanent location, it becomes a systemic part of the institution. Following are examples of some systemic programs which an institution can focus on to improve campus climate.

For each policy or program, ask yourself:

In what ways is this policy or program systemic? How can this policy or program be used to improve campus climate and reduce microaggressions and bullying? What's missing?

For example, FMLA is a systemic policy that is available to everyone at the institution. The FMLA, however, has been used at many institutions to support people who birth a child; meanwhile, some institutions tell faculty they cannot take FMLA time when they bring home an adopted child. People who adopt often feel institutionally microaggressed through policies like this, because their families "don't count." One way institutions can improve campus climate and reduce microaggressions is to examine their FMLA policies to see if they apply equitably to all families.

Consider how this program or policy is systemic:
- Family and Medical Leave Act (FMLA)
- Hiring policies
- Raises and merit increases
- Annual leave
- Faculty promotion and tenure
- Annual evaluations
- Holidays
- Interview processes
- Standing and official meetings
- Application processes

What are other systemic policies and practices at your institution?

Choose one unit or department. Take a moment to list all the policies and programs that you can recall. How much does each further diversity, equity, and inclusion (DEI)? How could they do an even better job at DEI?

Individual means the programs and policies that are connected to an individual's learning opportunities on campus. These can be one-on-one sessions with someone who has been accused of microaggressions or bullying. They can be campus-wide learning opportunities that individuals can opt into to learn about different identities.

These learning opportunities often focus on one identity category, defining it and exploring the academic and social needs of people with that identity. Programs and policies like these can be reactive or proactive and are often systemic.

TAKE FOR ACTION

For each program or policy ask yourself:

In what ways is this policy or program individual? How can this policy or program be used to improve campus climate and reduce microaggressions and bullying? What's missing? For example, the Center for Students with Disabilities (CSD) is systemic and applies to all students with documented disabilities. But it is also individual, because it is meant to meet the needs of specific individuals who have needs unique to themselves. This program can be used to improve campus climate by conducting audits of students' experiences to see if their accommodations are well-enacted and academically meaningful in classrooms.

These audits can also check if there are any "hot spots" where students' needs are met, but the emotional turmoil they experience in order to have their needs met takes away from their educational experience in certain classes. Then the CSD can target conversations with professors who put up emotional barriers to student success.

Consider how this program is for individual growth:

- The Center for Students with Disabilities (learning about and supporting students with disabilities)
- Undocupeers (learning about and supporting students who are undocumented)
- Power, Privilege, and Difference (learning about and supporting power and privilege on campus)
- Veteran's Boot Camp (learning about, supporting, and working with students who are veterans)
- CAMP (learning about and supporting students from migrant backgrounds)
- Fostering Success (learning about and supporting students who have experienced foster care)
- First Generation (learning about and supporting students who are the first in their families to go to college)
- My Brother's Keeper (learning about and supporting male students of color)
- LGBTQIA+ Center (learning about and supporting students who self-identify as gay, lesbian, bisexual, transgender, queer/questioning, …)

Proactive means programs and policies that are put in place to foster learning about diversity, equity, and inclusion in order to create a more positive campus climate—before problems happen. Hopefully, the campus becomes more welcoming as people become knowledgeable about what different groups need to thrive on campus—thus, leading to a reduction of microaggressions and bullying. The programs listed fit into the proactive category.

MYRON R. ANDERSON AND KATHRYN S. YOUNG

TAKE FOR ACTION

For each program or policy ask yourself:

In what ways is this policy or program proactive? How can this policy or program be used to improve campus climate and reduce microaggressions and bullying?

For example, a Center for Faculty Development is created as a proactive program to support faculty to improve and enhance their teaching. Many faculty do not have teaching experience prior to teaching at institutions of higher education and need support to be good educators. A CFD can have programs in place for new faculty to learn how to teach undergraduates and graduate students alike. There can be programs in place to encourage teaching from a Universal Design perspective and/or a Culturally Relevant perspective. Enacting proactive programs that enhance high-leverage teaching practices improves students' experiences in class because these practices help faculty address students as complex beings with complex identities, rather than focusing only on the content in their courses, thus reducing microaggressions that happen in classes.

Consider how this policy or program is proactive:

- A Center for Faculty Development (CFD)
- Support groups for new faculty and staff
- Affinity groups for faculty and staff
- Professional Learning Groups related to Diversity, Equity, and Inclusion
- Office of Equal Opportunity
- Professional Learning Conferences related to Diversity, Equity, and Inclusion
- Diversity Initiative Grants

- Supervisory Professional Development related to Diversity, Equity, and Inclusion
- Ombuds Office

And policies like:
- Clear and objective tenure guidelines
- Clear and objective hiring guidelines
- Clear and objective promotion guidelines
- Supportive bullying reporting policies

For example, clear and objective hiring guidelines are proactive policies, because they are created to be transparent to people seeking to be hired by the institution. Deans can require that hiring criteria use observable objectives in the hiring language, that these objectives apply to a wide pool of candidates, and can require departments to create rubrics related to these criteria that hiring committees complete individually prior to meeting with each other about candidates. This reduction in subjectivity reduces possible microaggressions that often occur within the hiring process.

Reactive refers to programs and policies that are put in place to foster learning about diversity, equity, and inclusion in order to create a more positive campus climate after microaggressions and/or bullying have occurred. When you look at these elements, they are oftentimes initiatives that arise after microaggressions or bullying have become public and people are asking for changes from the institution. They are not a part of the fabric of the institution and, as a response to an incident, typically carry a one-year shelf-life.

These initiatives include things like an Implicit Bias Task Force that arises after students of color accuse faculty of implicit bias in grading on social media, Civil Discourse Initiatives after a campus has experienced an invited speaker who was booed off stage, and a campus signage committee initiated by a group trying to change campus perceptions of who is included as a student in the campus community.

TAKE FOR ACTION

For each program or policy ask yourself:

In what ways is this policy or program reactive? How can this policy or program be used to improve campus climate and reduce microaggressions and bullying? What's missing?

For example, the Dean of Students Office is often tasked with talking to students about Code of Conduct violations. Therefore, they often act in a reactive capacity. The Dean of Students office can collect quarterly data about the types of offences they receive most often and build programs for students to stay informed about these sorts of misconduct from the outset of students' educational experiences. So, the Dean of Students takes their reactive data and creates proactive educational opportunities to reduce issues related to microaggressions and bullying on campus.

These offices and policies are often in charge of reacting to microaggressions and/or bullying in a public way.

Consider how these offices and policies are reactive:

Offices
- Ombuds Office
- Office of Student Life

- Dean of Students Office
- Office of Diversity and Inclusion
- Human Resources
- Equal Opportunity Office

Policies
- Referral and Complaint Processes
- Personnel Improvement Plans
- Bullying Policy
- Required, interactive workshops for individuals, departments, units, etc.
- One-on-one mediation
- Other institution-sanctioned interventions

Take a moment to think about programs and policies at your institution. Think about how comprehensive and effective your programs and policies are in efforts to improve campus climate. Campuses that are welcoming are better for recruitment and retention of faculty, staff, and students. Campuses that are welcoming are better able to respond to microaggressions and bullying. Campuses that are welcoming emotionally shore up people who work and learn there so that, when those same people experience microaggressions or bullying, they are better able to cope and can experience the discrimination with less intensity.

TAKE FOR ACTION

Ask yourself: How comprehensive are our programs and policies in regards to campus climate?

- Do our programs welcome all racial groups on campus?
- Do our programs welcome all gender groups on campus?
- Do our programs welcome all language groups on campus?
- Do our programs welcome all age groups on campus?
- Do our programs welcome all sexual orientations on campus?
- Do our programs welcome all religious groups on campus?
- Do our programs welcome all (dis)ability groups on campus?
- Do our programs welcome all types of students (traditional, transfer, non-traditional, etc.) on campus?
- What other groups do you need to think about specific to your campus?

How effective are our programs and policies in regards to campus climate?

- Do our programs improve campus climate according to internal and external measures? Examine each program and policy with this lens.
- Do we offer programs at a variety of cultural developmental levels, from novice to expert?

- Do we include diverse perspectives, even ones we disagree with, as long as they are supported by research?

What is missing? (Make sure to involve group representatives when answering these questions.)

- What groups or individuals have we heard from that feel disenfranchised?
- Why do they feel like they do not belong?
- What would belonging feel like to them?

Using the 4-Way Implementation Model to help evaluate program effectiveness

The 4-Way Implementation Model can also help your institution examine each of the programs and policies periodically to determine effectiveness of programs and also to determine gaps in policies and in programs that can be addressed.

When you are thinking about starting a new equity-focused program or policy, STOP! Before starting a new program or policy, START with the end in mind. Much like teaching a class, you must know why you want to do what you want to do and what success will look like before you even start planning. It's important to be able to measure success and share those measures with interested stakeholders. At some institutions, if you can't measure success, it did not happen and will lose its funding. Don't let that be the fate of your new equity-focused program or policy.

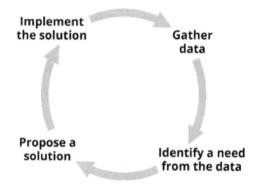

TAKE FOR ACTION

Equity-Focused Program or Policy Planning Tool:

1. What is the proposed program or policy?

2. What is the objective or desired outcome?

3. What steps will it take to get to that objective or outcome?

4. What needs to be in place (resources, staff, time, room, etc.) to even get to the first step?

5. How will you know when you have met your objective or outcome? What measures will you use?

Use an instructional design model that works for you and apply it to new policies and practices. One well-known instructional design model is the ADDIE Model:

Analyze

Design

Develop

Implement

Evaluate

Data driven decision-making is at the core higher education. You must find a way to align with current measurement strategies or develop new ones to measure success. Some easy ways to evaluate milestones at the beginning of a new program are to start with the numbers. How many people attend the first meeting? The second meeting? Each meeting until the end of the year? How many people keep coming back? How many new people are now attending? Attendance is a great first measure of interest in a program, and continued attendance is a good measure that the program is fulfilling a need. Then the program can develop other measures to internally evaluate its effectiveness based on approaching the desired outcomes.

An informal, internal rating tool

Use the following tool on your own, or with a steering committee with knowledge of the program, to list and internally and informally evaluate how a new or existing policy or program is meeting an agreed upon definition of equity and equity effectiveness for your institution.

TAKE FOR ACTION

Informal Internal Equity Assessment Tool (IIEAT)

Our Definition of Equity:

Our Definition of Equity Effectiveness:

Name of Policy or Program	Internal Equity Effectiveness Rating 0-5 (0 = not effective; 5 = very effective)	Improvement Ideas	Need for a Formal Effectiveness Tool (yes/ no)

Barometer checks – or climate audits

Use the 4-Way Implementation Model to conduct your own internal campus barometer check/ climate audit/ or gap analysis of barriers or resistance to improving campus climate. For each program you list on the worksheets in this chapter, you can apply assessment strategies (also found in this chapter) to those programs. Find out if the programs are really working like you think they are, and if not, gather information to make meaningful changes.

In addition to internal checks, institutions also need external checks on their climates. If your institution does not have a campus climate survey completed by an external third party every 2-5 years, we suggest you start one. This is like a wellness check-up or a physical with the doctor. You need to know how you are doing so that you can decide if you should do more of the same or make changes to improve the overall climate.

Climate surveys solicit opinions broadly related to the overall campus climate and help a campus to know how to better use its resources in the future. They assess:

- Job satisfaction and support from the institution to conduct job-related work
- Participation in institutional governance
- Attitudes toward diversity
- Feeling of comfort and belonging
- Treatment by various groups
- Inclusiveness of institutional workforce for multiple identity groups (e.g., age, race, gender, ethnicity, national origin, disabilities, sexual orientation, religion, etc.)

- Internal communication
- Career development, research, and scholarship
- The teaching environment
- Faculty, administration, and staff relations
- Professional development
- Collaboration
- Compensation, benefits, and work/life balance
- Supervisors, department chairs, and senior leadership
- Respect and appreciation
- Facilities
- Other related issues to your specific institution

How else do you know if your programs work?

Much as a barometer helps you see when the weather is going to change, institutions of higher education should incorporate a DEI assessment piece that aligns with the ongoing structural institutional assessment strategies rather than creating new ones wherever possible. Tying diversity data to large scale, already-valued assessment data uses resources wisely and gains credibility as the collection tool is already seen as valid and reliable. Someone in Human Resources or the Office of Diversity and Inclusion can take existing institutional data and apply an equity lens. This data is one of the first places that will alert you to changes in the climate and possible microaggressions and bullying taking place in a department or unit.

For example, if the institution collects data on how many faculty earn tenure, an inclusive-minded leader can then break that data down by race, gender, disability, etc. If they find that a certain racial group is earning tenure at lower rates in a department, they can investigate to see what the climate is like for people from different racial groups in the department. They can learn if microaggressions or bullying are impacting the tenure process and people's ability to feel safe and productive in the space where they work. If the institution collects trend data from the Ombuds office, an inclusive-minded leader can then break that data down by race, gender, disability, etc. If they find that students in a certain department are all staying away from a certain professor's course, they can investigate to see what the climate is like for students in that professor's course. They can learn if microaggressions or bullying are impacting the students' learning experience and ability to feel safe and productive in the classroom. If HR collects Exit Interview data, an inclusive-minded leader can then break that data down by race, gender, disability, etc. If they find that staff in a certain department are leaving at higher rates than from other departments, they can investigate to see what the climate is like for staff in that department as opposed to other departments. They can learn if microaggressions or bullying are impacting staff's work experience and their ability to feel safe and productive in the space where they work. An equity lens can be applied to any systemic assessments used at the institution. Other places where you might collect data and disaggregate by race, gender, disability, etc. are: complaints filed with any units within the institution, EO complaints, Employee Relations complaints, police reports, and student code of conduct violations.

When executing large-scale assessments through an equity lens, all senior leadership should be on board. Buy-in is important. You might have to "sell" them on the idea (See "Get the Boss to Buy In" by Ashford and Detert, *Harvard*

Business Review, 2015). The process should be completely transparent. They need to know the purpose, the timeline, how results will be shared and with whom, and be able to know when they will receive reports on future progress that came about because of the results of the assessments through an equity lens. Even small scale, internal, formative assessments through an equity lens need stakeholders to know the purpose, the timeline, how results will be shared and with whom, and be able to know when they will receive reports on future progress that came about because of the results of the assessments.

Use the following tool to make a plan for incorporating an equity lens into existing assessments.

TAKE FOR ACTION	
	Name of Assessment
Purpose	
Timeline	
People to share results with	
Format of sharing results	
Future programs and policies	

How often should you check if programs and policies actually improve the climate?

First, it is important to say that most institutions do not check on their climate as often as they check on other Key Performance Indicators (KPI). They check on climate when climate surveys happen—every 2-3 years—or when an institutional crisis is underway, and people are demanding accountability. As with most other institutional functions, being proactive and systemic about checking on climate is way more helpful than only checking when damage has been done.

Institutions should examine the data annually or at similar times to when the larger data set is being analyzed. For example, if Exit Interview Data is shared annually, then breaking it down by race, gender, disability, etc. should be analyzed and shared annually, as well. Departmentally, chairs and deans should examine more local data semester by semester to see if there is an uptick in absenteeism – absenteeism on the rise is a good indication of climate problems in a department or complaints about specific staff members or specific faculty.

Chairs and Directors can take this one step further and, like instructors who offer mid-semester course evaluations in order to change course and better meet students' needs, chairs can evaluate their local climate mid-semester as well.

TAKE FOR ACTION

Mid-Semester Departmental Check-In

I enjoy going to work.
Strongly Agree| Agree | Neutral | Disagree | Strongly Disagree

I feel valued in the department.
Strongly Agree| Agree | Neutral | Disagree | Strongly Disagree

I have the resources I need to get my work done.
Strongly Agree| Agree | Neutral | Disagree | Strongly Disagree

I have the time I need to get my work done.
Strongly Agree| Agree | Neutral | Disagree | Strongly Disagree

The chair is there to make things better for me.
Strongly Agree| Agree | Neutral | Disagree | Strongly Disagree

I get adequate support from the chair if I have a problem.
Strongly Agree| Agree | Neutral | Disagree | Strongly Disagree

Would you like me to come talk with you about your results? If so, include your name below.

For departments where you think people will write in feedback, the following tool might be useful.

Mid-Semester Departmental Check-In
(from the Chair or Director)

What am I doing that is helping you get your job done?

What am I doing that is getting in the way of getting your job done?

How can I better support you?

Would you like me to come talk with you about your results? If so, include your name below.

Tools like these can also be adapted for formative use with new or existing programs so that the program be nimble enough to pivot to meet the needs of its constituents.

MYRON R. ANDERSON AND KATHRYN S. YOUNG

Who should be in charge of barometer checks?

Colleges and universities must balance internal and external evaluation of programs and policies. It is sometimes difficult to decide who should conduct these audits. These decisions break down into two questions: Is the evaluation of climate formative or summative? And how much trust is there? If there is no trust, no type of internal evaluation will be useful. People will not be honest and may not fill out climate surveys.

How valuable is it to work with an outside entity for climate assessments?

The four reasons to use a 3rd party for climate and other DEI related assessment data:

- Trust
- Budget
- Scale
- Anonymity

If you have the budget, utilize a third party when conducting such assessments. This promotes anonymity, delivers objective analysis, and is best in the case of a large-scale survey. The third party should review the data before sharing it with the leadership, who is then free to also review the data. Hopefully, formative climate assessments, like mid-semester climate evaluations, can be completed internally and informally. But if a department is experiencing a toxic climate, even this sort of feedback might best be collected by an outside party.

An outside entity often leads to truthful, authentic results and a rich data set, which allows you to have robust information to inform the institution's thinking in regards to developing processes and policy.

Trust – By using a third party to implement and analyze the data, you create an environment of objectivity where the participants can see from the onset that their voice will be heard and that the data received will be truthful. This is important because having this understanding at the onset will lead to increased participation.

Budget – There are many companies that perform campus climate surveys, and there are some independent consultants that do this work, as well. The cost of executing a campus climate survey can vary, ranging from low-cost, standard templates to high-cost, customized surveys. It is recommended that you do your research and have a clear understanding of the goals and outcomes of your survey. Then align them with your budget and the third party who will be administering your survey. The takeaway is to strive for a third-party survey process that fits your budget.

Scale – It is important to have a survey that can be executed, analyzed, and presented to your institution in a way appropriate to the scale of your institution. It is important to be timely, accurate, and transparent throughout the process. The third party who executes your survey must have the capacity to deliver on all aspects. There are many moving parts to implementing a campus climate survey and having elements of this process not meet campus expectations can start to erode the trust factor.

Anonymity – Anonymity goes "hand-in-glove" with trust. If your goal is to hear your campus community's authentic voice then your climate survey process must be designed to protect anonymity. Having a third party execute, analyze, and deliver the objective analysis of the survey is the most important step. However, within the survey process there should be additional anonymity protectors (i.e., if you are a part of a small department with less than five employees, your responses will be rolled up to the next reporting level to collect your responses and protect your anonymity). Another anonymity protector is for the third party to redact specific names and comments that people intentionally or unintentionally disclose in the open-ended question section. Finally, there needs to be careful thought in collecting demographic data so that this information protects anonymity.

Trust, scale, anonymity, and aligning them with your budget should be at the forefront of the climate survey process. Incorporating these elements with the overarching goal of hearing everyone's authentic voice will increase your survey response rates and provide you with a rich data set to use to develop programs and policies to improve your campus climate.

Note: Trust is the biggest barrier. If you do not have much trust in the organization, you will need to lean more toward third-party involvement in data assessment related to climate.

What do you do when there is no budget for working with a third party in your climate assessment?

If you do not have the budget to commit to a third party, convene a group of constituents from across campus and ask that group to develop a plan for trust, scale, and anonymity. Then share that plan with the larger constituent group to make sure that the campus community feels trusting of the process.

TAKE FOR ACTION

Questions to think about, related to trust, scale, and anonymity:

- How much would people trust an internal climate survey at our institution?
- What are some reasons people might not believe the results of an internal survey?
- What can we do to increase trust in the results?
- Who is going to be responsible for creating and disseminating the survey?
- Who is going to analyze the findings?
- Who gets to see the results first? Can they ask for changes? If so, of what sort?
- What are you doing to do about identifiable information in responses to the survey?
- How will the results be shared with the campus community?

- What resources are needed to complete a campus survey?
- Are there resources that can be used to support this endeavor?
- Where are the resources coming from?
- What is the timeline from creation of the survey to dissemination of results?
- How will you preserve individual responses while also protecting anonymity?

Who should see the results of barometric climate data?

All appropriate leadership areas should receive their area's data and should be charged with using the data to improve the climate. This will allow for the entire organization to move in a positive direction. If the data remains centralized or hidden the movement to improve climate will be very slow or nonexistent. If meaningful action to improve climate is not taking place, people will lose interest and stop trusting in the process of collecting data to make systemic improvements.

Should you make the findings public?

This one is easy. If the climate audit is not about a personnel issue, then the results should be made public to all institutional constituents.

Awareness through Education + Policy Support = Reduction of Microaggressions and Bullying

When attempting to reduce microaggressions and bullying throughout a campus it is important that each institution's framework has both systemic and individual paths. Having this dual approach allows for an institution to be both proactive and reactive in the development and implementation of policies and programs that promote equity and reduce microaggressions and bullying. Both paths are needed to move the needle. Additionally, because of the fleeting nature of microaggressions and the entrenched nature of bullying, the better the institution educates faculty, administrators, staff, and students ahead of time, the greater the self-reduction of these behaviors. And the greater the ability for an organization to intervene quickly when microaggressions and bullying happen, maximizing the reduction of microaggressions and bullying on campus.

More and more institutions are adopting workplace bullying policies which provide a corrective action framework to remove bullying actions from the workplace if the education strategy is not successful. Higher education has not adopted policies to execute corrective action when someone received a microaggression because microaggressions are much more contested than bullying and much harder to prove. Microaggression reduction relies on education.

Self-correction as part of that educating process is an important element in reducing microaggressions and bullying. If you are not aware that your actions are microaggressions or bullying, then you do not have a chance to self-correct. Except for the most egregious cases, people must have the opportunity to self-correct.

Education about microaggressions and bullying reduces the behavior. At Metropolitan State University of Denver (MSU Denver), we experienced a 15% reduction in workplace bullying (as evidenced by changes to campus climate survey data) after we implemented an education program and corresponding workplace bullying policy. We also saw similar reductions in microaggressions across campus.

The first part of this chapter focused on describing the 4-Way Implementation Model and offering examples of programs and policies found on many campuses. The next part shares examples of successful policies and practice at MSU Denver in Denver, Colorado.

Specific examples of helpful programs and policies

We support a parallel approach where you implement a comprehensive microaggression and anti-bullying education program as well as develop and implement an institutional bullying policy to address the climate systemically, proactively, individually, and reactively, accelerating the improvement of your campus climate. Following, we provide several examples from MSU Denver to share real efforts to improve campus climate at a Colorado university.

Proactive and Systemic Policies and Programs

Tenure Track Supper Club

Senior faculty of color voiced concerns over the differing rate of African-American faculty (65%) and white faculty (95%) receiving tenure at MSU Denver. Drawing on the positive outcomes of mentorship in realizing other significant milestones, the Office of Diversity and Inclusion led the development of the "Tenure Track Supper Club," a mentorship program for pre-tenure African-American faculty. At the onset, the program was piloted for African-American faculty, then grew to include faculty of color, then faculty from other underrepresented groups, then welcomed all tenure-track faculty to join the program.

The Tenure Track Supper Club (TTSC) is a faculty retention program that relies on mentorship and building community as the foundation to increase the retention of underrepresented faculty. Retention of underrepresented faculty leads to improved campus climate for faculty, staff, and students. As a faculty of color who has gone through the tenure process, and has benefitted from mentorship, as well as having become a senior leader who has developed and participated in many mentorship programs, I (Dr. Myron Anderson) became the ideal person to lead this initiative at MSU Denver.

Earning tenure is an achievement milestone as well. One might argue that the complexity, pressure, and unknown within the process is as equal if not greater to other academic milestones. With this understanding and that of being a person of color who has gone through the tenure-track process, I realized there was no "How to Earn Tenure 101" class or program for junior faculty that would provide greater understanding on how to earn tenure. We needed a mentorship program specifically designed to demystify the tenure process, build community, sharpen tenure achievement skills, and educate the leadership involved in the tenure process, more specifically the journey faculty of color take to earn tenure.

The TTSC has a three-tier approach that: 1. Introduces tenure-track faculty to tenured faculty who serve as mentors and provide insights into the hidden steps in the tenure process, 2. Introduces tenure-track faculty to a "How to Earn Tenure" curriculum, including the "9 Insights to Earning Tenure" from *Winning Tenure Without Losing Your Soul* by Kerry Dr. Ann Rockquemore and Dr. Tracey Laszloffy (2008), a text that grounds the processes and experiences in theory for evidence-based planning, and 3. Provides a space for the organic building of community, allowing for just-in-time and longitudinal support throughout the tenure-track journey.

The TTSC provides a safe environment to share knowledge with new faculty and, in turn, allows faculty to enlighten administrators in promotion and tenure review leadership positions about the subliminal inequities in the tenure process that are experienced by faculty in the classroom and in the office. These inequities range from differently valuing areas of scholarly activity, to having different expectations for in-service days, to requirements around advising, to daily interactions with students, other faculty, and staff at the institution. This three-fold education environment (mentorship, knowledge sharing, and community building) arms the faculty (of color) with additional tools to combat received inequities. However, just as important, the TTSC educates the university system, namely the decision-makers in the promotion and tenure process, about inequities experienced by faculty of color and provides an avenue for removing inequities from the tenure process.

This program promotes collaboration from multiple fronts and promotes inclusive efforts to remove inequity and promote excellence, thus increasing the diversity of the faculty. Today, African Americans are earning tenure at 95% and white faculty are earning tenure at 95%. This mentorship program is an example of a reactive program that quickly became a systemic and proactive effort designed to increase the diversity of the tenured faculty, which then promoted a diverse and inclusive institution, which then promoted a welcoming climate for everyone.

CREATE YOUR OWN

If you want to create your own Tenure Track Supper Club, here are some tips to make it successful:

1. Find out your university's policy on affinity groups. For example: Are you allowed to host a women's only event—an event where anyone can come, but it is clear you will be speaking about women's issues, prioritizing women's voices, and purposefully inviting women, etc.

2. Poll people who could benefit from a supper club to learn what they would want in a supper club.

3. Once you know the policy, find out what on-going funding and rooming you can secure for the group.

4. Decide on facilitators and a schedule.

5. Decide on an anchor text to support conversation throughout the year.

6. Develop a mentoring pool of senior administrators and faculty to support the club.

MYRON R. ANDERSON AND KATHRYN S. YOUNG

As you read through the description of the TTSC, what was on your mind?

1. What would have been an ideal supper club for you when you first started in academia?
2. What are the benefits in having a race-based supper club, like one for only African-American faculty?
3. What are the drawbacks in having a race-based supper club, like one for only African-American faculty?
4. Do you think including other faculty from under-represented backgrounds added to the experience or took away from it? For whom? What about when the supper club changed again to include all new faculty? Did that newest change add to the experience or take away from it? For whom?
5. What might be some push back (implementation challenges and opportunities) you would anticipate from administration? Work ahead to imagine their concerns and have answers ready.

A note on the concept of push back

We'd like to reflect for a moment on the concept of push back. We all know that there will be some people more or less willing to try out new ideas, practices, and policies. Often, these people have a (legitimate concern) even if they have not figured out how to voice it yet. We like to reframe the idea of push back to "implementation challenges and opportunities" because, when someone is reticent, they are thinking through implementation challenges (conceptual and/or practical). Their concerns deserve to be considered and responded to—often these moments of push back can turn into opportunities to make the idea, program, or policy stronger by considering these implementation questions.

Administrative push back—implementation challenges and opportunities—can come in many forms as the goal for everyone is to provide a safe and welcoming environment for faculty, staff, and students to thrive. The administrative collective brings professional perspectives and specialists from various areas (i.e. legal, risk management, student services, academic affairs, diversity, finances, development, marketing and communication, and the president, to name a few). These collective perspectives that are typically engaged in decision-making come into play when developing and implementing campus-wide programs especially if they have a direct impact on people, the environment and their relationship to policy and procedures within.

Administrative push back - implementation challenges and opportunities - typically come from lack of knowledge, risk management, budget, and possible amplification of these issues if brought to light. Look at the following in relation to the concept of creating a Tenure Track Supper Club and think through answers to these concerns.

Knowledge:

1. **Disbelief** - Is this program really necessary?

2. **See no evil** - I think your program will make things worse because everything is fine as is. Do not fix a problem if it is not already stated as a problem.

3. **Deflect** - Programs like these are not needed. There are too many "snowflakes" who just have to learn what work is like.

4. **Denial** - This is not a good use of funds. No one needs this program.

5. **Acceptance** - People will just learn these things on their own. This is the norm.

Risk and Budget:

1. **Required action** - Once we identify that we have an issue, we are then required to take action.

2. **Resources** - Do we have the resources to take action individually and systemically?

3. **Repetition** - We already have an on-boarding process; no need not develop an additional program or policy.

4. **Legality** - There is no federal law to make us do this.

5. **Amplification** - Having a TTSC will be a place to air small problems. But when listened to in these spaces, these problems will become big and needlessly overload our system with unnecessary complaints.

When preparing to embark down the important climate improvement road, it is extremely important that you do your homework and have a complete understanding of new programs and policies along with their effects on an organization's climate and their ability to connect your solution with the documented problem. Your ultimate goal is to communicate to the administration that micro-aggressions and bullying are real, and they are taking place at your institution right now. Proactive programs can create the culture needed to lessen the effects of microaggressions and bullying and help improve the overall climate.

Supervisory Training Program

To foster the development of diversity champions throughout the institution, the Office of Diversity and Inclusion developed a 90-minute interactive workshop on diversity and inclusion that's woven into a mandatory two-day supervisor training program for all faculty and staff who supervise employees. The Diversity and Inclusion workshop is designed to introduce the concepts of cultural identity, implicit bias, microaggressions, and inclusive excellence. This interactive session breaks supervisors into groups to share their own experiences of microaggressions on campus. These experiences are incorporated into a larger discussion on diversity, inclusion, and equity and their relationship to campus climate.

The workshops also covered topics like the Family Medical Leave Act (FMLA), hiring processes, succession planning, etc. This administrative decision squarely places issues of cultural competence within the broader framework of supervisors' responsibilities in their leadership. It asks them to be problem solvers for diversity-related questions linked to the goals and mission of the institution.

This training is an example of a systemic and proactive program that provides knowledge and tools for supervisors to improve campus climate.

CREATE YOUR OWN

If you want to create your own Supervisory Training Program, here are some tips to make it successful:

1. Find out the agenda for the current professional development (PD) for supervisors. What topics are covered?
2. If there is no Diversity Equity and Inclusion (DEI) component, ask to speak with the person who plans the PD.
3. Talk about the need for integrating DEI into the PD, even if there is stand-alone DEI professional development. Leaders need to know that DEI is part of supervision.
4. With the current facilitator (usually from HR), co-plan the DEI component and make sure to link the content to the rest of a supervisor's roles.
5. Deliver the DEI component.
6. Have participants complete a post-survey about the integration of the DEI component and improve as needed.

YOUR THOUGHTS...

As you read through the description of the Supervisory Training Program, what was on your mind?

1. What would have been an ideal PD program for you when you first started in a supervisory/ leadership role?
2. What are DEI topics at your institution that you think all leaders need to know?

3. What are the benefits in having DEI incorporated into a general supervisory PD program?
4. What are the drawbacks in having DEI incorporated into a general supervisory PD program?
5. What might be some implementation challenges and opportunities you would anticipate from administration? Work ahead to imagine their concerns and have answers ready.

HIGHER EDUCATION DIVERSITY SUMMIT

The Higher Education Diversity Summit (HEDS) is an annual campus initiative that promotes and increases professional development opportunities through the lens of inclusive excellence. HEDS acts as a catalyst to understand diverse experiences on campus and provides an additional opportunity to raise the cultural intelligence of the institution. It opens communication about how to be supportive to groups and individuals who traditionally feel marginalized at institutions of higher education. HEDS educates the campus in the areas of implicit bias, diversity and inclusion, LGBTQIA+ issues, disability, race, gender, socioeconomic status, ageism, organizational climate, microaggressions, workplace bullying, and much more.

This conference keeps the diversity and inclusion conversation at the top of the institution's agenda and provides dialog via education related to equity objectives in order to prompt space for conversations about change throughout the institution. This program is an example of a systemic and proactive approach to increase the cultural competence of your university.

CREATE YOUR OWN

If you want to create your own HEDS program, here are some tips to make it successful:

1. Find out what conferences related to DEI already happen at your institution.
2. List the gaps that exist.
3. Convene a steering committee to plan and market the event.
4. Consider the goals for the conference. Use these goals to plan the type of sessions, topics of sessions, and who you hope will present.
5. Send out the call for proposals.
6. Have your HEDS conference.

YOUR THOUGHTS

As you read through the description of HEDS, what was on your mind?

1. What would be an ideal DEI conference at your institution?
2. Who would you like to see present, and who would you like to see attend the event? What would it take?
3. How will you know if this conference makes more space for DEI conversations?
4. What might be some challenges and opportunities you would anticipate from administration? Work ahead to imagine their concerns and have answers ready.

FACULTY FELLOW

The Office of Diversity and Inclusion receives funding from the institution to secure a faculty member's time, in the equivalent of one course release per semester, to work with the office on both systemic and individual projects to positively impact the university in the area of diversity and inclusion. The Chief Diversity Officer administers the institution's internal search process to identify and confirm faculty to serve in this role.

This Fellow is charged with being a liaison between administration and faculty and lends scholarly expertise to the office. The Fellow's responsibilities change as the needs of the institution change. The Faculty Fellow has been co-responsible for developing and conducting professional development on and off campus, co-writing articles for academic consumption, and for participating in a variety of institution-wide initiatives related to diversity and inclusion. Contributions from the faculty fellow position have been proven to be systemic, proactive, individual, and reactive - all contributing to improved climate at the university. There are plans to extend the position from one faculty from the institution to one faculty from each college or school so that each Fellow can reflect the DEI needs of their constituent group and be a spokesperson for their groups.

CREATE YOUR OWN

If you want to create a Faculty Fellow at your institution, here are some tips to make it successful:

1. Talk with someone in leadership or the whole leadership team at the institution about the need for not only an administrator to encourage a positive campus culture but also a faculty member to act as a diversity champion.
2. Write up a job description for someone in this role.
3. Conduct an internal search for this person.
4. Hire the person and co-write the plan for working together for the year. Make sure the plan draws on this person's research, presentation, and content strengths.
5. Work with the person on institution-wide programs.
6. Evaluate the plan and the person's work on the plan to make sure the person is able to complete the charge.

YOUR THOUGHTS....

As you read through the description of the Faculty Fellow, what was on your mind?

1. What role could a Faculty Fellow play at your institution?
2. What would be the benefits of a faculty versus a staff member in this role?
3. What would be the drawbacks of a faculty versus a staff member in this role?
4. What might be some challenges and opportunities you would anticipate from administration? Work ahead to imagine their concerns and have answers ready.

STUDENT ORGANIZATIONS TO PROMOTE SENSE OF BELONGING

Every institution has organizations to help students feel welcome, supported, and like they belong at the institution. Research has shown that students who have a stronger sense of belonging persist longer in higher education and that students who have a strong sense of belonging are better able to handle discrimination that they experience at the institution.

At MSU Denver, we have many programs to help students find people they are most comfortable spending time with and learning from, since most of their time on campus is spent with students who are different from them in meaningful ways. Some are part of national programs and others were created in-house to support specific needs for specific groups of students. Some student organizations we have include: "Brother 2 Brother" (and a new program called "Sister 2 Sister"), a national mentorship program to promote a sense of belonging and provide tools for young men of color to navigate the academic environment; CAMP, a national mentorship program to promote a sense of belonging and provide tools for students from migrant backgrounds; and Roadrunners First, a local mentorship program to promote a sense of belonging and provide tools for first-generation students.

CREATE YOUR OWN

If you want to create more student organizations that focus on sense of belonging at your institution, here are some tips to make it successful:

1. Talk to students about what they think is missing.
2. See if what students want exists at other institutions to use as a model.
3. Develop a steering committee to think through the design component (ADDIE from earlier in this chapter).
4. Develop measurable outcomes for this new group.
5. Recruit champions to advocate for the group.
6. Start!

YOUR THOUGHTS....

As you read through the description of student organizations related to sense of belonging, what was on your mind?

1. What student group do you think would benefit from having an organization to support their sense of belonging that does not already exist on campus?
2. What would be the benefits of specific student organizations versus one organization to help all students feel a sense of belonging?
3. What would be the drawbacks of specific student organizations versus one organization to help all students feel a sense of belonging?
4. What might be some challenges and opportunities you would anticipate from administration? Work ahead to imagine their concerns and have answers ready.

Conversation Circles

Some institutions proactively make time and space for students to speak with leadership about a variety of topics. This might include talking with leadership about diversity on campus, ways to make the campus more inclusive, and ideas students have for new programs. Students browse the list of conversation circle topics and who from leadership will be attending and can then choose to join the circle they have the most interest in. Circles often meet at more informal spaces, like coffee shops or restaurants, and might even have an interactive component like playing games or coloring together while chatting about important diversity-related institutional issues.

People who are supposed to be the beneficiaries of programs and policies on campus need to have informal spaces to speak to how welcoming the campus feels for them. Circles support the 4-Way Implementation Model as they often help leadership see what they are missing by hearing from the people who are supposed to be supported by systemic and proactive programs and policies but might not always feel the support that is intended. They act as a sounding board and are also places where leadership can learn new and innovative ways to better support students, staff, and faculty—ways that those in charge of creating programs and policies might not have thought of for the campus community.

TAKE FOR ACTION

If you want to create conversation circles related to diversity issues at your institution, here are some tips to make it successful:

1. Talk to students about what topics they think need to be listening to more closely. Ask for specifics if generalities are shared. So, if students say we need to talk more about race, then ask, "What about race? Which races? What is actively not talked about in relation to race? Etc."

2. Talk with senior leadership to find people to attend each Conversation Circle. Explain to people in senior leadership what you are asking of them, what role you expect them to play, what sort of feedback you want from them, how they can act to best listen, etc.

3. Develop a steering committee to think through the design component (ADDIE from earlier in this chapter). This steering committee should come from different departments and different roles at the institution. Make sure to include people from all the schools and colleges, as well as people who can represent staff, student and faculty perspectives.

4. Find welcoming spaces and activities to complete during each Conversation Circle. Ask people where they would like to meet and then provide a variety of spaces. Classrooms and spaces in the library may feel very welcoming for some and very alienating for others. Think carefully through the spaces where you seek to hold these events, so the space itself does not drive people away. Think also about activities you might have and if they are inclusive and diverse.

5. Start!

As you read through the description of Conversation Circles, what was on your mind?

1. What student groups do you think would benefit from having Conversation Circles?
2. What would be the benefits of Conversation Circles?
3. What would be the drawbacks of Conversation Circles?
4. Could the same idea of listening to students be implemented in a better way at your institution? How?
5. What might be some challenges and opportunities you would anticipate from administration? Work ahead to imagine their concerns and have answers ready.

These programs are examples of systemic-proactive initiatives that have both short-term and long-term impacts on implementing activities that led to positive changes to our campus climate as evidenced by changes reflected in our climate surveys. MSU Denver used this model and achieved a 15% reduction in bullying activity, received an exceptional rating in university pride from university employees by ModernThinks "Great Colleges to Work for" program, increased African Americans earning tenure by 30%, and developed an overall increase in the university's cultural competence - all because of promoting a strong sense of belonging and improving the overall campus climate.

Using the 4-Way Implementation Model as a guide will allow you to properly inventory your policies and programs and regulate their percentages generating the greatest yield in improving your campus climate. It can also help you spark conversations, such as figuring out when a situation calls for systemic versus individual change, proactive versus reactive change, etc.

Reactive and individual policies and programs

Despite all the systems in place to reduce microaggressions through systemic and proactive policies and programs, campuses will still contend with microaggressions and bullying. Each institution needs a first point of contact to respond to referrals from organizational units that work directly with issues related to microaggressions and bullying daily. The first point of contact might be Counseling Center Hotlines, Climate Intervention Response Teams, Human Resources, the Ombuds Office, the Equal Opportunity Office, Restorative Justice Offices, Student Life Offices, and more.

If a climate issue arises via referrals from one of these units and/or the complaint process at MSU Denver, the point of contact then meets with the person who entered the referral (most often a faculty or staff member) to decide a course of action. When deemed appropriate, they will provide an interactive workshop on microaggressions or bullying based on what is needed. These workshops are often facilitated by faculty or administrators from the Office of Diversity and Inclusion or a similar office.

Other microaggression and bullying issues are resolved through one-on-one mediation or through other university-sanctioned interventions respectively.

A REMINDER: REACTIVE AND INDIVIDUAL PROGRAMS ARE NOT ENOUGH

Often, when an institution is trying to move the needle in creating a welcoming environment, the mistake they make is focusing their efforts on individual-reactive programs and not on systemic-proactive policies and programs. This is natural because newly created and visible programs receive an immediate reaction; however, the positive effect of that reaction is typically not sustainable. The long-term effect of individual-reactive programs is not realized.

We often equate the effects of individual-reactive programs to a campfire analogy. When you build a campfire using paper (individual-reactive programs) as your main heating source, it creates a big fire, but it only lasts for a short time. Once the paper burns out, the fire is gone. This often is the case with situational program activity. In the moment, the program produces a good amount of heat. However, once the program is complete, the heat starts to leave. The effectiveness of the program reduces, and things gravitate back to the status quo.

Continuing with the campfire analogy, systemic-proactive programs are more like logs. They produce excellent heat and are sustainable, because the policies and programs implemented will have a long-lasting effect, like the heat from a glowing log. The more systemic-proactive policies and programs that an organization has, designed to reduce and remove microaggressions and bullying, the greater the improvement in your institution's campus climate.

If you find that you have more of your programs falling into the individual and reactive areas, then you'll see that you have a lot of paper in the fire. It's going to burn strong for

115

a minute, but this sort of fire might not be sustainable. If you have more proactive and systemic policies and practice, you'll see you have more logs on the fire. They will burn longer and stronger in regards to the institution's campus climate goals.

How do you know when a situation calls for a proactive versus a reactive strategy?

Reactive strategies are better for rare events like a sensitive issue that gains media attention or hosting a remembrance after a campus tragedy elsewhere in the country. Proactive strategies should be put in place for issues that might happen again. The whole idea of putting systems in place is that there are less things to react to and less scrambling when issues need to be responded to quickly. Individual strategies are best for rare events with individuals and events that can be linked to specific individuals. Events that can be linked to individuals, but have a local or national pattern, also need systemic strategies because then the individual events are actually impacting whole student populations and need systemic responses. In reality, many events begin as reactions to specific events by individuals and then the specific event prompts a systemic look at the need to be more proactive and systemic so that reactive events are unnecessary in the future. We advocate for trying to preempt this cycle by putting in place as many systemic and proactive policies and practices that will improve climate from the outset. Happy institutions have less need for reactive solutions.

Flexibility within the 4-Way Implementation Model

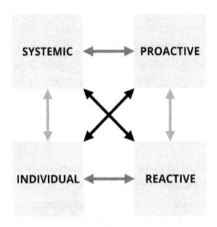

The 4-Way Implementation Model is also very nimble. When reviewing this model, you will see that, although it's broken up into four categories, the model is not linear in its application. There are four distinct categories: systemic, proactive, individual, and reactive; however, within the four categories, there is also the ability for policies and practices to move cross-functionally.

For example, a program or activity can originate in the systemic category and then move to a reactive or proactive category in the future. Further, an institution may embark on a reactive program approach, maybe due to a campus crisis. Then over time, and due to campus need, the program may undergo multiple transitions moving the program to the systemic category and allowing for greater institutional effectiveness. An example of this follows.

MYRON R. ANDERSON AND KATHRYN S. YOUNG

How an Ombuds Office can flex to be systemic, proactive, individual, and reactive

MSU Denver conducted a campus climate survey and received concerning findings in the areas of conflict resolution, institutional code of conduct, interpersonal relations, and trust. These survey findings informed campus leadership that they needed to react. The reaction needed to be systemic as these issues directly correlated to negative campus climate. The systemic action that the institution took was to develop an Ombuds Office. The Ombuds Office provides an alternative channel of communications that is voluntary, informal, neutral, unbiased, and confidential. The Ombuds Office supports self-determination as well as collaborative conflict engagement in understanding institutional policies and procedures, developing suitable options to conflict and finding fair and equitable outcomes for all concerned parties. The Ombuds Office is now a systemic part of the institution.

Evidence from the survey informed leadership that there was a need to resolve issues and problems at the lowest level, and there were numerous complaints regarding the understanding of institutional policies and procedures. The development of this office would allow the institution to reduce complaints, decrease miscommunication, and provide expedient and accurate information to members of the campus community. Improving these areas had a positive effect on the institution's climate. This effectiveness was measured in the reduction of complaints to the Equal Opportunity Office, the Office of Inclusive Excellence, the President's Office, and the Office of

Human Resources. It was further realized via the next campus climate survey that indicated an improved sense of belonging, more positive experiences at the institution, and a reduction in overall institutional conflict. An additional proactive impact of the office was that the faculty and staff at the institution developed additional skills to resolve conflict and engage with one another in a respectful way.

A safe space like an Ombuds Office for all members of the institution to privately engage takes a proactive approach in resolving conflict and individually promoting a welcoming environment. The Ombuds Office can resolve many issues individually by providing accurate and unbiased information to the employee. A specific example of how the Ombuds Office helped improve an individual's experience with campus climate follows.

EXAMPLE 1

Pay: Is my pay fair?

An affiliate faculty member was concerned about the rate of pay they were receiving for their work. They thought they were being paid less than peer faculty. This lesser pay equated with feeling like they were less important, less valued than their peers. They were worried it was a hierarchical microaggression due to their part-time role at the university. The Ombuds person performed research to identify the proper pay scale for the affiliate faculty member related to their credentials and years of service. The Ombuds person was able to go back to the faculty member

MYRON R. ANDERSON AND KATHRYN S. YOUNG

> and confirm that they were getting paid fairly and appropriately. Once the faculty member heard this unbiased information, they were satisfied, left the office with a positive outlook, and re-assumed their faculty duties.

ASK YOURSELF

- What did the Ombuds Office do to alleviate the faculty's concerns?
- What might have happened has the office not been there to address the faculty's concerns?

This is just one example where having an unbiased and safe space for individuals to communicate concerns can lead to the resolution of some issues in their infancy, reducing the engagement of the traditional complaint and compliance areas and reducing the involvement of multiple offices and multiple resources. More importantly, having this issue resolved quickly and directly provided a greater opportunity for affiliate faculty to enjoy their experience at the institution rather than going through multiple institutional compliance processes which take time, resources, and emotional energy—oftentimes leading to a similar or sometimes less satisfying result. Having the faculty work with the Ombuds Office reduced the ongoing impact of the microaggression as the faculty member learned that their pay was not a personal attack, which helped the faculty member feel better. The Ombuds Office could also use this opportunity to encourage personal action like joining the union to lend support to equal pay for equal work.

With this example as a backdrop, the involvement of the Ombuds Office saved the involvement of multiple institutional resources, provided quick, accurate, and unbiased information to the employee allowing for the issue to be resolved quickly and at the lowest level while promoting a positive interaction with the institution. This one example reflects an institutional reaction from a systemic program, like a climate survey, leading to the development of an Ombuds office. It also shows how a systemic program provided the ability to resolve an individual issue, leading to the improvement of the campus climate. Further, this example demonstrates the fluidity and flexibility of the Ombuds Office as part of the 4–Way Implementation Model.

Because the Ombuds Office was in place (systemic and proactive), there was an opportunity to be quickly reactive to this faculty's individual issue. Because the Ombuds Office functions systemically within the institution, the office also can work systematically and proactively by delivering workshops on conflict resolution to interested members of the campus community, going to departments throughout the campus, and delivering workshops when requested. The office also delivers additional programs (like developing a proactive Courageous Conversations Program about how to resolve conflict and increase communication). It continues to provide additional tools and resources throughout the campus to better problem solve.

EXAMPLE 2

Working: I am working out of my job description.

There were a number of administrative employees who visited the Ombuds Office to raise concerns about working outside of their job descriptions. The employees felt that they were working additional hours, performing duties that were not a part of their jobs, and were given added responsibilities that were unreasonable. This made it difficult for them to perform their written job duties and affected their annual evaluations. In addition, the employees felt that if they worked outside of their job descriptions, they should receive additional compensation. They also worried that they were asked to do things that others were not and wondered if some sort of hierarchical preferencing was at play.

ASK YOURSELF

- What did the Ombuds Office do to alleviate the employees' concerns?
- What might have happened had the office not been there to address the employees' concerns?

These issues connected to more than equity concerns and possible microaggressions, they related to annual review, compensation, and possible unfairness in the process. Employees felt that it was unfair to be evaluated for work that was not within their job descriptions and that the additional duties were not considered in their annual evaluation. Further, the employees felt that the additional duties were unfair, added stress to the supervisor-supervisee relationship, and created unreasonable expectations resulting in a hostile work environment.

In this situation, the Ombuds officer performed a "concerned persons inquiry" and met with each employee's supervisor to ask questions related to their evaluation process. The inquiry brought the issue to the forefront. In some cases, the supervisor would state that they can lead how they want, and "the employee must do what I need them to do." The Ombuds then asked the supervisors what sort of management training they had experienced. Some supervisor indicated that they had little experience and no training managing others. This was the opportunity point for the Ombuds officer to provide some education and guidance regarding the institutional rules as they relate to supervising employees.

The Ombuds concerned persons inquiry provided an opportunity for the supervisors to reflect on their understanding and implementation of linking the employee job descriptions to employee compensation and annual evaluations. Moreover, the Ombuds was able to communicate the adverse effect that this issue may have on the department's climate and the interactions between the supervisor and supervisee, potential favoritism, and the collateral interactions among the many employees within the department. These discussions led to the supervisors realizing that the practice of using the job description as the foundation for their employee's work plan and evaluation is very important to promoting positive and fair working relationship. Creating these shared and understood expectations provided a systemic infrastructure for the promotion of a healthy work environment. After the "concerned persons inquiry" sessions, many of the supervisors indicated that they would benefit from attending management professional development.

This example reflects, at first glance, an individual reaction to individual experiences. Having a systemic program in place like the Ombuds office provided an avenue for employees to receive answers to their concerns. Because the

Ombuds Office was in place (systemic and proactive), there was an opportunity to be quickly reactive in regard to these employees' individual issues and address hierarchical microaggressions early so they did not become institutional bullying. Because the Ombuds Office functions systemically within the institution, the office also can work systematically and proactively to develop or work with HR to develop management professional development for anyone who enters a management position. The Ombuds Office can push to make sure people receive this sort of professional development before they move into a leadership position or, at the latest, in the first weeks of a new position.

Conclusion

This chapter focused on the relationship between the 4-Way Implementation Model and microaggressions and bullying. Although people who commit a microaggression might just prefer to let the "small" slight go, to the person who experiences the microaggression, the pain lingers. Individually, as leaders, we often want to solve the immediate problem of a microaggression without thinking through the systems that have allowed the space for microaggressions to be committed.

We must act on several fronts at once. We must act individually to address the harm caused in the moment. This is forcibly a reactive action. We must then act proactively and systemically to change the institutional conditions so that we reduce the possibility of future microaggressions and bullying actions. This is a multifaceted approach that will yield greater success in improving your institution's climate. Institutional leaders must not just see microaggressions as one-time occurrences. We must go one step further and work to reduce the organizational conditions that allowed for the microaggression or bullying to occur in the first place. The 4-Way Implementation Model is a tool to evaluate existing policies and programs and to plan for future policies and programs so that the institutional focus is on a diverse and inclusive space for all.

Think about it – Talk about it

This is an opportunity to think about and discuss some of the concepts in this chapter. On your own, with a few colleagues, or in a departmental or unit meeting, discuss one or more of the questions below.

1. What is one program or policy that has arisen at your institution because of a reaction to an event? How did it come about? How did the program affect campus climate?

2. What is one program or policy created proactively before a negative event happens? How did the program affect campus climate?

3. What program or policy would you like to see at your institution that does not currently exist?

Cultural Shift Challenge

This is an opportunity to do something! On your own, with a few colleagues, or in a departmental or unit meeting, (individually and/or collectively) select one of the following forms that you (individually and/or collectively) can use as a tool to start to improve the culture in your sphere of influence.

FORM 1: BALANCING YOUR PROGRAMS AND POLICIES

Use this tool to list policies and programs that exist within your institution. You can choose to complete this sheet at the institutional level, departmental level, school or college level, or unit level.

Systematic	Proactive
Individual	**Reactive**

Now, examine your lists. Where do the bulk of programs and policies fall? If they fall mostly into the individual and reactive boxes, convene a task force to create more systemic and proactive policies and practices to better address DEI.

FORM 2: SYSTEMIC EFFORTS

Ask yourself about **systemic** efforts to reduce microaggressions and bullying on your campus. You can also complete this activity in a department, school, unit, college, or institution-wide level.

	Does this process result in a more diverse institution? Evidence?	Does this process result in a more inclusive institution? Evidence?	Does this process result in a more positive campus climate? Evidence?
FMLA			
Hiring			
Promotion			
Annual Leave			

Tenure			
Evaluations			
Holidays			
Meetings			
Interview process			
Application process			

For anything that you answered "no" to above, ask yourself what it would take to turn the "no" into a "yes." Choose one "no" and make a plan to turn it into a "yes." What is the first step? Do that step this week.

FORM 3: PROACTIVE EFFORTS

Ask yourself: Does my institution have ways for individuals to **proactively** learn about the needs of social identity groups in relation to power, privilege, and advocacy? You can also complete this activity in a department, school, unit, college, or institution-wide level.

Category	Programs to support learning about this category
Accessibility	
Gender Identity	
Sexual Orientation	
Culture	
Race	
Class	
Age	
Nationality	
Language	

Veterans	
First Generation Students	
Intersectionality	
Other	

What is one more proactive effort you would like to see? What would be the first step in getting this up and running?

Take initiative and send the email, pick up the phone, or go and talk to the appropriate person to complete your first step.

FORM 4: REACTIVE EFFORTS

How are these programs, policies, and offices used in your organization to REACT to microaggressions and/or bullying? You can also complete this activity in a department, school, unit, college, or institution-wide level.

Office/ Policy	Way it is used/can be used to respond to microaggressions and/or bullying
Ombuds Office	
Equal Opportunity Office	
Office of Student Life	
Referral and Complaint Processes	
Personnel Improvement Plans	
Bullying Policy	
Interactive workshops for individuals, departments, units, etc.	
One-on-one mediation	
Other university-sanctioned interventions	

What is one more reactive effort you would like to see? What would be the first step in getting this up and running?

Take initiative and send the email, pick up the phone, or go and talk to the appropriate person to complete your first step.

CHAPTER 3: HIERARCHICAL MICROAGGRESSIONS AT THE SENIOR LEADERSHIP LEVEL

SUMMARY

The previous chapters explained how to spot and remove microaggressions and bullying. We also explained how to use the 4-Way Implementation Model to examine an institution's policies and programs. This chapter and the next will put these ideas into practice by providing stories of microaggressions that happen in higher education. Each story explains why something is a microaggression and what might the intent and impact of the action be. Then each will provide steps to address the microaggression. Following each story and solution is a reflective tool to use in your own practice. At the end of the chapter, you will be able to create your own stories and put them through the same process.

Introduction

The first chapter defined microaggressions, microbullying, and bullying. The second chapter provided a tool called the 4-Way Implementation Model so that your institution can purposefully examine its policies and programs through an inclusive lens. The hope is that a more inclusive campus with more purposeful policies will lead to the reduction of microaggression and bullying. The reality is that it will be nearly impossible to remove all microaggressions and bullying from any campus. This chapter takes the theoretical underpinnings of the first two chapters and puts these ideas into practice. At the end of the day, everyone wants to know what to do about microaggressions right now. And people in leadership should be thinking, "How can we keep microaggressions and bullying from happening in the future?"

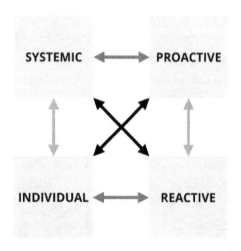

This chapter focuses on those in senior leadership— presidents of the institution, vice presidents, directors, deans, and associate deans. You are in a unique role where you act individually, but your actions impact large groups of people in the present and in the future. Your roles relate to policy and program goals, so you are in a unique position to put your personal mark on institutional decisions—which also means your roles in addressing microaggressions is paramount for impacting the institution's culture on these issues. Modeling how we want others to act through our own actions is one of the biggest ways we can change the institution's culture. How we address microaggressions sends a very strong message to our schools, departments, and units about how we expect others to address microaggressions.

This chapter provides you with real stories from real institutions to inspire you to think how you might make the same or different choices as the people mentioned. Interspersed throughout this chapter are conceptual and practical tools to use in your own practice. Think through what aspects of the 4-Way Implementation Model will help you respond to the microaggressions in the stories that follow.

Listening: Whose ideas matter the most?

Imagine you are a vice president running a meeting with senior leaders of the institution. You know Mark can be counted on to come up with good ideas. You also know that Kiko does not usually share anything in meetings but does listen attentively. There are also a few other senior level colleagues in the meeting. In this meeting, you ask for feedback on how a new policy will impact students. Kiko tries three times to mention concerns she has related to the impact on students. Then Mark repeats what Kiko says. You say, "That is a great point, Mark. Thanks for bringing it up." You leave the meeting happy that Mark was there to provide his insight. Later, you hear grumblings through the grapevine, though no one tells you this information directly, that you do not listen in meetings to anyone but Mark.

What is the microaggression?

Kiko is experiencing being devalued because she is not being heard, and the information she is presenting is not being received. This makes Kiko feel like her contributions are not important, and she does not feel that her contributions and her input matter to the goals and directions of the institution.

There is a gender microaggression in that Kiko is a female, and historically, due to the intersections of micro-aggressions between identity categories, negative experiences keep piling on to people with more marginalized identities. The gender biases (where women are listened to less than men in meetings) and a bias against Asian faculty (where Asian faculty are presumed to be quiet, so they will not participate in group meetings) manifest into societal and organizational microaggressions which then have a negative accumulation effect on Kiko.

What would you do in a similar situation?

A. Do nothing. Kiko did not come talk to me, so the problem must not be that important.

B. Go directly to Kiko and tell her that you heard about her feelings, and you want to explain yourself so that she understands you weren't trying to not listen to her.

C. Respect Kiko's decision not to come to you and instead work to create better systems for strong sharing of information in meetings.

Which option is best?

A. Do nothing. Kiko did not come talk to me so the problem must not be that important.

    No. There are always power dynamics going on in colleges and universities, no matter how open a leader you may be. Many people will not feel comfortable talking to you, no matter how approachable you think you are. Doing nothing is a good way to maintain the status quo – but the status quo is not working for Kiko and probably not working for others either. Eventually, when more and more people think you only listen to Mark, they will also stop speaking up. An issue like this is like a rolling snowball and gets worse with time.

B. Go directly to Kiko and tell her that you heard about her feelings, and you want to explain yourself so that she understands you were not trying to not listen to her.

    No. Again, because there are reasons that Kiko did not come to you initially, going to her does not usually make sense either. It might be an awkward move given that you learned about your microaggression through the grapevine. This might send the message to Kiko that she is being watched and reported on, not a good feeling if you are trying to increase transparency, comfort, and approach-ability.

    Also, if you are going to someone to try to explain yourself, usually you are doing this to try to make yourself feel better. Their feelings are a side effect of getting yourself to feel better. Even though you were not trying to ignore her, the effect was that she felt not listened to, and the harm was already done (See more on intent versus impact later in this chapter).

C. Respect Kiko's decision not to come to you and instead work to create better systems for strong sharing of information in meetings.

Yes. Read a more detailed response below about why this was the best option in this case.

HOW CAN THE MICROAGGRESSION BE MORE EFFECTIVELY ADDRESSED?

Frequently, a person in leadership who presents with identities from dominant backgrounds does not even know a microaggression has happened, because they are looking at the world through their own lens and personal experiences (this can also happen in leadership with people who do not hold dominant identities, but, because of their leadership role, the microaggression happens due to their abuse of power in relation to their place in the hierarchy). We often do not know when we call on the same person over and over, we just know that person is competent and has good ideas. We do not realize the effect it might have on others in the room.

What can be done to solve a microaggression you hear through the grapevine that you've committed? In this situation, the person leading the meeting has the greatest opportunity to promote a welcoming climate in the future. The VP can develop different ways for people to provide input and create a mechanism that will promote feedback equally throughout the meeting. One way to do this is by following the "rule of threes." Place people in groups of three to talk about the impact of the new initiative on students. This smaller grouping provides a smaller space for people to present concepts and for ideas to be generated by those who might otherwise be overlooked and ignored. This also provides an opportunity for people to work more independently at one stage then bring the independent work to the larger group for consensus.

Another strategy is when engaging in a brainstorming exercise to be intentional about placing all ideas on a board or space that the entire group can see. This promotes equity in ideas and ensures that all ideas have an equal chance to be reviewed by the group. Along with this exercise, you may incorporate an anonymous element to it and provide opportunity for ideas to be written down and placed in a basket to be added to the board (electronic versions of this exist). Again, this promotes equity, increases access, and takes into consideration the fact that people have different comfort levels in sharing ideas in group settings.

Placing ideas on the board seems simple, but if you put all of the ideas on the board, everybody has an opportunity for their idea to be reviewed and be a part of the consideration process.

If you execute this process in the typical call out way, there are many variables that come into play that derail the process. The person who talks the loudest gets heard more. The person who does not talk fast enough or loud enough gets their points heard the least. If someone is shy, they may not present any ideas, even if they want to share. And you might not hear all ideas or may be implicitly filtering out ideas of different people allowing for subjectivity to enter into the process at the onset.

Develop a system to make sure you do not inadvertently make the same mistake.

Not developing a system to allow for equity in group meetings can lead to many brilliant ideas not making it to the board for consideration. Implicit bias is at the core of microaggressions and developing mechanisms to reduce bias can also lead to reducing microaggressions thus improving your university's climate.

The following tool helps you track meeting engagement. Use this occasionally to see how you are doing in leading a meeting. Gather the data, analyze it, and evaluate what changes you need to make to ensure meetings are more inclusive. You can also do this informally by asking yourself after a meeting ends who you can name that shared input today. Once you finish naming people, review the list of people who attended and mentally think of ways to engage with them in the future.

TAKE FOR ACTION

Notice interactions in your meeting (or have someone else take note of):

- Who is talking?
- Who is quiet?
- How are people reacting nonverbally?
- Whose ideas are getting considered?
- Whose ideas are being discounted? Ignored?
- Who interrupts others? Who gets interrupted?
- Who do people look at when they are talking?
- Who do people look at when others are talking?
- Who is asked to take notes?
- Who is waited for in order for a meeting to begin?

Self-assessment in soft skills

If you have heard that people question your ability to read a situation well and respond in ways that are supportive, or that you come off as too aggressive instead of assertive, Chapter 4 provides a short list of self-assessments (1. Soft-Skills; 2. Concerns, Strengths, Needs; 3. Emotion-Specific Strategies) for you to think through the socio-emotional tools you will need in order to be able to address microaggressions in your role.

Intent and impact

We shared this initial story from Kiko to talk about the difference between intent and impact in the case of microaggressions. Notice, the VP did not even know a microaggression happened, but Kiko still felt pain. She still did not know if he ignored her due to her race, gender, role at the institution, or a combination of things. Even though the VP had no intent to hurt, the impact remained – Kiko felt devalued.

Intent and impact are easy to understand through the example of texting while driving. Imagine I am texting the babysitter to make last minute plans while driving, and I run over a pedestrian and break her leg. I apologize; I did not mean to break her leg. I only meant to send a really quick text. Unfortunately, the impact is that she still has a broken leg and is still mad about the fact that my inattention led to her broken leg. My intent was good; my impact was bad.

You might wonder in many of these stories about how much of someone's behavior is an accidental oversight or on purpose and then weigh the actions based on intent rather than impact. That is wrong. The impact is the critical point for someone who experiences a microaggression. Intent is often used to justify the action in hopes that it will reduce the impact. But the impact has already happened; the pain has already been felt.

Knowing about intent helps you talk with the microaggressor about their possible intent. If they really intend what they say they intend, then they need to find a better way to share their message. The way they have chosen is hurtful and harmful. If they did not mean what they said, then they need to find a better way to share their message. The way they have chosen, maybe unintentionally, is hurtful and harmful. Wouldn't you want to know if you hurt someone so you could address it and try not to do so in the future?

INTENT CLARIFICATION QUESTION

A diplomatic strategy that a person receiving a microaggression might want to try is what we call the "Intent Clarification Question." The reason this is an important question is that it gives a way to voice the pain of a microaggression and allows for the possibility of it being addressed. The question communicates to the micro-aggressor that a microaggression took place, but it does so in a non-threatening way. It provides an opportunity for the microaggressor to recognize that their intent may not have been to do harm, provides them with a way to understand the event, and opens the door for bringing up the point that the impact is still the same and addressing the microaggression is still very important.

WHAT YOU COULD SAY

Say this:

If someone says or does a microaggression to you: "When you say X, I hear Y, was that your intent?

Or this:

If someone brings a microaggression to you that you are not involved in, but you are in a leadership role: "Thank you for telling me about this. It sounds like when s/he/they said X, you heard Y message, is that right? I can hear the (pain, frustration, etc.) you feel. (What) would you like me to do about it?"

When a person receives a microaggression, sometimes it is difficult to address the microaggression, especially if it is from someone in leadership. Diplomacy is important in a work environment when addressing a microaggression, for the microaggressor and for the microaggressee. Being respectful in your dialog when addressing the microaggression can go a long way in creating a dialog that will lead to a greater understanding and future removal of microaggressions. This is important as the removing of future microaggressions has a positive influence on your university's climate.

Emotions related to microaggressions

Although we encourage respectful dialog about the event, it is also important to note that since microaggressions hurt, the microaggressee might not feel like it is their job to contain their pain. They might be angry, sad, shocked, or ashamed, and these feelings might come out in relation to the microaggression. That is OK. Those are their feelings; they were harmed. It is important to not discount someone's feelings and to make space for their feelings.

In your leadership role, you can make space for them to emote—just do not add to it. Your job is to be a good listener, not emote back. Leaders who can achieve this balance of letting people speak through their emotions but holding their own emotions in check provide a powerful example of how to maintain composure in difficult conversations. This sort of listening without sharing one's own emotions allows the person harmed to share their concerns without managing yours.

Note: Various social identities can come into play in these moments and leaders in a power/dominant role can impact how safe a person feels in the conversation. So, even when someone feels pain, they may not want to show vulnerability in front of a leader and could suppress their pain or deny their pain, leading you to believe that they did not experience any pain. Remember, just because someone is not telling you about their pain does not mean that they aren't experiencing any.

REBUILD, AFTER THE STING

One of the biggest things you can do for someone who comes to you and shares that they have experienced a microaggression is to bring their value back up a little, since so many microaggressions relate to feeling devalued or undervalued. Through how you talk to the person, you can help them see their worth in their department or unit and in the institution. You can help rebuild their feelings, after the sting of the microaggressions.

Learning through stories

Has Kiko's story or something similar ever happened to you or to someone you know? Have feelings been hurt, and you were the last to know? Are you the one who hurt someone's feelings and made them feel lesser in their role? Could there be role, race, or gender biases in your interactions? How do you know and how do you stop these occurrences in the future?

The following sections of this chapter provide you with real stories from real institutions to help you think how you might make the same or different choices. The headings group the stories into lessons about unintentionally invoking privilege in relation to data, invoking privilege in relation to policy, and examining how biases affect the environment. These stories are often compilations of several similar stories from different institutions merged together in order to protect anonymity and provide clear examples of microaggressions. If you read the story and it feels like it could be a story from where you work, good. We intentionally draw on real situations that really happen.

Each section will begin with a story then lays out why it is an example of a microaggression, the possible intent of the person who committed the microaggression, the possible impact on the person who felt harmed, and then some ways to address the microaggression, both individually as a reactive measure and systemically as a proactive measure, so the microaggression does not occur again in the future. Following each story and solution, you will find a reflective tool (called "Take for Action") to use in your own practice.

First, we want to provide you with some general tools and ways of being that will serve as a reminder in your interpersonal interactions with others.

Microaggression Reduction-Removal Instrument

The Microaggression Reduction-Removal Instrument was designed to provide a strategy for a person being confronted after committing a microaggression to have tools to reduce the impact of the microaggression, increase their knowledge of the microaggression, and take action to reduce and possibly remove microaggressions in the future. This instrument promotes a positive, educative exchange between the microaggressee and the microaggressor which, in our experience, leads to a more beneficial outcome for everyone.

> **MICROAGGRESSION REDUCTION-REMOVAL INSTRUMENT (MRRI)**
>
> Acknowledge
>
> Understand
>
> Empathize
>
> Develop
>
> Implement

STEP 1: ACKNOWLEDGE.

If a microaggression is brought to your attention, you should acknowledge that the person coming to you has received a microaggression. This can be done by thanking them for bringing it to your attention. Acknowledgement is a significant first step as, in many cases, it takes a big effort for a person receiving a microaggression to bring it to your attention. Many times, the microaggression may be related to emotions or pain and can be a part of an accumulative effect of receiving many microaggressions over time. That can be a very difficult conversation to start. Another reason why this is an important step is because the norm (which we believe should not be the case) is for microaggressees to keep the microaggression to themselves. Keeping the microaggression internal will not allow for the microaggression to be addressed, which then leads to poor interactions between you and paves the way for the microaggression to be repeated in the future.

STEP 2: UNDERSTAND.

It is very important that you "listen for understanding" in this stage. Listen to the "why" when the microaggressee explains what they are receiving. This is their truth and their feelings, and they should not be criticized or dismissed in any way. This is not the time for you to justify your behavior, either. The person receiving the microaggression is the judge and jury of confirming the microaggression. It is not for the person that is delivering the microaggression to decide if the microaggression is real. When you listen critically to the "why" and you do not place yourself in a defensive or a justification mode (typically done as a self-serving attempt to prove why this was not a micro-aggression), you will be able to gain information to develop a strategy to address the microaggression in the present and in the future. In Chapter 1 we addressed what to do if you still think the person is wrong about being microaggressed by you.

STEP 3: EMPATHIZE.

It is important to thank them again for bringing this to your attention. Also, indicate that they have provided you with additional insight and understanding on how you will learn from this experience. You can say something like, "Going forward, I will work on not delivering this microaggression. Please keep me honest, and, if I unintentionally deliver this microaggression again, bring it to my attention. Please know, this is a priority for me to remove microaggressions from our engagement."

5-STEP APOLOGY SCRIPT

When someone indicates to you that you communicated a microaggression to them we recommend the 5-Step Apology Script:

1. Tell them you are sorry.

2. Thank them for trusting you enough to bring this to your attention.

3. Ask them if they would be willing to share more context about the microaggression to increase your understanding. Again, you must be non-defensive.

---

4. Thank them for sharing this experience with you and increasing your understanding about the micro-aggression they received.

5. Indicate to them that you will work toward not delivering this microaggression in the future.

Step 4: Develop.

Once you have completed Steps 1-3 in the process, you have acquired knowledge, gained a deeper understanding, helped the person know that you have heard them, and have brought calm and clarity to the situation. This is the ideal time to put this knowledge to work. Start thinking about "What can I do going forward to remove this microaggression from the environment?" This strategy may be individual or systemic, simple, or complex, but it is important to give it some thought. For example, if the microaggression is because of a comment you made in a meeting, then simply making the decision not to make that comment is a strategy to remove that microaggression. However, if the microaggression is about a process or policy, then the developmental step is more involved and might involve more people. It is your responsibility as a leader to champion this development and communicate to the powers that be that the current policy or process harms the institution's climate. In this case, it might involve setting up additional meetings, committees, meetings with senior leadership, etc. The developmental stage may differ from institution to institution. However, the important question to ask yourself, which can serve as your developmental guide, is, "What can I and the institution do, going forward, to remove this microaggression from our environment?"

Step 5: Implement.

The execution step is paramount to microaggression reduction and removal success. Institutions of higher education are littered with great ideas, processes, and policies that have not been placed into action. Reducing microaggressions are no different if you don't implement the strategy you developed in Step 4. Executing your microaggression reduction and removal strategy will improve your institution's climate at individual and at systemic levels.

It is important to note that with each removal of a microaggression there is some marginal improvement in the climate. Whether it is individual or systemic, the recipient receives an immediate positive impact which is an incremental improvement. As your institution moves to remove more microaggressions, you will see a greater improvement in your institution's climate.

As a reminder, you can use the 4-Way Implementation Model along with the Microaggression Reduction-Removal Instrument (MRRI) to address microaggressions at your institution.

For each story that follows, you will see an individual reactive way of addressing the problem since people often want to know, "What do I do about this microaggression today, right now?" Then, you will also see systemic and proactive ways of addressing the microaggression. Even though microaggressions happen in the moment, the overall goal is to reduce them throughout campus in the future—and the overall reduction takes systemic solutions to create a more positive climate so that the space where we work and learn sends a message of awareness and inclusiveness. It must be a space where microaggressions do not thrive.

The role of deans, directors, vice presidents, and presidents in creating, removing, and addressing microaggressions

Senior leadership is so important in removing and reducing microaggressions and bullying on campus. Senior leaders often have the opportunity to shape budget, policy, and programs in important and impactful ways. They also, often inadvertently, can hurt campus climate through these same budget priorities, policies, and practices that reflect hierarchical microaggressions.

Hierarchical microaggressions represent the everyday slights found in higher education that communicate systemic valuing (or devaluing) of a person because of the institutional role held by that person. These happen in four different ways, through:

1. Actions related to role, where the same action can be deemed appropriate or not depending on the role the person holds.

2. Changing accepted behavior depending on the role of the person doing the behavior.

3. Changing terminology related to work position.

4. Valuing/Devaluing opinions of people based on their role, not on the quality of the opinion. (This was addressed in more depth in Chapter 1).

For example, if a dean wants everyone in a school or college to attend a meeting, calling the meeting a departmental or school-wide meeting makes sure everyone knows they are included. When the meeting is called a faculty meeting and staff are still required to attend, staff feel like they are invisible and not noticed for the contributions they bring. Staff might then disengage and become less productive due to the disrespect enacted by the dean.

Deans, directors, vice presidents, and presidents have an opportunity as institutional leaders to pay attention to the systems in place and to change systems that send devaluing messages. Changing these systems changes the climate. When the climate is more welcoming, fewer micro-aggressions occur. The ones that do, often cause less harm.

TAKE FOR ACTION

If you are in a position of leadership:

Notice interactional dynamics.
Understand the differing perspectives.
Talk to constituents to see what they want in a positive campus climate.
Talk to constituents to see if they have ideas about how to implement positive change.
Develop a team to make the climate better.
Enact the systemic changes.

Deans, directors, vice presidents, and presidents can also lead cultural shifts in departments, units, schools, and colleges. You need to get all employees (faculty and staff alike) to leverage their talents to contribute to the success of the institution. They will only do this if they feel respected. Acknowledge that the faculty and staff have many skills, dispositions, and experiences to offer—skills, dispositions, and experiences that can make the culture of departments, units, schools, and colleges better.

Microaffirmations

Microaffirmations are "tiny acts of opening doors to opportunity, gestures of inclusion and caring, and graceful acts of listening. Microaffirmations lie in the practice of generosity, in consistently giving credit to others, and in providing comfort and support when others are in distress, when there has been a failure at the bench, or an idea that did not work out, or a public attack" (Rowe, 2008). Acts of kindness, genuine understanding, human connection, and solidarity can improve the climate.

Behavior change works better with behavior replacement instead of extinguishing a behavior. Microaffirmations help you change your behavior rather than stop a behavior and set the tone for the whole school or college. If you are someone who likes to talk to staff but you use sarcasm that sometimes hurts others' feelings, instead try to still talk to people but use your efforts to notice something positive about others in your sphere of influence.

- You can recognize people of a different rank across the institution by speaking to people kindly, instead of ignoring them.

- You can comfort a faculty member who is teased for their size in a fashion design department.

- You can encourage a faculty member with an accent that sometimes people need to do better listening rather than the faculty try to speak clearer.

You have so much you can do as a leader to impact climate. How you treat people in your sphere of influence on a day-to-day basis matters to the overall climate and to everyone who comes into contact with you. Here is a list of small actions and microaffirmations that you can do to improve people's experiences with you.

HOW TO CREATE A WELCOMING DEPARTMENT, UNIT, SCHOOL, OR INSTITUTIONAL CLIMATE:

Learn names and pronunciation – ask if needed. "I want to ensure that I say your name correctly, could you tell me again? I will write it down phonetically, so I get it right."

Inquire about things individual people value most. Inquire about your colleagues as people with needs and interests.

Don't change the rules of respectful behavior depending on who is in the room. If you have a colleague with a disability, for example, it is still wrong to question their competence when they are out of the room. It doesn't matter who is in the room – what matters is that it is against departmental norms to put others down, and our goal is to create a respectful department, no matter who is currently in the room.

Notice people! Say hi when you see people – or at least a head nod.

Engage in casual conversation with a variety of people before and after meetings.

Thank and genuinely praise a broad range of people.

Ask opinions and value those opinions by acting on them or explaining why you are not acting on them.

Ask follow-up questions of a broad range of people [double check that you are not only asking follow-up questions from people (or ideas) you like or people (or ideas) that you do not like].

Admit and apologize if you mess up. If you mess up publicly, then also apologize publicly.

Positive Inquiry

Positive inquiry (also called appreciative inquiry) is an approach to organizational change that focuses on strengths of the organization and the people in it, rather than on their weaknesses. This does not mean that you do not notice what is wrong; you focus on the skills and dispositions of people in the institution to make things right. It focuses on "asking questions that strengthen a system's capacity to apprehend, anticipate, and heighten positive potential" (Cooperrider and Whitney, 2005).

Leaders can also engage in Positive Inquiry. Look back at the list of how to create a welcoming climate. You might usually say, "I am not very good with names, and I would like to ensure that I have your name correct for pronunciation." Instead reframe this to, "I want to ensure that I say your name correctly." This frames the exchange positively. This will place you in a position of not having to state, "I am not good at something," and simultaneously, it places a positive indicator to the person that they are respected and that their name is respected, which often links to people's comfort with their identities on a campus.

In this case, framing the question to someone whose name you are working to pronounce creates a microaffirmation since they know you want to learn to say their name correctly. It is important to you. It moves asking about names to a positive interaction. Positive inquiry links to diplomacy as well. We know when addressing microaggressions with people in our work worlds, we must use diplomacy. How this is done can affect the results as well as alter the tenor of the exchange and the relationship going forward. Coming from a positive inquiry disposition will yield greater results in rectifying a microaggression between two people.

Addressing microaggressions from a positive approach and working to hold the least dangerous assumption about the person is fair, because frequently microaggressions are unintentional (although still harmful). As a member of the institution's leadership, you can make the exchange into a more positive, educational experience.

TAKE FOR ACTION

Ask the department, unit, school, or institution to respond to the following prompts. Think about how people will respond best in an authentic way (as a whole group, as a small group, on paper, etc.).

Prompts:
- Talk about a time when you felt you really mattered in the department. What was said or what happened that helped you feel that you mattered?
- What does an inclusive department, unit, school, or institution mean to you?

- What practices have helped create and maintain an inclusive department, unit, school, or institution? List them.

- From this list, which one or two practices can we implement tomorrow? If none, what do we need to do to be able to implement some of these? What can we get started on?

How do people invoke their privilege when looking at data?

We operate under all sorts of assumptions every day. These assumptions often lead those of us in leadership to have internalized processes about how we do things at work, including how we look at data. This could be as simple as valuing qualitative data over quantitative data. Or it could be as complex as unconscious biases we have when looking at data so that we read data results in a certain way to forward our own agendas, often without us even knowing about it.

One aspect we might not think of is how microaggressions creep into data and budget meetings. Every institution must juggle many budget lines and many programs that need funding. The dance to meet the needs for every program is a very real part of the life of deans, directors, vice presidents, and presidents at an institution. However, deans, directors, vice presidents, and presidents are often unaware of how their own implicit biases creep into these decision-making

157

processes. They might favor some programs over others, some people over others, or even some data over others, which leads to inequities related to programming and funding—and can lead to microaggressions.

The following stories highlight some of the (un)intended consequences of people who invoke their privilege when evaluating data in making budget decisions, deciding whose job it is to do what at the institution, and deciphering how to use data to attract a more diverse pool of applicants.

An inclusive environment: What role does the budget play?

A dean has asked all the chairs to a budget meeting. You bring data about the progress of African-American students in the program and their persistence to graduation. Although a small group of students, you feel like they are often overlooked in budget decisions, and you are ready with the data to show that their progress is important, too. The dean asks everyone how to spend the funds in the upcoming year. You mention that more needs to be done to support African-American students and have supporting data. She says, "Thanks for sharing," and quickly moves onto the next chair, without giving you a chance to share the data.

What is the microaggression?

This story feels like the chair has been dismissed right away, does not having an authentic voice in the meeting, and is not valued at the institution. Additionally, there is a figurative swatting away of a pesky insect that impacts the messenger and the group the messenger represents.

There are a few things taking place in this story that lead to microaggressions. First, in looking at the feelings of the chair, they are monetarily defeated before they have a chance to present the budget information. This might parallel a past experience directly related to African-American student needs being ignored in budgeting. It could be from past experiences on issues related to students with marginalized identities and/or to the overall tenor on issues related to these students.

Second, context plays a big part in the delivery of microaggressions. There is a historical context of people from marginalized backgrounds being underrepresented in higher education, and there are on-going struggles for this student population, including societal and institutional factors that already indicate a lack of positive attention to this group. This established bias may magnify the actions that are taken by the dean in the meeting.

Third, there is the situation itself. Time can be a quantifier of importance. Not providing a platform for the position to be explained is a direct indication of the importance of the issue. The dean heard the statement but did not allow for the chair to have the floor for a fair amount of presentation time. The short time period, the denial of presentation time, and the quick, dismissive response further communicate lack of importance of the chair and of the topic of African-American retention.

What might be the microaggressor's intent?

She might just feel rushed, feel she knows the issue, or even feel that the chair brings this issue up a lot. She might even feel like she has enough information from the chair to decide on the budget, so she moves on.

What might be the impact on the microaggressee?

The chair is angry and hurt. The very lack of engagement about this topic is so painful and parallels the experiences of African Americans on campus—brought to the conversation but not given space in the conversation, nor allowed input, and then ignored.

What would you do in a similar situation?

A. Nothing. That is just the nature of busy, high-level meetings.

B. Chastise the chair for repeatedly bringing up the same issue.

C. Plan meetings to allow all who are invited ample time to make their programmatic cases.

Which option is best?

A. Nothing. That is just the nature of busy, high-level meetings.

No. People attend high-level meetings because

they are expected to be there. They also attend because their voices are supposed to be crucial to informing leadership about the goings-on from their own departments, schools, or units. So, if you really value the voices of the people in the meeting, you will need to show it through your actions.

B. Chastise the chair for repeatedly bringing up the same issue.

No. If you publicly chastise someone, expect that they will stop speaking up in future meetings as well. This type of public shaming is powerful in stopping you from hearing important voices. It also sends the message to others that if they are not talking about what you want to be talking about, then they should remain quiet, or you might publicly chastise them, too. So, if you really value the voices of the people in the meeting, you will need to show it through different actions.

C. Plan meetings to allow all who are invited ample time to make their programmatic cases.

Yes. Read the more detailed response that follows about why this was the best option in this case.

HOW CAN THE MICROAGGRESSION BE MORE EFFECTIVELY ADDRESSED?

Use the Microaggression Reduction-Removal Instrument (MRRI).

1. Individual-Reactive:
Acknowledge, Understand, Empathize.

Although it would be good to use the 5-Step Apology Script here, the problem is that the dean does not even know that the chair felt slighted in the meeting. It is hard for someone else to correct the wrong when they do not even know it has been committed. If the chair ever does come forward to the dean, the chair can say:

"I felt like you dismissed my budget issue in the meeting by not giving me any time to present and not asking any follow up questions. Was that your intent?"

This gives the dean an opportunity to acknowledge the concern, understand where the chair is coming from, and hopefully empathize with the situation.

2. Systemic-Proactive: Next Steps to Develop and Implement.

When leading meetings, it is important to recognize that your visual actions and the time that you allow for each member to present their points can be received as hierarchical and sometimes as an identity-based microaggression—especially if your time allotment correlates with existing race and gender biases.

Allowing for appropriate presentation time, but also being engaged and actively listening to the information, sends a positive message and reduces the potential microaggression of the person feeling unimportant, devalued for their work and for information being presented to the group.

As you develop your meeting schedule, have an agenda. For each section, provide an equal amount of time for chairs to present their reports. If they choose to use less time, then let them communicate that to the meeting participants. Do not decide for each chair the amount of time they have to communicate their point once they have started speaking.

When you cut one person off but not another, this allows for more subjectivity to enter into the decision-making process, and the increase of subjectivity allows for the increase of bias (i.e., cutting short the presentation about African-American students but then not cutting off a chair that supports a different group might send the wrong message from you).

In rectifying this microaggression, implement a system in which each chair would have five minutes to present on a topic of their choice related to the mission of the institution or topics on the agenda for the week. This would allow for their voice to be heard completely by all in attendance of the meeting. With the presentation being heard by everyone, learning can take place, and the exchanging of ideas as they relate to the issue can take place as well.

Again, allow for a caveat that if chairs choose to use less time or yield some time to the group, that is the individual's choice. However, each person knows they had an equal opportunity for their presentation to be heard, and the potential microaggressions are removed before they are ever delivered. When you allow the voluntary yielding of time from some, all attendees leave the meeting feeling heard.

AGENDA PLANNING TOOL

Ask yourself:

- What are the important topics in this meeting? Order them.
- How long does each topic need?
- How long should I allot for each person to speak on each topic?

163

- Ask team members for other salient topics. Slot them into the current ordering and timing before the meeting begins.

Topics in order of necessity	Time per topic	Time per person per topic	New items suggested by team

Hierarchy: Whose job is it?

The Assistant Director of Human Relations (Carlyle) started to notice a trend with exit interviews of people who were voluntarily leaving the institution. Many were people of color leaving from one particular administrative unit. He brought this up to his director who said, "Dig in, find out what is going on." Carlyle went through all the exit interviews and created a matrix of who had left the institution in the last three months, their race, ethnicity, gender, and administrative unit. Carlyle went back to the director and said, "85% of people leaving from the

Continuing College Program are people of color, and they all reported to Samantha. These interviews are not giving me enough information to know why they are all leaving, but there is definitely a pattern. Can I call these people to find out more?" The director thought it was a good idea but needed the provost's approval. The provost called in the director and assistant director and asked, "Why are you looking at this information? Are you even the right person to be looking into this? Is it part of your job description to be asking these questions?" Both the director and assistant director were shocked. Isn't this what they should be doing in HR? Why were they being questioned and "put in their place?" What was going on?

WHAT IS THE MICROAGGRESSION?

The Assistant Director of Human Relations felt that his ability to perform his job was in question. The fact that his qualifications were now in question devalued his abilities to perform his job. Second, the provost, who was not in his supervisory chain of command, called Carlyle's supervisor and him into a meeting to address the issue. This action created a meeting atmosphere in which Carlyle felt he was being reprimanded, even attacked, for performing his job. Because of the hierarchical positioning of the provost in relation to Carlyle and the director, they felt unsure about if they were even "allowed" to explain their decision-making process.

What might be the microaggressor's intent?

The microaggressor's intent might be to simply understand the process since a person from their staff had been identified and linked to negative retention data related to employees of color. However, questioning this data and the way that it was done, set off multiple hierarchical microaggressive actions that were received by the assistant director and by the assistant director's supervisor.

What might be the impact on the microaggressee?

The microaggressee might feel devalued as a professional in relation to performing his job duties. The microaggressee might also feel vulnerable, because a person not within his supervisory chain of command called a meeting and challenged his skills, ability and scope of work. This could reflect a lack of job security and a conflict regarding who to consult when performing his job duties. It might encourage inequitable checks and balances in the institution. Finally, the assistant director might develop lack of systemic trust in the institution. As roles, systems, and chains of command were broken, this might make the assistant director wonder what could take place if a related incident occurred in the future. Can he trust the system to do the just thing and support his professional actions going forward?

What would you do in a similar situation?

A. As provost, tell him to focus on his specific job description only.

B. As provost, call the director in privately to get a better sense of the project.

C. As director, show outward support for Carlyle's inquiry.

Which option is best?

A. As provost, tell him to focus on his specific job description only.

No. People need to have the latitude to work within the broader confines of their job, not the strict details. When people notice inequities at work, the whole institution should be there to support the inquiry, not to question it. There is room for the provost to ask questions in a supportive way to better understand the concerns. Coming down hard with pointed questions might send the message that Carlyle is being micromanaged at best, intimidated at worse.

B. As provost, call the director in privately to get a better sense of the project.

Pretty good. A provost's job should be to support the university's mission and to support those who work to maintain the mission. A provost's job should not be to cover tracks so things look good on the surface, while turmoil bubbles below. Provosts often become provosts because of keen interpersonal skills and clear qualifications. The provost in this case clearly has some unanswered questions but also needs to send the message that she supports inquiry for inclusiveness. She does need to be careful how to talk to the director to preserve the director's autonomy in supporting Carlyle. This might be a case where the provost can talk with a trusted friend first to make sure the tone and content send a supportive message to the director and to Carlyle.

C. As director, show outward support for Carlyle's inquiry.

   Yes. Read the more detailed response that follows about why this was the best option in this case.

HOW CAN THE MICROAGGRESSION BE MORE EFFECTIVELY ADDRESSED?

Use the Microaggression Reduction-Removal Instrument (MRRI).

1. Individual-Reactive:
Acknowledge, Understand, Empathize.

Because of power dynamics in the meeting, the director might be able to reframe the situation by using the Intent-Clarification Tool better than Carlyle can. In the meeting, the director could say something like, "When you ask if Carlyle is the right person to be asking these questions, I hear that you are wondering if he made these choices on his own without consulting me. Was that your intent? Because, I can assure you that this issue is important to our mission and our strategic plan, and I wholeheartedly support this inquiry so that we can continue to work toward a more inclusive university." The director has hierarchical power that she can use to inquire about the problem and restate the goal of Carlyle's undertaking in relation to the institutional mission (See Chapter 4 for more information on bystander interventions). This might help the provost see that Carlyle has backing and that the questions were well thought out.

2. Systemic-Proactive:
Next Steps to Develop and Implement.

In higher education, hierarchical microaggressions are the largest percentage of microaggressions that we found in our research, even greater than race or gender. To that end, it is important for institutions to look critically at systems, programs, and engagement opportunities that involve hierarchy as this is a prime place to reduce and remove microaggressions and have a significant positive impact on the climate.

This issue has many systemic microaggression concerns. Hierarchy is a concern. You have a provost, typically the second highest ranking employee at the institution, moving across supervisory lines to question an employee's authority to implement their job. Systemically, there should be protocols in place to address these issues. The provost could have talked first to the vice president linked to this area to ask initial questions and check if there's an issue present. Having a provost meet with an assistant director establishes a power imbalance that may (unintentionally) present hierarchical microaggressions. Individually, microaggressions were sent by the questions she asked, in the way she asked them, and through the challenges she made regarding the assistant director's job responsibilities. How these questions are asked, or not asked, is how these microaggressions can be reduced or removed. If the provost went through the proper chain of command, the questions may be unnecessary, because they would have already been answered by the vice president. The assistant director would not need to be involved at all.

Does the institution have processes or practices around protocol as it relates to senior level employees challenging non-senior level employees outside of their chain of command? If there is a policy, process, or even a culture that states this does not take place, then if the senior level employee followed the protocol, there would have been no issue.

Someone can also speak to the provost directly and say, "I appreciate your concern regarding the research undertaken by the associate director; however, at our institution, we follow the protocol of communicating with our leadership level supervisors when questions like these arise so as to not create a hierarchical imbalance." This communication from a neutral party (e.g., an Ombuds Officer, a colleague, or the senior employee's supervisor) said in a neutral way may be what it takes to implement the elements of the Microaggression Reduction-Removal Instrument.

If there is no existing policy, process, or cultural norm that discourages cross-unit challenges from senior level administrators to other employees, elements four and five (develop and implement) will be more involved. You will need to conduct research, look at best practices from other institutions, form a policy and corresponding procedure, and agree to promote a culture that does not support this activity. Connect this and other cultural shifts to the institutional mission and core values. This creates an accountability touchpoint and reminds everyone that there is a larger reason that this change is being made, not due to one interaction. This connects back to campus climate. The goal is always to develop an inclusive and welcoming environment. The value of respect and civility must be adhered by all.

SUPPORT WHISTLEBLOWERS

People who examine equity are often whistleblowers. They are sharing their concerns in the institution to make it a better place. And like other whistleblowers, there is often retaliation against them. Even when someone else in the institution has asked them to inquire into equity issues, the messenger often gets caught up in the messaging. Have a system that allows for equity and examining equity. Let people go up and down the institutional ladder to ask questions related to equity. Do not have only one person assigned with this task.

TAKE FOR ACTION

Make sure people can speak up:

- Have an institution-wide program with safe and structured channels for reporting equity issues.
- Make it easy for staff, faculty, and administrators to institutionally question and report in lowkey ways.
- Be prepared to provide protection and confidentiality to those who question or report.
- Examine issues employees raise even if delivered in an unwelcomed way.
- Look for possible institutional failures. Are there lots of complaints from one area? Do lots of people leave one area? Investigate, learn, and change something.

- Find and dismantle formal and informal value systems that encourage or allow retaliation to those who question or report.

- Provide PD on what constitutes questioning, reporting, and retaliation.

- Understand that sometimes people do try to counteract questioning and reporting by creating their own stories to discredit the concerned person.

- Investigate concerns promptly, thoroughly and with transparency. Make sure to circle back to the person who brought forward the initial concern.

(Adapted from *Best Practices for Protecting Whistleblowers and Preventing and Addressing Retaliation,* WPAC of OSHA, 2015)

Data debacle: How will we get a diverse pool?

The Department of Education has a policy stating that in order to be qualified for a position, the candidate must have five years of K-12 teaching experience. The dean is surprised that they have only hired three African-American faculty in the last 10 years. When she asked each of the chairs, she was told time and again about the importance of teaching experience for people who will be training future educators. She agrees, but still wonders if the five-year requirement is part of the problem, as statistically in the US only 7% of teachers are African American. So then, how many people in the pool of applications will ever be African Americans? Is there racism built into the policy that people are defending?

WHAT IS THE MICROAGGRESSION?

The microaggression is an institutional microaggression when there is a policy that was developed without an inclusivity lens, a policy that people challenge with data showing why they cannot create a more diverse workforce. In this case, it is important to look at the national data on the diversity of K-12 teachers and also look at some of the reasons that draw people to the profession. What are the economic factors that allow a specific population to be drawn to the profession? What are the professional steps you must take to get there? If you take a deeper dive on these issues, you might find that it may be more difficult or not as attractive for African Americans to meet the five-year K-12 teaching experience requirement as part of eligibility for hire. This creates a de facto policy that discourages African Americans' ability to meet the qualifications for the position.

African-American families have a lower total family income than white families. More specifically the family "bread winner" makes much less in the African-American family then the white family. Most K-12 teaching positions are nine-month positions, and the salaries are not very high. This comes down to basic economics. If your total family income surpasses your needs, then you are in a better position for a second income level to provide less money. However, if your family income does not meet the income needs of your family, then you are more likely to select positions and professions that will allow you to generate the most money collectively to sustain your family. This fundamental economic decision matters for African Americans' considering the K-12 teaching profession and, if entered, their ability to stay in the profession for a minimum of five years. (There are many other systemic reasons African Americans are not prominent in the teaching field, but that is outside the scope of this example).

Therefore, an education department that will only review applicants with five or more years of teaching experience will systematically recruit far fewer African Americans than it says it wants to recruit. This is an institutional microaggression that basically tells African Americans that they will have added barriers to becoming teacher education professors.

WHAT MIGHT BE THE MICROAGGRESSOR'S INTENT?

There may be no intent regarding this microaggression. The intent is to get the best teaching talent in the country.

WHAT MIGHT BE THE IMPACT ON THE MICROAGGRESSEE?

The impact is that many potentially excellent EdD and PhD candidates will not enter the teacher education profession. The African-American K-12 teachers who did enter the profession are more likely not to have the five years' experience needed to qualify for advanced positions, resulting in a shortage of African-American college professors. This microaggression multiplies as college students will see less African-American professors, which may implicitly discourage their desire to go into this profession.

WHAT WOULD YOU DO IN A SIMILAR SITUATION?

A. As dean, track down African-American PhD and EdD completion rates, knowing that some people in this pool will not have taught for at least five years. Show faculty the data that, even though African Americans earn less than 7% of all doctoral degrees across all fields (data from 2017), the faculty should try even harder to get those candidates in the door.

B. Faculty know best. Do not challenge them on this topic.

C. Convene a thinking team to tease out the important components related to teaching. Ask the committee to think creatively about this recruitment problem and to propose novel solutions.

Which option is best?

A. As dean, track down African-American PhD and EdD completion rates knowing that some people in this pool will not have taught for at least five years. Show faculty the data that, even though African Americans earn less than 7% of all doctoral degrees across all fields (data from 2017), the faculty should try even harder to get those candidates in the door.

Pretty good. Data can be your friend in asking people to explain their actions and to help you see if your "ask" is out of line. If less than 7% of all PhDs are awarded to African Americans, there will most likely be less than 10% of applications coming in from African Americans. This might help you see some of where faculty frustration is coming from. However, just telling people to try harder with the current systems in place only leads to cynicism and failure as the current application system has racism embedded into it.

B. Faculty know best. Do not challenge them on this topic.

No. Faculty may know best about many things. But faculty, like anyone else, gets complacent in following how things have always been done, and they do not always try to solve a problem in a different way. Faculty, like anyone else, can also have biases infused into their decision-making. In this case, the deep and long-standing tradition of the five years of teaching has led to a stalemate. Faculty want to hire African Americans but then put up roadblocks to their own desires. They need to deconstruct their logic to get past this roadblock.

C. Convene a thinking team to tease out the important components related to teaching. Ask the committee to think creatively about this recruitment problem and to propose novel solutions.

Yes. Read the more detailed response that follows about why this was the best option in this case.

HOW CAN THE MICROAGGRESSION BE MORE EFFECTIVELY ADDRESSED?

When a department is trying again and again to recruit more diverse faculty, and it is not working, it is important to look at each aspect of the hiring process for possible biases and address them.

In this case, the department really needs to look at required versus preferred qualifications for the position. For the required qualifications, ask why that qualification matters to the job. For some qualifications, they really must remain the same. For others, thinking more creatively about the goals of this position might help move some required qualifications to the preferred category, which might help create a more diverse pool.

In the case of teacher preparation, why is five years an important amount of time in the classroom? What does it indicate? Time spent with students? Time spent developing curriculum? Time spent in a bureaucracy? If those parts can be teased out, then the specifics can be more transparent, and a wider variety of applicants would fit the requirements.

It is also important to get as many eyes as possible on the job posting. Following is a list from the University of Pittsburgh Diversity Recruitment Resource Guide about how to share job listings to wider audiences.

TAKE FOR ACTION

The University of Pittsburgh Diversity Recruitment Resource Guide is a comprehensive guide for sharing job postings to a wide audience. This especially helps when the percentage of people from marginalized identities receiving doctorates in the field is low.

It includes:
- What universities offer what doctoral degrees
- Specific schools that have received designation for having a significant percentage of different under-

represented groups: Alaska Native and Native Hawaiian-Serving Institutions; Historically Black Colleges and Universities; Hispanic-Serving Institutions

- POC alumni groups and professional organizations
- Diverse job posting websites
- Publications and journals that attract diverse audiences

How do people invoke their privilege when making policy decisions?

In our work, many people who share microaggressions with us share examples of policies where they felt like they were not included, policies that ignored explicit advice by important constituents, and/or policies that actually made matters worse by not talking with the right people from the start.

The following stories share examples of people who invoke their privilege when making policy decisions through who is invited to a meeting, how to ensure those who are invited attend, and how to make practice match policy.

Decision-making: Who is at the table?

The Council of Deans is meeting to decide how best to help support Latinx across the institution in the new strategic plan. Many centers and units are represented at the table. The group talks at length about how to better support Latinx students. They come up with policy recommend-ations for the new strategic plan and feel very pleased with the progress they have made.

Later, one of the deans speaks with the Director of the Latinx Association on campus about something related to the new policy initiatives. The director is shocked and hurt. Why was her unit not involved in the conversation? She finds out that no Latinx were at the meeting. Was she left out on purpose, or was it an accidental oversight? What other Latinx-serving units were included or left out? How did they make policy without considering the Latinx point of view?

WHAT IS THE MICROAGGRESSION?

There is a racial and a gender microaggression here. The Latina director felt left out as she was not involved with the developmental process. She was not hurt because she was personally left out but because Latinx representation mattered and was overlooked. Even though the Council of Deans may be feeling good because they are developing a policy to support the Latinx community, they did not reach out to anyone in that community. The lack of involvement from the community at the onset sends a paternalistic message that "we know what is best for you." The director also feels this message personally as woman and as a Latina. She feels like her opinion is not valued and/or the deans do not feel that she has the skills and abilities to contribute to the development and implementation of the decision.

What might be the microaggressor's intent?

The intent of the action is positive from the Council of Deans as they want to show concern and make improvements in this area. However, what is being received is the opposite.

What might be the impact on the microaggressee?

Her input is not valued. She may feel like she is implicitly being told that she does not have the skills and ability to be a part of the solution. An accurate voice was not heard. The perspective she brings as a member of the community is not incorporated in the solution development. This may impact the effectiveness and sustainability of the policy and/or program. There is also a larger societal context where marginalized groups are often not included at the decision-making table (i.e., government, institutional strategic planning, senior leadership, and legislative processes). This one experience is mirroring a larger societal action and adds further negative impact to this issue.

What would you do in a similar situation?

A. Apologize and make sure she, or someone from her identity-group, will be included in the future.

B. Tell her not to worry. Other people from underrepresented groups on campus were there, so her concerns were definitely covered.

C. Tell her that meetings can only get so big, and she should trust the people who were there.

Which option is best?

A. Apologize and make sure she, or someone from her identity-group, will be included in the future.

Yes. Read the more detailed response that follows about why this was the best option in this case.

B. Tell her not to worry. Other people from underrepresented groups on campus were there, so her concerns were definitely covered.

No. All diversity is not the same. All groups' histories and current relations with dominant society are not the same. Lumping everyone you consider as "other" into one category sends a second microaggressive message that you do not see the similarities and differences among groups and are not honoring what each group brings to the policy-making table.

C. Tell her that meetings can only get so big, and she should trust the people who were there.

No. This is one of those times when people from dominant backgrounds often do not understand the long-standing distrust people from non-dominant backgrounds have of those in power. There are so many examples, both historical and current, which demonstrate that those in power are not good at knowing what is best for anyone except themselves. So, telling her to trust, when she is already experiencing distrust by being excluded, is exactly the wrong thing to say.

MYRON R. ANDERSON AND KATHRYN S. YOUNG

HOW CAN THE MICROAGGRESSION BE MORE EFFECTIVELY ADDRESSED?

Use the Microaggression Reduction-Removal Instrument (MRRI).

1. Individual-Reactive:
Acknowledge, Understand, Empathize.

In this example, the dean can use the 5-Step Apology Script for Steps 1-3 with the director.

1. Tell her you are sorry.

2. Thank her for bringing this to your attention.

3. Ask her if she would share more context about the microaggression to increase your understanding. Again, you must be non-defensive.

4. Thank her for sharing this experience with you and increasing your understanding about the microaggression she received.

5. Indicate to her that you will work with others on the Council of Deans toward not delivering this microaggression in the future.

2. Systemic-Proactive:
Next Steps to Develop and Implement.

This issue relates to the fundamentals of inclusion, how input and a "seat at the table" communicates value and respect to the group. It is important that leaders are intentional and inclusive in developing committees and task forces to engage with issues, discussion, and decision-making processes throughout the institution. This is critical when engaging in discussions around policy that affects a specific group.

An example of how an institution might handle a similar issue might be: if the institution created a policy or initiative to better include Latinx faculty, staff, and students throughout the institution, then they should engage affinity groups, diversity councils, the Student Government Association, and other appropriate groups that can provide insight at the beginning of the process and as the initiative is developed.

You should include a greater representation of constituents around an initiative at the initiation of decision-making versus inclusion of those constituents at the end of the process. This can be accomplished by the leadership first asking, "Who does this policy or program affect?" And with an inclusive mindset, "Who should be at the table as we embark on this important initiative?"

Including these groups and organizing a committee to provide input in the development and planning process will serve as a platform for more voices to be heard. It will also communicate respect and value for all involved. In addition, this allows for a diverse exchange of ideas and leads to a better product and more thoughtful outcomes.

Frequently, leadership wants to get started so fast that they never ask these questions. Typically, the vice presidents, deans, and/or unit leaders meet and start going down the planning and implementation road without taking a step to include the ideal constituent groups that would have additional skills, perspectives, and expertise. If included, those constituents could most certainty add value to the final outcome. Sometimes titles can serve as a roadblock for maximizing skills and expertise.

TAKE FOR ACTION

Reflect before a meeting invite goes out:

- Who is currently on the invite list?
- Who do I ask to make sure I get the right people on the list? (Name at least three.)
- Who else would it be good to have input from—if time and space were not considerations? How could I get that input?
- Who do I think does not belong here? Why? Is that the right assumption?
- What could be the impact on those included and excluded?
- How might being at the table advantage some and disadvantage others (e.g., people, programs, etc.)?
- How can we make this group of thinkers more inclusive?

Policy: What to do when policy does not equal practice?

I walked into the History Department as a guest speaker asked to speak on diversity. I looked around the room and noticed that I was the only person of color, and there was only one woman in the room. I began with "I see you have a clear policy that does not allow African Americans and women to be employed here." They said, "We do not have a policy that excludes women or minorities." I replied, "I hear what you are saying; however, judging by the results of the people in the room, something must be going on to indicate the lack of value for diversity." The dean was quick to remark, "We do. We want to. Valuing diversity is in our strategic plan." I then asked, "Is your plan working?" and left a long silence. I then mentioned, "You cannot really 'value diversity' with no diverse people. If you want to value diversity, how must your plan change?"

WHAT IS THE MICROAGGRESSION?

This is an example of an organizational microaggression. At first, it might seem like no one is harmed by a lack of diversity in an institution, but when prospective new faculty walk around the institution and see no one that looks like them, they may feel unwelcome, suspicious, uncertain, curious, or like they will have to work hard to be welcomed into the environment—even before anyone talks to them. All faculty want to feel like they can see themselves at an institution. Without that representation, they begin the interview process knowing that they would be "the only one" if hired. It is scary and uncomfortable.

WHAT MIGHT BE THE MICROAGGRESSOR'S INTENT?

The intent is actually lack of intent. Because of having a homogeneous faculty and dean, no one has thought about what the institution might "feel" like to someone who is not represented in that space. No one has thought about the strength of the policy and how to change it. In fact, people might think the space is very welcoming as it is a welcoming space for themselves.

What might be the impact on the microaggressee?

The impact is harm through omission and harm through thinking, "if the space works for me, it will work for everyone. If this space does not work for someone, it is a personal problem, not a systemic one." The person who enters a space feeling like they are "the only one" has already started to gauge the possible experience of working at this institution. If they decide this is a good place to work, then they are already thinking about their own social supports they will need to be successful in a homogeneous institution. And if they are not, they might be worrying about what their day-to-day interactions will feel like.

What would you do in a similar situation?

A. Ask the invitee to be respectful and not start fires where they are not needed.

B. Take the invitee on a departmental tour to show him every person of color you can find that works in the department in some capacity.

C. Ask the invitee if he or his organization can come again and do an equity assessment of policies and practices that get in the way of your mission.

Which option is best?

A. Ask the invitee to be respectful and not start fires where they are not needed.

No. You did ask the invitee to come and talk about diversity. He is doing what you asked him to do. Noticing who is represented in a department is not disrespectful. It is quantifiable.

B. Take the invitee on a departmental tour to show him every person of color you can find that works in the department in some capacity.

No. This option is problematic in several ways. First, showing off someone because of their race or ethnicity is dehumanizing. Staff do not like to feel like "animals in a zoo," being shown off for their diversity. Second, this would reinforce the fact that there is a hierarchical problem here, since staff come from a variety of backgrounds, but not faculty. This shows what sorts of jobs people of color hold at this institution. Third, you are deflecting that there is a problem, and you will not increase your faculty diversity if you don't recognize the problem.

C. Ask the invitee if he or his organization can come again and do an equity assessment of policies and practices that get in the way of your mission.

Yes. Read the more detailed response that follows about why this was the best option in this case.

How can the microaggression be more effectively addressed?

Use the Microaggression Reduction-Removal Instrument (MRRI).

In this case, the individual harm comes through an organizational lens, so you would not need step 1 of the MRRI. People who do not see themselves represented sometimes feel like they will have to work harder to be welcomed into a new space. The dean has an opportunity to acknowledge that there is a lack of diversity, understand that this is a systemic problem, and empathize with the guest speaker that something needs to be done differently in the department.

2. Systemic-Proactive:
Next Steps to Develop and Implement.

This story asks you to take a look at your policies and procedures. Frequently, policies and procedures have been developed many years in the past. When they were developed, often they did not have a diversity and inclusivity lens. You don't know what you don't know. If there is no diversity at the policy and process developmental point, then typically this perspective is not included.

In this case, you would have to think that there may be something in the hiring policy or process that may be deterring faculty with marginalized identities from applying or accepting positions at this institution.

- Are the hiring processes inclusive?
- Has the institution worked systemically to reduce implicit bias from the application and interview process?
- Does the institution intentionally recruit faculty with marginalized identities by being involved in recruitment fairs, marketing their positions in diverse publications, and infusing the value of diversity within the job descriptions?

These are just a few policy and process measures that an institution can take to promote the hiring of a diverse workforce.

Retention policies and procedures also need to be considered. Without clear and intentional retention policies, the faculty with marginalized identities who are hired will not stay at your institution very long. A welcoming and inclusive climate is critical to the retention of faculty with marginalized identities.

- Does your institution perform a climate survey to inform the leadership of the climate within the institution?
- Do you have active affinity groups to provide outlets for people from marginal identities to connect with people like them?
- Are the ongoing institutional programs and initiatives inclusive? To whom?

- Do you have policies and programs that promote diversity and reduce poor conduct between constituents?
- Have you ever done an equity audit?

Developing policies and programs in this realm does much to send a message that the institution is inclusive and values diversity. Developing clear, inclusive policies in both the recruitment and retention space will send a message and provide a framework for the institution to recruit a more diverse workforce. Promoting a strong sense of belonging will allow for greater workforce retention as well.

Inclusion: Whose job is it?

In a policy seminar for the whole department about upcoming changes in the next year, one of the few staff members present mentioned that the seminar did not feel very inclusive as not many staff were invited to the event. The dean said, "Why don't you plan the next event and make sure to invite more staff?" and then continued on with his planned lecture.

WHAT IS THE MICROAGGRESSION?

The initial microaggression may have been in the statement, "not many staff were invited to the event." When meetings are designed to be inclusive, it is important to be intentional throughout the process. As there are so many hierarchies within higher education, we need to go the extra mile in our communication to ensure that the appropriate message to the appropriate constituent group is delivered. The invitation needs to be inclusive in the writing and delivery. As the organizer, if the plan is to hold a second event, then the organizer should plan the meeting but be more intentional regarding inclusivity.

Asking a staff member who brought the issue to the table to organize another meeting presents this new meeting as an afterthought to hear second tier comments. It is kind of like sitting at the kids' table at a big family event. Of course, you are welcome and valued; however, some of the discussion at this table is for grown-ups. We will fill you in on the decisions later.

Hierarchical microaggressions are received by multiple people in multiple ways. First, the invitation was the first microaggression, because it was not inclusive in planning a meeting that staff could not actually attend. Second, the dean decided to wash his hands of setting up another meeting. Tasking the staff member with it sends an additional hierarchical microaggression to the staff that the dean cannot be bothered to be inclusive to staff. This is a non-inclusive process that promotes separation and the feeling that staff perspectives are an afterthought to the department. Third, there is the microaggression to the staff member that brought the issue up. There was little empathy from the dean as he quickly acknowledged the issue and then said you set up the next meeting and invite more staff. Quickly brushing the issue off communicated that it was not of great importance.

What might be the microaggressor's intent?

There may be no intent to deliver a microaggression. The dean might just have not thought this was a big issue and felt like he had a good way to move forward - have the staff plan the next meeting.

What might be the impact on the microaggressee?

The impact of the microaggression was that the dean was not truly interested in everyone's perspectives. The concern of the staff member that the dean be more inclusive was not valued. Hearing all voices was not important to the departmental functioning. Staff hear loud and clear that they are not important.

What would you do in a similar situation?

A. Decide to hold separate meetings for faculty and staff and attend only the faculty meetings as their views need to be the most prioritized.

B. Let it go. Staff get upset about all sorts of things and move on. Asking more about it will just give attention to a non-issue.

C. Ask for a rewind. Redo the interaction with the staff member by stopping and really listening to the issues. Brainstorm inclusive meeting strategies in the future.

Which option is best?

A. Decide to hold separate meetings for faculty and staff and attend only the faculty meetings as their views need to be the most prioritized.

    No. If you call it a departmental meeting, and you need everyone to know the same information, then you need to be able to make the meeting so staff and faculty can attend. If you hold two different meetings and only attend the faculty one, you send a clear message that you value the input of faculty over staff.

B. Let it go. Staff get upset about all sorts of things and move on. Asking more about it will just give attention to a non-issue.

    No. If a staff member is brave enough to speak up in a meeting where, by the virtue of their role, they are considered less powerless, then that person really wants to be heard. They are not speaking up just to make a point. This means they really want to be heard about the lack of voice for staff in a department and are willing to put out their workplace neck to be heard.

C. Ask for a rewind. Redo the interaction with the staff member by stopping and really listening to the issues. Brainstorm inclusive meeting strategies in the future.

    Yes. Read the more detailed response that follows about why this was the best option in this case.

How can the microaggression be more effectively addressed?

Use the Microaggression Reduction-Removal Instrument (MRRI).

1. Individual-Reactive:
Acknowledge, Understand, Empathize.

In this case the dean will probably not hear about the microaggression. Staff will likely talk amongst themselves, and, if these oversights continue to happen, the department will start to lose staff. The dean has shown a lack of acknowledgement, understanding, and empathy. Clearly, the microaggression will not be addressed quickly.

If this story could be rewound and done again, the dean would first acknowledge the issue. Then the dean would thank the staff for bringing this to his attention. Lastly, the dean would ask questions to ensure understanding which can also serve to empathize with the person.

A NOTE TO DEANS AND DIRECTORS

When you notice a lot of people leaving from your department or unit in a short amount of time, it is time to examine your culture more closely. Happy and satisfied employees stay; unsatisfied and frustrated employees leave.

2. Systemic-Proactive:
Next Steps to Develop and Implement

In looking at the information received under phases 1-3, the dean can develop a personal strategy to ensure that the invitations for future department meetings are inclusive in the language, inclusive in being sent to the invitees, and inclusive in the time and location. Further, if it is known that participation levels will be low, then under the dean's purview an additional meeting should be planned following inclusive principles, taking in additional information regarding time and place to get the most participants. Finally, when executing the meeting, the dean should be inclusive in every aspect of running the meeting and follow-up.

Incorporating these actions and being able to communicate them to the staff member who raised the concern may reduce the microaggression "sting." This larger systemic action will reduce and possible remove microaggressions like this from happening in the future.

TAKE FOR ACTION

Planning Checklist: Representation matters.

- Make sure enough seats are reserved for all categories of people who work in the department.
- Make sure if you invite people from all categories that they can actually make the meeting, seminar, etc. If they are teaching a class or have to be in the office, then they are not really invited.

- Make sure if you invite people from all categories that the date does not fall on someone's religious holiday or a day when public schools are closed.

How do biases affect the environment?

Leaders in multicultural education often talk about people's experiences being like fish in a fish tank. Fish do not realize they are in water until you take them out of water. Then they struggle to breathe. People do not realize how their actions or inactions can be harmful if they are not thinking about another group of people. For example, faculty will often not have a problem with something called a Faculty Club where faculty and staff can go to eat. Faculty are included, so they do not even notice that others might be excluded because of the club's name. Staff might find the title exclusionary as they are not explicitly named in the title. Higher ups might not take the same offense as someone lower down on the institutional ladder because a small slight to someone in power does not reflect on their position at the institution; the same slight to someone else does often reflect on their lack of power.

Forgetting about others because we are focused on ourselves is very natural. But in institutions of higher education, and especially at institutions that value diversity and inclusivity, we have to do better. We have to think about organizational and environmental aspects of the institution to ensure these parts of the institution send a welcoming and inclusive message to both people who teach in and work in this space.

The following stories share examples of how our biases affect how we engage with our environment through who we think belongs where and how we mete out praise.

A welcoming environment: Where does everyone belong?

In her second week as dean, Dr. Obi saw that the institution was hosting a math symposium. "I walked over a few minutes early," she explains, "And in the room two men were already seated." One saw her and immediately asked if she was looking for the English department's guest speaker event that was being held down the hall. The men had assumed she was in the wrong room.

WHAT IS THE MICROAGGRESSION?

This is a gender microaggression that is linked to implicit bias. The man who asked if Dr. Obi was in the wrong room had a bias that women typically have careers in English and not in math. This bias led him to ask the question, "Are you looking for the English Department guest speaker event that was down the hall?" Dr. Obi received a gender microaggression linked to societal stereotypes that indicate that women do not belong in math.

MYRON R. ANDERSON AND KATHRYN S. YOUNG

WHAT MIGHT BE THE MICROAGGRESSOR'S INTENT?

The intent was to be helpful and assist Dr. Obi in getting to what the man thought was the desired room. However, the impact was quite the opposite.

WHAT MIGHT BE THE IMPACT ON THE MICROAGGRESSEE?

The microaggressee received an incorrect assumption from a person regarding her professional credentials. Because of societal biases about women in math, this may be a microaggression that has happened often in the past to Dr. Obi, and there is a possibility of an accumulation effect from this and similar (possibly repeated) microaggressions related to gender and professional paths.

WHAT WOULD YOU DO IN A SIMILAR SITUATION?

A. Watch her walk in and sit down, but then avoid eye contact at all costs so that no one is uncomfortable.
B. Make a joke about why there are few women in math to lighten the mood.
C. Apologize for your assumption. Let the dean know you are using this as a personal learning opportunity and will work to improve on what you know about gender at work.

Which option is best?

A. Watch her walk in and sit down, but then avoid eye contact at all costs so that no one is uncomfortable.

    No. When you say you want to make no one uncomfortable, what you really mean is that you do not want to be uncomfortable. More useful than ignoring someone is making eye contact, so you acknowledge they exist. Then offer a quick friendly smile, so they feel welcome in the space.

B. Make a joke about why there are few women in math to lighten the mood.

    No. In Chapter 1, we provided a flow chart about jokes. Refer to it here. If you are in the dominant group, do not make jokes about a group considered less well represented in your field. It will often come off as crass and uninformed at best, downright hurtful and sexist (in this case) at worst.

C. Apologize for your assumption. Let the dean know you are using this as a personal learning opportunity and will work to improve on what you know about gender at work.

    Yes. Read the more detailed response that follows about why this was the best option in this case.

HOW CAN THE MICROAGGRESSION BE MORE EFFECTIVELY ADDRESSED?

In looking at this story from an unbiased lens, instead of asking the dean if she was looking for the English Department guest speaker event, the man could have simply asked, "Hello, may I be of assistance?" This is an unbiased question that will allow for the person needing assistance to communicate their possible need.

TAKE FOR ACTION

Speak up.

The dean can address the men by saying, "I trust you did not to intend to say to me that women need to go to the English department, and only men belong in math. But the impact on me and on other women whom you assume do not belong in your space makes us not want to be in this space."

She can then encourage them to assume the Least Dangerous Assumption about people who enter their space—that everyone who enters a math space intends to be there.

TAKE FOR ACTION

Learn from your own biases.

The men, when noticing they were wrong about where the female dean belongs, can do work to learn from their biases.

Notice you have a bias.

Remember times when people have acted in a counter-stereotypical way. If you cannot remember any, work to imagine what this would look like. For example: Remember when women have been present at math meetings and conferences. Remember when men have welcomed people into the space.

Make an effort to think about people from this group as individuals. For example: It is OK to acknowledge someone is a woman if she is a woman, but also learn her name and see her as an individual, just as you would any other colleague.

An inclusive environment: Who is praised?

The associate dean sends recognition emails out to the whole staff and faculty whenever a faculty member publishes an article. For the last year the associate dean has forgotten to send out recognition emails when pre-tenured faculty published an article. One pre-tenured faculty member asked another one if they noticed the trend and if it was something to be concerned about? Did the associate dean only celebrate people once they were "worth it," meaning they made tenure?

WHAT IS THE MICROAGGRESSION?

A group, in this case pre-tenured faculty, feels devalued related to their publication accomplishments. Recognizing tenured faculty publication accomplishments and not recognizing pre-tenured publication accomplishments magnifies the separation between pre- and post-tenured faculty, resulting in hierarchical microaggressions against the worth and the accomplishments of pre-tenured faculty.

WHAT MIGHT BE THE MICROAGGRESSOR'S INTENT?

The intent might be to recognize faculty accomplishments. The impact is received negatively, and the pre-tenured faculty may be experiencing a microaggression from this action.

WHAT MIGHT BE THE IMPACT ON THE MICROAGGRESSEE?

The microaggressee may experience lack of value in the department. Their publication work does not matter, and they do not matter unless they have tenure. This can also make them feel jealous towards tenured faculty who seem to get all the kudos.

WHAT WOULD YOU DO IN A SIMILAR SITUATION?

A. Ignore the issue. If it is a real problem, someone will come and tell you about it.

B. Stop sending out kudos. It was too much work anyway.

C. Come up with a better system to acknowledge people. Apparently, your system has a lot of holes in it.

Which option is best?

A. Ignore the issue. If it is a real problem, someone will come and tell you about it.

   No. We have mentioned this before, and it is worth mentioning again. Ignoring problems does not make them go away. Ignoring problems makes them slide under the surface for a time but then they often bubble up larger than they were before. As with many things at work, gathering information first to decide the best next steps is always advised.

B. Stop sending out kudos. It was too much work anyway.

   No. You started sending these out for a reason. If that reason did not go away, then you probably should stick with your idea. It sounds like you just need a stronger system in place to make a good idea great.

C. Come up with a better system to acknowledge people. Apparently, your system has a lot of holes in it.

   Yes. Read the more detailed response that follows about why this was the best option in this case.

HOW CAN THE MICROAGGRESSION BE MORE EFFECTIVELY ADDRESSED?

Use the Microaggression Reduction-Removal Instrument (MRRI).

1. Individual-Reactive:
Acknowledge, Understand, Empathize.

Junior faculty are looking for affirmation of their experiences, even from each other. If a colleague brings this up to you, you can say, "Thank you for telling me about this. It sounds like when the associate dean leaves you and the rest us off the kudos list, you feel like you don't matter, is that right? I can hear how frustrated that makes you feel. What would you like done about it? Maybe we can go to the chair and ask what's going on?"

2. Systemic-Proactive:
Next Steps to Develop and Implement

It is so easy when you are in a position of leadership to forget how much your actions are examined and evaluated by everyone around you. People are looking to see who you favor or who they think you favor. They are looking to see what you say you value versus how you act on those values. You are in an amazing position to set the tone for the department or unit through your words and through your actions.

Because of this fishbowl effect on people in leadership, you need to develop tracking mechanisms of your own behavior so that you can begin to see what others see in you. This is not just a numbers game, but if you learn that you are not including someone or a group of people, or always interact and talk with only one person or only one group, you do need to rectify that. People are looking to you to be inclusive.

Think about procedures you have put in place to elicit feedback or to share kudos. Every term, spend a few minutes collecting data on who is highlighted in these experiences and who is not highlighted. Then the next term, go out of your way to interact with those you have not recognized. This level of intentionality will create a more welcoming campus climate.

Note: If you dole out praise for people just doing their jobs, that might come across as inauthentic as well. Meaningful and specific praise for events and experiences that are outside of the day-to-day work is the best sort of praise.

TAKE FOR ACTION		
Who have I publically noticed	**Date**	**Rank**

How do microaggressions show up at your institution?

In this last section of the chapter, we provide a template for you to work though microaggressions that occur at your own institution. You can use this tool on your own or bring it to your department or leadership meeting and ask people to fill it out then discuss. If you choose this latter option, please know that most people will not divulge wrongs that have happened to them when they do not feel 100% safe, such as if the person who committed the microaggression is in the room. Sometimes, they will not share in front of people they consider their "boss." We offer a broad prompt that can be used depending on the group of people, their personal and professional relationships, and perceived emotional safety in the environment.

If you want to share these with us, please tweet us: #higheredmicro.

TAKE FOR ACTION

"Please share a microaggression that has happened to you, in front of you, you have heard about, or you have committed." (For people in leadership and/or with several dominant identity categories, it often works better to share one you have committed to show that no one is immune to committing them, no matter how committed you are to an inclusive institution.)

Identify a microaggression.

Explain why it is a microaggression.

How did you resolve it? Did you use the MRRI?
   Acknowledge
   Understand
   Empathize
   Develop
   Implement

If you did not resolve it, how *could* you resolve it? Use the MRRI.

Acknowledge
Understand
Empathize
Develop
Implement

Have people practice talking about microaggressions. Provide scenarios (we provide some for you in Chapter 8) and have people practice sharing their experience with a microaggression and have people practice apologizing for one. You can use the following prompts for such role-playing exercises, to help people get used to talking about microaggressions. (Additional prompts are also found elsewhere in this and in other chapters of this book.)

TAKE FOR ACTION

Sharing a microaggression

If someone says or does a microaggression to you: "When you say X, I hear Y, was that your intent?"

TAKE FOR ACTION

Supporting someone who has experienced a microaggression

If someone brings a microaggression to you, that you are not involved in, but you are in a leadership role: "Thank you for telling me about this. It sounds like when (s/he/they) said X, you heard Y message, is that right? I can hear the pain (frustration, etc.) you feel. (What) would you like me to do about it?"

Conclusion

This chapter provided a series of microaggression stories that you might experience in your own institution. You may have had quick responses that you hoped would address the microaggression and permit all to move on. You may have wondered why anyone would get upset by that?! You may have wondered what the right course of action was. Or you may have wanted more context to better know how to address the microaggression in the moment and to implement systemic next steps to prevent microaggressions in the future. So much of reactively addressing these microaggressions comes through in how you prepare yourself before speaking, how you speak in the moment, and how you respond after. The rest of how you address microaggressions revolves around how you examine your policies, programs, and practices so that you can put proactive systems in place to reduce and remove future microaggressions from your institution.

Think about it – Talk about it

This is an opportunity to think about and discuss some of the concepts in this chapter. On your own, with a few colleagues, or in a departmental or unit meeting, discuss one or more of the questions below.

1. If you are now in a director, associate dean, dean, vice president, or presidential role, think back to some of your early experiences when you were not in charge? How did the people in charge treat you? What did that teach you about how to treat others?

2. Where did many of us learn that "doing nothing" is the best way to address small workplace problems? When has it worked to "do nothing," and when has it backfired for you?

3. How do you feel about the intent versus impact argument? Can you think of times when paying more attention to intent than to impact is the right answer? Is there a way to fairly pay attention to intent and to impact in your role?

4. Talk through 3-5 things you do to model an inclusive climate in your sphere of influence. Talk through 3-5 things you see other leaders doing to model an inclusive climate. Try to add one of those into your repertoire.

5. When do you think it is appropriate for someone to be a whistleblower in higher education? When is it inappropriate? Would people feel safe whistle-blowing at your institution?

6. When does representation matter in your sphere of influence? When does it not seem to matter? How do you balance people at the table with getting the work done?

Cultural Shift Challenge

This is an opportunity to do something! On your own, with a few colleagues, or in a departmental or unit meeting, select one of the following forms that you (individually and/or collectively) can use as a tool to start to improve the culture in your sphere of influence.

1. Look into your institution's mentoring programs. Who is mentored, who is not? Who participates as a mentor? Who does not? What opportunities are afforded through these relationships? If you do not currently mentor someone, challenge yourself to take on this role in the next year.

2. Think about how many times people have come to you with climate-related concerns. What is your gut reaction to these concerns? What is your secondary reaction once you have had a minute to digest the information? What steps have you taken to address these concerns? What are three steps you could take next time to address these concerns?

3. Think about a time when you could have apologized but did not as you did not think you needed to because of the role you hold at your institution. Look through the 5-Step Apology Script and practice what you would have said. Now, be on the lookout for the next time you could apologize and do it.

4. People in leadership have been often socialized to tell rather than to ask. Print out the Intent Clarification Question and use it the next time someone comes to your office to share a microaggression.

5. Print out a copy of the Microaggression Reduction Removal Instrument. Talk through its possible use in your next leadership meeting.

6. Make a list of five microaffirmations you want to share with people in your department. Share each of them in the next week.

7. Study your unit or department and see how much you need to change your recruitment and retention plan for faculty and staff. Convene a thinking group to consider more creative ways to attract a diverse faculty and staff pool. Share the *University of Pittsburgh Diversity Recruitment Resource Guide.*

8. Use the agenda planning tool in one of your upcoming meetings.

9. What would an ideal meeting look like to you? How long would it take? Who would be involved? How would you gather information from others who are not there and disseminate information back? What is holding you back from making meetings closer to your ideal? Now think about the person who you see to be the least similar to you in meetings. Ask that person these questions, too. Where are possible overlaps? Strive to change two things that you agree on.

MYRON R. ANDERSON AND KATHRYN S. YOUNG

Food for Thought

We work at colleges and universities, places of learning. Reducing and removing microaggressions and bullying is first and foremost an educational practice. Removing these actions from our organizations promotes a welcoming and inclusive climate thus allowing faculty, staff and students to thrive. Below is a list of readings to continue your learning in these areas.

Berk, Ronald A. "Microaggressions Trilogy: Part 1. Why Do Microaggressions Matter?" *The Journal of Faculty Development*, vol. 31, no. 1, 2017, pp. 63-73.

Berk, Ronald A. "Microaggressions Trilogy: Part 2. Microaggressions in the Academic Workplace." *The Journal of Faculty Development*, vol. 31, no. 2, 2017, pp. 69-83.

Cooperrider, David, and Diana D. Whitney. *Appreciative Inquiry: A positive revolution in change.* Berrett-Koehler Store, 2005.

Fuller, Robert W. *All Rise: Somebodies, nobodies, and the politics of dignity.* Berrett-Koehler, 2006.

Rowe, Mary. "Micro-Affirmations and Micro-Inequities." *Journal of the International Ombudsman Association*, vol. 1, no. 1, 2008.

CHAPTER 4: HIERARCHICAL MICROAGGRESSIONS AT THE DEPARTMENTAL LEVEL

SUMMARY

The previous chapters explained how to spot and remove microaggressions and bullying, how to use the 4-Way Implementation Model to examine an institution's policies, practices, and programs, and how deans, vice presidents, and others in senior leadership can address microaggressions. Each story in Chapter 3 had individual and systemic ways to respond to microaggressions. Chapter 4 provides more of the same but focuses on the role of the chair and departmental influencers in responding to microaggressions at the departmental level. Each story in this chapter asks why something is a microaggression, asks what might the intent and impact of the action be, and provides steps to react after the microaggression. Following each story and solution is a reflective tool to use in your own practice.

Introduction

Institutions of higher education need everyone at every level to be working to reduce microaggressions. It takes all of us. Chapter 3 focused on deans, directors, and vice presidents and the things they can do to support programs and policies in fair and equitable ways. Their institutional support leads to a better campus climate and to a reduction in micro-aggressions.

People often think it's senior leadership that sets the tone for a campus – and this is true. But for the day-to-day work that happens between students, staff, and faculty, the chair is actually the person who has the most day-to-day engagement with fluctuations in the climate. This is like voting in national elections versus local ones. National elections matter a lot, especially for big picture issues. Local elections matter for our everyday: our roads, our schools, our parks, and our libraries. The chair matters for interpersonal disputes, scheduling, rooming, etc.

The role of a chair is so important to departmental climate. They have great influence systemically in how policies are enforced: how classes are allotted, how departmental meetings are run, how tenure guidelines are interpreted, etc. They influence the department individually as well. Faculty and students come to the chair first when they have a concern. The chair acts as a sounding board for many. People can leave the chair's office satisfied that their concerns will be addressed or concerned that they are being ignored, devalued, or not taken seriously.

The role of faculty who act as departmental influencers is just as important. These people work behind the scenes to change institutional conditions, open doors, and share resources in order to make the department a more welcoming and inclusive space. These people often understand institutional structures and where to find wiggle room in existing policies, practices, and programs. They are the ones who will explain the unwritten policies as well as the written ones to new people. They understand people—

who to go to and who to avoid. They also undertake personal work to learn more about those in their community and beyond. They proactively ask, "How can we make this department feel like a place to thrive for anyone who is here and anyone who might come here in the future?"

The role of staff cannot be understated in creating a welcoming climate. Departments do not function without the people who show up every day. Staff are often gate keepers to knowledge and resources. Staff interact with faculty and students in so many large and small ways that they can make or break someone's educational and workplace experience at the institution. They can be incredible diversity and inclusion champions, too.

Did the chair do enough?

A faculty member who identifies as transgender, Jesse, is hired to teach in the department. Several hours into their first day in the departmental suite, they enter the chair's office and ask, "Where is the All Gender Restroom?" The chair blinks and says, "Can't you just use the male restroom? You look enough like a man. It is just down the hall." Jesse hesitates and says "Yes, if I have to, but is there a way to fix this in the future?" The chair says, "Probably not. Bathrooms are never going to change around here. Chairs can't do anything about that. And you are fine, you can use the men's room." Jesse walks away, stunned.

Jesse experienced a hierarchical microaggression through being the new faculty on campus and feeling silenced by the chair. They also experienced a gender expression microaggression from the chair in the dismissiveness of Jesse's concern.

The chair missed an important opportunity to make a new faculty member feel welcome and feel like they have an ally in the fight for transgender rights in the institution. Instead, the chair alienated the new faculty member, letting them know that the department was not trans-friendly, is not literate towards issues that the transgender community experiences, and that the chair is not someone to be counted on to make things better. The chair is not even someone who is going to look into things to see how difficult or easy change is to make happen. The chair accepts the status quo and the privilege and oppression that currently exists in their system.

> Jesse then walks into an office of a faculty member, Hodari, who seemed very kind and asks if they can share about a situation that they did not know how to take, a situation that made them worried they took the wrong job. Hodari says, "Yes, please do share. We want you here and want you to be happy." Jesse then relates the situation they experienced with the chair. Hodari says, "Oh, no. That is not acceptable at all. Let's problem solve to figure who to talk to on this campus. We hired you because we want you, and we need to make this place into a place where you feel like you can work."

Hodari is an example of a departmental influencer—someone who does not have power through their role or title—but does have power through their knowledge and relationships. Hodari knows how to get things done. Jesse starts to feel like "the bathroom issue" has a chance of getting solved. Hodari understands that everyone deserves to use a restroom where they feel safe and Hodari seems like a guy who will have Jesse's back.

If the chair had approached the conversation with Jesse differently, here is a tool that might have been useful.

TAKE FOR ACTION

Chairs can ask themselves this set of questions:

- Is there a reasonable way I can accommodate the person's request?
- Is my decision in compliance with institutional policy?
- Is my decision fair and equitable?
- How can I best explain this decision to others who may ask about it?
- If I cannot accommodate the request but it relates to equity, what is my next step to be able to improve departmental climate?

Why you, as a chair, might not engage in conversations about microaggressions

Avoiding conversations about microaggression can come from our own fears. This does not absolve you from needing to confront microaggressions and from making a safe space, a brave space, for people to come to you to talk about the culture of the department and about microaggressions they have experienced. After all, you are the chair, and sorting out faculty-related conflict is part of your job. Following is a short list of self-assessments (1. Soft-Skills; 2. Concerns, Strengths, Needs; 3. Emotion-Specific Strategies) to help you to think through the socio-emotional tools you will need in order to be able to address microaggressions in your role as chair.

First, you need to be able to have empathy, flexibility, strong listening skills, appreciation for multiple cultural perspectives, and have skills in cross-cultural communication in your job as chair.

TAKE FOR ACTION #1: SOFT-SKILLS			
	Very well	**Sort of well**	**Not so well**
Empathy			
Flexibility			
Listening without judgment			
Appreciation for multiple cultural perspectives			
Appreciation for cross-cultural communication			

After you ask yourself each of these, if you are brave, ask others in your circle to answer these about you as well – perhaps anonymously. Then make a plan to get better at the skills with which you still struggle.

Next, you need to be brave enough to hold hard conversations. All of us have areas where we need to grow, and interpersonal communication is often one of these.

Ask yourself: What will a discussion about microaggressions potentially expose about me? List:

- 3 areas of concern that you worry could limit your effectiveness in having these discussions.

- 3 strengths you believe will help you to lead open and honest dialogues.

- Lastly, list specific needs that, if met, would improve your ability to have successful hard conversations.

TAKE FOR ACTION #2: CONCERNS, STRENGTHS, AND NEEDS		
Areas of Concern	**Strengths**	**Needs**
Example: I don't know enough about the issues people bring to be. Am I "allowed" to lead a discussion while I also have so much to learn?	Example: I am a really good communicator in general.	Example: I need clearer ground rules for knowing when I might offend someone accidentally.

Areas of Concern	Strengths	Needs

(Adapted from *Teaching Tolerance: Difficult Conversations: A self-assessment.*)

Now make a plan to get each of your needs listed above met. Ask for help if needed.

Third, you need to be ready to know what strategies to use depending on the emotion the faculty member brings with them into your office. When someone comes into your office looking to talk about a microaggression, listen carefully. Listen for what emotion they bring to you and then choose a strategy to help you develop a plan to make the situation better. Use what you know about the faculty member and the rest of the department to inform your plan. Sometimes the plan is just to listen, sometimes it's to ask the person if they plan to follow up with the microaggressor or if they would like you to, sometimes the plan is a more systemic effort like a new program or policy. Listen, learn, and act, depending on the emotion, the person, and the context. Your goal is to make, or re-make, the department into a safe place for all faculty.

Emotion	Strategy to Use in the Moment	Your Plan
TAKE FOR ACTION #3: EMOTION-SPECIFIC STRATEGIES TO USE IN THE MOMENT		
Pain/ Suffering/ Anger	Check in with faculty. Model the tone of voice you expect from faculty who come to you. If crying or angry faculty want to share what they are feeling, allow them to do so. If they are unable to contribute to the discussion, respectfully acknowledge their emotions and either wait for the emotion to subside and ask if they prefer to talk another day, or finish up your side of the conversation.	
Blame	Remind faculty that microaggressions are everywhere because of our common socialization through family, media, friends, etc. We all breathe microaggressions in and are harmed by them. Faculty did not create the system, but they can contribute to its end.	

Guilt	Have faculty specify what they feel responsible for. Make sure that faculty are realistic in accepting responsibility primarily for their own actions and future efforts, even while considering the broader past actions of their identity groups.	
Shame	Encourage faculty to share what is humiliating or dishonorable. Ask questions that offer faculty an opportunity to provide a solution to the action, thought or behavior perpetuating their belief.	
Confusion or Denial	When faculty appear to be operating from a place of misinformation or ignorance about a particular group of people, ask questions anchored in accurate and objective facts for consideration.	

(Adapted from *Teaching Tolerance: Responding to strong emotions.*)

Rebuild, after the sting

We shared this in Chapter 3, but it is worth repeating here. One of the biggest things you can do for someone who comes to you and shares that they have experienced a microaggression is to bring their value back up a little since so many microaggressions relate to feeling devalued or undervalued. Through how you talk to the person, you can help them see their worth in their department or unit and in the institution. You can help rebuild their feelings, after the sting of the microaggressions.

Thinking about students

Just as much as a chair's job is to support faculty, the chair's job is also to support students. There is a lot of research that shows that how we think about someone affects how we act towards someone. Following is an activity you can use with faculty to help each member of your team think differently about students.

TAKE FOR ACTION

Thinking and Teaching

Ask each person to:

1. Write about one time you had an issue/an altercation with a student.

2. Print or project this example.

    I had this student last semester. From day one, she looked like she hated me and everyone else. She wore a baseball hat inside,

    low over her face, and a necklace with bullets on it. She gave short answers to questions, never smiled, and looked completely disinterested in everything.

3. Ask everyone to underline the words you would not like being used about you, your loved one, or your child in the example. These might be some phrases that people underline:

> *I had this student last semester. From day one, she <u>looked like she hated me</u>, and everyone else. She wore a <u>baseball hat inside, low</u> over her face, and a <u>necklace with bullets</u> on it. She gave short answers to questions, <u>never smiled</u>, and looked completely disinterested in everything.*

4. Ask people to share what they underlined. Then ask why those comments might be problematic.

5. Ask people to go back to their own writing and underline the words you would not like being used about you, your loved one, or your child in the example.

6. Share this rewrite:

> *I had this student last semester. From day one, I knew I would have to work hard to develop a relationship with her. I could feel my negative feelings about her, and she had not even done anything yet. I wonder what supports she will need to be successful?*

7. Ask them to rewrite their own stories from the beginning of the exercise.

8. Ask what is different about the two descriptions. Ask which student they would be more inclined to want to teach.

This is an exercise that people can do on their own or in groups to help them develop a growth mindset about students. A growth mindset means believing students' talents can be developed (through hard work, good strategies, and input from others), and we can develop our own growth mindset about students by writing about them and rewriting about them. The act of writing and rewriting helps surface our unconscious biases (See Chapter 3 for more on unconscious bias) about students. Once surfaced, these biases can be confronted.

Note: You can do this exact same exercise when thinking about colleagues that you find difficult. Just change the word student to colleague and start writing.

More learning through stories

The following sections of this chapter parallel the sections of the previous chapter. We provide you with stories from real departments to inspire you to think how you might make the same or different choices. The headings group the stories into themes about what power has to do with tenure, who can speak freely and safely, and whose opinion matters.

These stories are often compilations of several similar stories from different institutions merged together in order to protect anonymity and to provide clear examples of microaggressions. If you read the story and it feels like it could be a story from where you work, good. We intentionally draw on real situations that really happen.

Each section begins with a story and then lays out why that story is an example of a microaggression, discusses the possible intent of the person who committed the microaggression, reviews the possible impact on the person who felt harmed, and then provides some solutions. As a reminder, you can use the 4-Way Implementation Model to address climate through addressing microaggressions at your institution.

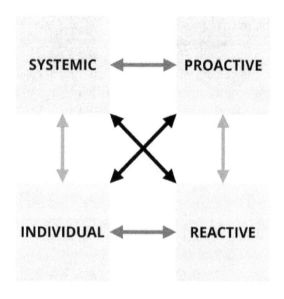

For each story that follows, you will see an individual and reactive way of addressing the problem since people often want to know, "What do I do about this microaggression today, right now?" Then you will also see a systemic and proactive way of addressing the microaggression since, even though microaggressions happen in the moment, the overall goal is to reduce them overall throughout campus in the future. The overall reduction takes systemic solutions to create a more positive climate so that the space where we work and learn sends a message of awareness and inclusiveness, a space where microaggressions do not thrive.

What does power have to do with tenure?

Faculty often like to think that we work in an egalitarian space where everyone can be heard; we also know that there is much power in attaining tenure at an institution. Although tenure is no longer a "job for life," it is still very difficult to fire a tenured faculty member—and people know it.

Most people do not take advantage of this strong job position and work hard every day. Others take advantage of their earned position and do not treat newer colleagues, staff, or students well—all because they have tenure. This becomes an abuse of the position. Tenured faculty need to make sure that they do not take advantage of their valued positions at colleges and universities and need to continue to treat others with respect. Chairs have a responsibility in helping faculty focus their energies in positive ways with students, staff, and colleagues.

Because of the role of tenure and the autonomy and longevity associated with it, faculty and staff often feel like they work in different worlds, even though they work in the same space.

Myron R. Anderson and Kathryn S. Young

Rank: When does your degree matter and when does it not matter?

There is a new task force with faculty from across campus coming to the table for the first time. People go around and introduce themselves. The first three people mention their department and if they are an assistant, associate, or full professor. The fourth person shares his department only. The chair of the meeting, a full professor asks, "Do you have a doctorate?" And then follows up with "Are you full-time or affiliate?"

WHAT IS THE MICROAGGRESSION?

This microaggression has to do with hierarchy and implicit bias. The task force was developed from faculty across departments. This means that the faculty members at the meeting have met the requirements to serve as a faculty member at the institution and have already been chosen for the task force for a reason. The three faculty members who introduced themselves first elected to give their rank as assistant or associate professor and the fourth person only shared their department. This was the choice of the people introducing themselves. However, the questions from the chair of the meeting started the microaggressive process, and it focused on the fourth faculty member.

The follow-up questions were not even necessary. Rank had no bearing on the purpose of the meeting, so why was the question asked? Was it designed to subtlety establish a hierarchy for the flow of the meeting? Second, the specificity of the follow-up questions, "Do you have a doctorate?" and "Are you full-time or affiliate?" goes further to establish hierarchy. It assumes that the fourth person may be at a lower faculty rank and that they may not have a doctorate credential, sending the message that they should not be listened to in the meeting.

Having to explain your credentials, especially when others need not, adds to the hierarchical microaggression and challenges your sense of belonging. The microaggression in this situation reduces someone's sense of belonging in a meeting and perhaps even greater, at the institution.

WHAT MIGHT BE THE MICROAGGRESSOR'S INTENT?

The leader may have been unintentional in delivering this message to the faculty member. He might have been just trying to fill roles in his head since the fourth member did not state their role outright.

WHAT MIGHT BE THE IMPACT ON THE MICROAGGRESSEE?

The recipient may have felt like a second-class faculty member, and this would lay a foundation for them to be less engaged in future meetings, reducing communication, ideas, and strategies to reach the task force goals. Not only does this create a less than welcoming climate for the individual, but it reduces organizational outcomes as well thus reducing the university's ability to be innovative and inclusive in promoting the mission. This hierarchical microaggression harms the individual, the organizational climate, and organizational productivity.

WHAT WOULD YOU DO IN A SIMILAR SITUATION?

A. Everyone should turn and look at the person who did not state their rank. Expect an answer to this question.

B. In a forceful tone, ask the full professor who initiated the query, "Why do you care?"

C. Speak up and show your support for the person who did not state their rank.

Which option is best?

A. Everyone should turn and look at the person who did not state their rank. Expect an answer to this question.

No. People have choice in how they decide to answer a question, unless it is required for some reason. Institutions of higher education are full of rankism, where people "pull rank" and think that because they have attained a certain status, they have the right to treat others poorly. This will not help the institution function, nor will it help this new task force function well. Institution-wide task forces do better when they are cross-functional, flatter in hierarchy, and include perspectives from all over campus. Enforcing hierarchy beginning with the newcomer will reduce sharing of perspectives and reduce productivity in the task force.

B. In a forceful tone, ask the full professor who initiated the query, "Why do you care?"

   Pretty good. It is good to speak up. It helps flatten the hierarchy. It is good to question problematic motives. However, how you flatten the hierarchy is just as important. Using aggression to respond to aggression does work in some circumstances. In other circumstances, you will just become the person others think is acting uncivilly, and people will forget about the originator's offense to focus on your forceful tone. As mentioned in Chapter 3, diplomacy goes a long way when addressing microaggressions. Being respectful in your dialog when addressing the microaggression can go a long way in creating a more welcoming space. It will hopefully lead to a greater understanding of how to treat each other on the task force to get the work completed.

C. Speak up and show your support for the person who did not state their rank.

   Yes. Read the more detailed response that follows about why this was the best option in this case.

HOW CAN THE MICROAGGRESSION BE MORE EFFECTIVELY ADDRESSED?

The resolution to this situation may have been to not single out the fourth faculty member by asking any of the follow-up questions. That simple action would have removed the microaggression that impacted the faculty member and quite possibly improved the overall outcomes of the task force.

The secret to removing microaggressions is to think before you act. Place yourself on the receiving end of your actions to envision the possible impact before you even speak. This is difficult, and you may miss some possible microaggressions you might still commit. However, each microaggression that you catch prior to commitment is one microaggression removed from the environment and one positive check towards improving the climate within your sphere of influence.

BYSTANDER INTERVENTION

Other people at the meeting witnessed the interaction. Often other people can intervene when someone feels like they cannot do so. Frequently, the person who experiences the microaggression is in shock, feeling shamed or like they might lash out in an unprofessional manner. Others in that space can speak up. This is called being a bystander, or increasingly, an upstander (notice, even though this is equity-focused language, it still has disability bias in it as standing is equated with being strong).

TAKE FOR ACTION

Bystander intervention

State the behavior you want to see.

Set limits.

Reiterate a welcoming comment to the person who was microaggressed.

In the preceding story, one of the other faculty members can use the Intent Clarification Question shared in Chapter 3 to give voice to the pain of a microaggression and allow for the possibility of it being addressed. Then you can say to the full professor, "We aren't like that here. We want to hear everyone's opinions no matter their degree or where it came from. They were invited here because of their expertise in this area. Do not ask people if they have a doctorate or if they work full time here. That is not part of the criteria that was used for this task force."

Then the same person can say to the fourth member, "We want you here. Your perspective is valuable." If this seems uncomfortable, remember that we need to prioritize the pain of the person who was harmed over that of the person who caused the harm.

The next story highlights how students might experience events with faculty differently than faculty do.

Immigration services: Student voice versus faculty prerogative

A faculty member wrote on a student's paper: "Your writing needs a lot of help. Please go see Immigration Services." The student was shocked. She was not an immigrant. Her parents were not immigrants. Her grandparents were not immigrants. Why did the faculty member think she needed to go to Immigration Services? The only thing she could come up with is that the faculty noticed her last name is Lopez, a Latinx last name. The student went to talk to the faculty about the comment. She reiterated that Ms. Lopez's writing needed help. Ms. Lopez mentioned to the faculty that assuming she was an immigrant was hurtful. The faculty said she did not mean the comment "that way." The student then went to the chair, trying to get someone to see that assuming she was an immigrant was a problem. The chair sided with the faculty. Who would see the pain the student was experiencing?

WHAT IS THE MICROAGGRESSION?

The faculty member is assuming that the student is an immigrant because of her last name. Everyone just wants to belong on a college campus, and people who are American want to be counted as American. This is one of the classic tropes of microaggression research—that the student is a perpetual foreigner in her own country to some people because of her name. The second microaggression relates to hierarchy. Within academia, we encourage students to talk to faculty about their problems, yet we do not acknowledge the power imbalance in these interactions. We expect faculty will act civilly towards students, and problems will work themselves out. Sometimes though, faculty are not held accountable for their actions and use their relative positions of power to make a problem with a student go away. In this case, the student cannot get anyone to take her concern seriously, primarily because she is a student.

WHAT MIGHT BE THE MICROAGGRESSOR'S INTENT?

The intent in this scenario was to be helpful and to improve the student's writing and her grade, but the path chosen caused harm and actually derailed the student's success. This took the conversation to a negative space causing no improvement in the student's writing and damaged the relationship.

WHAT MIGHT BE THE IMPACT ON THE MICROAGGRESSEE?

The professor does not recognize her as a U.S. citizen. This contradicts her cultural identity leaving her with a feeling of invalidation. The student may disconnect and disengage from the professor. This will reduce learning. Also, she now feels an unwelcoming climate in the classroom and in the department. It is situations like these that sometimes lead students to change majors as they feel misunderstood and unsupported in the departmental atmosphere. There is pain when the microaggression is received and added pain when no one realizes why the statement is harmful.

WHAT WOULD YOU DO IN A SIMILAR SITUATION?

A. Ask the student to explain what you are missing, what is making her feel like this is a big deal.

B. Tell the faculty this is a non-issue, and the student is being too sensitive – you will handle it.

C. Listen to the student. Then tell her that you have no control over faculty and send her back to talk to the faculty member again.

Which option is best?

A. Ask the student to explain what you are missing, what is making her feel like this is a big deal.

   Yes. Read the more detailed response that follows about why this was the best option in this case.

B. Tell the faculty this is a non-issue, and the student is being too sensitive – you will handle it.

   No. This sends the message to the faculty that harming, even if inadvertent, is OK. Also, reinforcing that the student is the problem, that the student is too sensitive, absolves the faculty from having to do any reflection of the incident. It precludes any future learning from the event.

C. Listen to the student. Then tell her that you have no control over faculty and send her back to talk to the faculty member again.

   No. You are the chair. You are right that you cannot actually control faculty; however, in your role, you do have some responsibility for addressing faculty actions and improving the climate in the department. Also, if the student has tried with the faculty member and felt like the conversation went nowhere, how will it help for the student to go back? She is already at a power disadvantage as the faculty member is a person in leadership and a person who will issue her grade. She already found out her professor will not willingly engage with the topic to even learn why her comments were hurtful. The student needs your help and your mediation skills.

HOW CAN THE MICROAGGRESSION BE MORE EFFECTIVELY ADDRESSED?

How do you address this individually?

We hope, individually, that the student can diplomatically bring her identity to the professor's attention. She can ask, "Why are you recommending me to go to immigration services?" This would open the door to further understanding the recommendation without making an assumption of the professor's intent. This might not always work given the power dynamics and possible lack of openness of the professor.

In order to address this, the professor or the chair would need to see this is a problematic statement first. But let's say the chair really does not know why sending a student to immigration services for a writing problem is the wrong place at best and insulting at worst. The chair can start with acknowledging the pain the student is feeling, acknowledging that they must be missing something important here and ask for clarification. It is an adaptation of the Intent Clarification tool.

TAKE FOR ACTION

Intent Clarification Script

Thank you for being brave enough to come in here and voice your concerns. I see you are in a lot of pain over this situation. Please forgive me. I try to stay on top of microaggressions that may happen, but in this case, I do not understand the problem. Can you tell me more about why this statement is so hurtful to you?

This script gives you space to acknowledge the student's pain and also helps put the onus of understanding on you. You want to help. You want to understand and just need a little more information. This might then open the door to discuss the microaggression and develop strategies for removal. This is diplomatic and takes the conversation away from intent and moves it to impact to get to resolution. Additionally, if you are starting to explain away some action that might have caused harm, pause. Think what an apology might accomplish over a justification, sometimes even when you are right and especially when you are wrong.

HOW DO YOU ADDRESS THIS SYSTEMICALLY?

For every specific microaggression that you know is problematic, you can probably work on a way through the harm. But you will continually be confronted with new and problematic speech patterns in academia. You also need a way to respond systemically to these. First of all, the administration needs to have a commitment to engage in ongoing professional development about microaggression and bias at the institution. This PD needs to be up to date so that faculty, staff, and administrators are prepared to address the ongoing and shifting nature of these issues, depending on different contexts and time periods. A reactive strategy is to implement a Microaggression Awareness institution-wide campaign. This would bring awareness about microaggressions to the workforce. A systemic strategy is to incorporate cultural intelligence PD within a mandatory supervisory PD program. This would provide awareness to the leadership and possibly open the door for a train the trainer strategy further providing the workforce with awareness abilities and tools to remove microaggressions from the environment.

You also need a systemic mechanism so people can feel heard, especially people who feel less powerful around leaders of the institution. Faculty might not think of themselves as leadership but in the classroom, they are the ultimate leaders.

TAKE FOR ACTION

Microaggression Receptacle

This can be electronic or could mirror a suggestion box. It is a way to allow for students to place received microaggressions in this "box." The contents of the box are reviewed by faculty and staff to increase their knowledge of possible microaggressions that are impacting students on the campus. Knowing that we commit microaggressions can help us reduce them.

RESTORATIVE JUSTICE

K-12 education, and increasingly higher education, is investing in Restorative Justice Practices. Restorative Justice has a history in informal communal justice strategies used by indigenous people throughout human history. It is a space where people (often when there is a power imbalance but not always) can come together with a facilitator to ensure that people are recognizing when they're doing something wrong and finding a way to make it right. Systems that are embracing restorative justice find that it helps student/faculty relationships, student/student, and even faculty/faculty relationships as needed.

If a chair is trained in restorative practices, here are some questions that might be asked in a facilitated meeting between the faculty member and the student. If not, the chair can bring in someone who is or adapt the script accordingly. It is important to note that these questions only work when there is a culture that allows for them to work.

Restorative Questions

1. The person who caused harm must provide their perspective of what happened and how their part would have affected other people.
2. The person who was harmed is asked to explain how the events have affected them and what they feel should happen to restore the harm done.

After the incident has been recognized, the person who caused harm (even if it is a faculty member) would answer the following questions:

1. What happened?
2. What were you thinking about at the time?
3. What have you thought about since?
4. Who has been affected by what you have done? And in what way?
5. What do you think you need to do to make things right?

The person who was affected by the harm would answer these questions:

1. What did you think when you realized what happened?
2. What impact has this incident had on you and others?
3. What has been the hardest thing for you?
4. What do you think needs to happen to make things right?

The next story highlights how staff might see experiences with faculty, even when faculty do not see the same slight.

Hiring: Who is included in decision-making?

The Department of Nutrition likes to have faculty on staff searches because faculty will have to interact with the staff. This has been the norm for several years. No one has spoken up about it. Last week, a chair mentioned to a faculty member that there was a new search for a new faculty member in front of one of the staff members. The staff member then asked, "Why are there faculty on staff searches but not staff on faculty searches?" The faculty member states emphatically, "They don't get tenure. So, they wouldn't understand the role we are hiring for," and walks away. The chair hesitated then walked away, too. The staff member was left standing alone feeling like the conversation still hung in the air.

WHAT IS THE MICROAGGRESSION?

The staff member feels that their opinion does not matter when hiring faculty, and typically this aligns with hierarchy as faculty tend to carry a higher rank within the organization. This creates a hierarchical microaggression that staff feel that their voices are not meaningful. Since the faculty are involved in the staff hiring but not the other way around, the faculty have a voice in departmental hiring, demonstrating that faculty's opinions are more highly valued than staff in the hiring process.

This microaggression relates to equity and inclusion at an institution. If the organization's goal is to have cross pollination of perspectives in the hiring of staff, why not do the same for faculty? The hiring of faculty and not including staff on the hiring committees goes towards establishing adversity in hierarchy and devaluing of the input of staff.

WHAT MIGHT BE THE MICROAGGRESSOR'S INTENT?

In this case, the intent may be to adhere to a process that has existed for a while.

WHAT MIGHT BE THE IMPACT ON THE MICROAGGRESSEE?

Staff may feel devalued and a reduced sense of belonging. They might even feel like second-class citizens at work. Feeling that they are worth less than others and their opinions do not matter in workforce decisions does not make people want to work their hardest for a place that does not value them.

WHAT WOULD YOU DO IN A SIMILAR SITUATION?

   A. Laugh at the interaction to diffuse the situation as you walk down the hall.

B. Say something like, "Don't be silly. That's not how things are done around here."

C. Say, "Huh, I never thought of that. Let's look into the feasibility of your idea."

Which option is best?

A. Laugh at the interaction to diffuse the situation as you walk down the hall.

No. Laughter is a great tool as a chair, but laughter can be seen as ignoring the problem. Laughter only works when everyone laughs, and laughs genuinely, which is difficult to ascertain.

B. Say something like, "Don't be silly. That's not how things are done around here."

No. Chairs are supposed to mediate between higher ups and everyone else. They are supposed to be advocates for faculty and students. When a chair does not entertain a change to policy, does not find out if it can be changed, or why it cannot, then the chair is not fulfilling the duties of their role. This response belittles the person and shows that you have no interest investing in questioning policy for possibly improving the climate within the department.

C. Say, "Huh, I never thought of that. Let's look into the feasibility of your idea."

Yes. Read the more detailed response that follow about why this was the best option in this case.

How can the Microaggression be more effectively addressed?

Use the Microaggression Reduction-Removal Instrument (MRRI).

1. Individual-Reactive:
Acknowledge, Understand, Empathize.

Let's say the chair was not speechless and knew what to say. They could enact the 5-phase process of the Microaggression Reduction-Removal Instrument (Acknowledge, Understand, Empathize, Develop, Implement) from Chapter 3. Some other statements the chair might use to help out the conversation are found in Chapter 8.

The chair can start by using the 5-Step Apology Script to acknowledge, understand and empathize with the staff member:

1. Tell the staff member you are sorry staff have been left out in the past.

2. Thank them for bringing this to your attention.

3. Ask them if they do not mind sharing more context about the microaggression to increase your understanding. Again, you must be non-defensive.

4. Thank them for sharing this experience with you and increasing your understanding about the microaggression they received.

5. Indicate to them that you will work toward finding a solution that will make staff feel like they belong and are valued in the department.

2. Systemic-Proactive:
Next Steps to Develop and Implement

By looking at this issue from an equitable and inclusive lens, the chair may choose to make a procedural change and include a staff member on the hiring committee. Or, the chair may choose to make a policy in which all potential hires deliver a presentation to the entire faculty and staff so that everyone can voice their choice in the hiring process. If this decision is not up to the chair, the chair can bring the idea to the leadership team and advocate for the change. Promoting equity and reducing rankism in institutional processes goes a long way in reducing microaggressions and improving the sense of belonging for everyone.

As this issue might also be occurring institution-wide, it is important to examine the policy at the highest levels as well. Often policies and processes have been in place for years and may not have been developed with an inclusive and an anti-microaggression lens. To that end, it is recommended that the institution take a systematic approach and review all departmental, unit area, and institutional policies and processes with this lens. This will allow for you to proactively remove microaggressions from your institution in a systemic way.

In this case, hiring authorities can look at who is on search committees and why certain groups are represented and other groups not represented. Make sure people who make institution-wide decisions about hiring include faculty and staff (and even students). You can ask if the groups that are represented are the ones who should be, and does it make sense to exclude the ones who are excluded. Sometimes it does.

Some institutions that prioritize collegiality and equity explain that it is important to have staff and students represented on searches as faculty do not only interact with other faculty. Other institutions that prioritize research may want faculty to choose their peers because of the possible future research relationships that may develop. It is important to be able to explain the reasoning behind the decision-making and to develop buy-in from affected parties.

Going forward, it is important to look at the development of your new policies and process in this way as well as these choices are setting the future for reducing and possibly removing microaggressions in your organization.

Micro-resistance

Instead of feeling like you have to "react" to micro-aggressions you can reframe this work. You can improve the climate. You can work to engage in micro-resistance. Micro-resistance is when you proactively work, every chance you have, to create an inclusive environment around you. This means that when you speak up, you are not trying to make people feel bad. You are working to address structural problems that have made hostility acceptable in the hallway, in a meeting, etc. Ganote, Cheung, and Souza (2015) use a technique called "opening the front door" (OTFD).

OPENING THE FRONT DOOR (OTFD)

Observe: Describe what you see happening, no interpretation.

Think: Explain what you think about the event.

Feel: Say how you feel about the situation or how others might feel about the situation.

Desire: State what you would like to happen.

If you, as chair, reframed the preceding story, you might say to the faculty in front of you, so that the staff member hears, too:

"When you respond to the fact that faculty do not have staff on searches with the remark, 'but they don't get tenure' (observation), it sounds like you think the time they spend and the services they provide in the department are not important. That makes it seem like they do not matter (think). I feel sad that you might think they don't matter (feel), and I would like us to discuss either how to include them in ours or take us off of theirs (desire)."

Your words do not have to be perfect, they need to communicate the possible impact on the harmed individual and possible solutions. The goal is to speak up for someone in a marginalized role since, often when they speak up, it will not fix the problem. They might lose face, get demoted, or even fired. Your daily choice whether to speak up or not to speak up contributes to the climate.

You can improve the climate. You can work to engage in micro-resistance.

TAKE FOR ACTION

Engaging in written reflection helps tease out our own personal reasons for acting or not acting.

Use this prompt if you did not react how you wished you had in a microaggressive situation. Perhaps you did not react well or perhaps you did not react at all. Write about it.

Free write:

Why didn't I speak up?

Why did I speak up in that way?

What might I say next time when I feel stuck in a situation?

Practice your new solution out loud a few times so that you will be ready to say it when needed.

The next story highlights how actions speak louder than words.

Being valued: When does ignoring become dismissive?

Everyone in the department knows a certain senior faculty member, a full professor, who only responds to emails if the dean is cc'd or if the email comes from another full professor at the institution. Otherwise, if junior faculty contacts him, he just ignores emails. The chair has been asked to speak with him. The chair is a little scared. This faculty member is also known to "bite the head off of the messenger."

WHAT IS THE MICROAGGRESSION?

The hierarchical microaggression is that people are being devalued by the actions of this senior faculty member. His actions demonstrate that ideas and communications are not important if the person sending the email is not a full professor or carry the title of dean.

WHAT MIGHT BE THE MICROAGGRESSOR'S INTENT?

The intent might be to prioritize personal workload, addressing only what they feel as the most pressing items first with the intent to communicate with the junior faculty at a later date. However, this is not the impression that is received.

Myron R. Anderson and Kathryn S. Young

What might be the impact on the microaggressee?

The negative impact is on junior faculty. They feel that their perspectives do not matter. They feel excluded within the faculty ranks and feel they are not complete members of the team until they receive a higher faculty status. This can provide a double dose of lack of sense of belonging for faculty from marginalized backgrounds as they may also receive this as an element of their marginalized status. They may be receiving this event from other elements of the institution as well. This will reduce the person's sense of belonging as well.

What would you do in a similar situation?

A. Meet with the senior faculty. Clarify the intent of his actions.

B. Make a systemic noticing plan.

C. Ignore it. Everyone knows that one faculty member will never change and might even become hostile to a chair who inquires about his conduct.

Which option is best?

A. Meet with the senior faculty. Clarify the intent of his actions.

   Yes. Read the more detailed response that follows about why this was the best option in this case.

B. Make a systemic noticing plan.

   Yes. Read the more detailed response that follows about why this was also part of the best option in this case.

C. Ignore it. Everyone knows that one faculty member will never change and might even become hostile to a chair who inquires about his conduct.

   No. This is definitely a human reaction. When someone is known to respond with negative energy, no one wants to approach that person. However, part of the chair's job is to help a department run smoothly. If this one faculty member is holding up the communication process, then he needs to be talked with and the interaction needs to be documented. The chair can make sure to have the conversation in a hallway as public spaces often blunt the force of hostile actors. The chair can talk to the dean to see what other sorts of back up are available. Doing nothing harms everyone involved and may lead to a bully ruling the department through fear. (More on micro-bullying and bullying in Chapters 5 and 6).

HOW CAN THE MICROAGGRESSION BE MORE EFFECTIVELY ADDRESSED?

Use the Microaggression Reduction-Removal Instrument (MRRI).

1. Individual-Reactive:
Acknowledge, Understand, Empathize.

When the chair calls the faculty in to chat, the chair can adapt a script from Chapter 3:

WHAT YOU COULD SAY

If you need to chat with someone about the microaggression they have committed you can say: "When you say X, I hear Y, was that your intent?"

Note: It is important with this strategy to be patient and wait for their response.

The chair can say to the senior faculty member, "When you do not respond to emails from anyone except the dean or other full professors, it sends the message that other people are not important, was that your intent?" Often the faculty will be surprised and say, "No, not at all." If the faculty agrees that other people are not important to respond to, the chair can then remind the faculty of departmental norms and that, in order for people to do their jobs, they often do need responses. Then the chair and the faculty can come up with a plan to respond better to emails. If the faculty member is not aware of his prioritizing of people, the following tool may help.

TAKE FOR ACTION

List the people that you have greeted or had a conversation with this week. Next, list what role they hold at the institution.

Name	Role

Note the roles of people that you have *not* interacted with.

Role	Put a check next to roles you have not interacted with recently
Dean	
Chair	
Full Professor	
Associate Professor	
Assistant Professor	
Affiliate Professor	
Administrator	
Student worker	
Other: _____	
Other: _____	

Make sure to genuinely greet or meet whomever you have not interacted with in the next week/month to help you get in the habit of noticing all of your colleagues.

WHOSE OPINION MATTERS?

Microaggressions also happen when people value some people's opinions over others at work. This sometimes happens explicitly and on purpose in higher education because of norms related to the built-in hierarchy. But these also happen inadvertently because of the norms built into higher education. The stories below show the impact of microaggressions that value some people's opinions more than others in higher education.

Hiring: Who decides what to expect of a man?

The Philosophy Department was preparing to hire a new faculty member. They had interviewed the three top candidates. The chair of the search started out the final conversation about who to hire by wondering aloud if the male knew how much he would be paid and if his wife would be mad about the low salary. Given that, maybe offering him the job would backfire, because he would say no to the low salary, and they should instead offer the position to a female candidate who is probably not the primary breadwinner so is better able to handle the low salary. The chair's comments were met with an uncomfortable silence from the rest of the committee.

Or: Hiring: Who decides what to expect of a woman?

> The Math and Computer Science Department was preparing to hire a new faculty member. They had interviewed the three top candidates, two men and one woman. The chair of the search started out the final conversation about who to hire by wondering aloud that all three were strong candidates, but would the woman stay very long as she was of childbearing age. Given that, maybe offering her the job would backfire, and they would need to do another search in two years.
>
> The chair's comments were met with an uncomfortable silence from the rest of the committee.

Above are two versions of hiring and how gender impacts conversations around the hiring process. Both stories lead to similar results and similar changes that need to be made internally.

WHAT IS THE MICROAGGRESSION?

There is bias towards the candidates through the form of a gender microaggression. These are also clear cases of gender discrimination, but since many such conversations happen and never rise to the level of formal complaints, we will address the microaggressive aspect of these comments here. Because of the conversation and the introduction of gender microaggressions, as well as the economic discussions related to salary, these conversations may sway the decision-making and change who the department offers the position to. These microaggressions are taking place behind closed doors and are not immediately felt by the people applying for the position.

What might be the microaggressor's intent?

The person making these comments might just be thinking how not to fail the search or how not to have to have a new search in a few years. They might be thinking how they would evaluate taking a new position within their own family dynamics.

What might be the impact on the microaggressee?

Although the person being hired may not directly receive the microaggressions, they may receive an external microaggression (and possibly be able to file for discrimination if they found out) after the committee has finalized their decision. This demonstrates how a microaggression, as little as it may seem to be to the person committing it, can have a significant impact on the outcome of a decision.

People on the committee may experience a hierarchical microaggression as the meeting is led in such a way that no one feels comfortable contradicting the search chair. People on the committee may also experience a gender micro-aggression wondering if the same conversations were had about them before they were hired, and this will have a negative effect on the climate. Women on the committee might start to wonder if their salary and institutional worth are tied to their gender in some way. Are their childbearing (lack of) desires brought into consideration when they are not in the room? What does this say about how their colleagues value their contributions to the department? There is also a heteronormative expectation of men marrying women which is problematic as well.

WHAT WOULD YOU DO IN A SIMILAR SITUATION?

A. Laugh it off.

B. Confront the search chair.

C. Stay silent. This feels so awkward. Hidden power dynamic challenges make this not something worth speaking up about.

Which option is best?

A. Laugh it off by saying something sarcastically funny.

   No. We talked about this previously. Humor is wonderful, but there is a time and a place. Be very careful of sarcasm as it is often a biting form of humor at someone else's expense.

B. Confront the search chair.

   Yes. Read the more detailed response that follows about why this was the best option in this case.

C. Stay silent. This feels so awkward. Hidden power dynamic challenges make this not something worth speaking up about.

As mentioned in previous chapters, we have to move from protecting the person who causes pain to protecting the person who was harmed. If someone hits someone else, our first response is not go to the hitter to see if they hurt their fist. We go to the person who was struck. Staying silent, in this case, shows tacit approval to the search chair that questioning gender in relation to hiring is acceptable. This does not mean you have to take a noble and loud stand. How you speak and when you say it has a lot to do with removing this sort of microaggression in the future.

HOW CAN THE MICROAGGRESSION BE MORE EFFECTIVELY ADDRESSED?

Use the Microaggression Reduction-Removal Instrument (MRRI).

1. Individual-Reactive: Acknowledge, Understand, Empathize.

This is a case where people are stunned into silence, but it would be great if someone was brave enough (perhaps a departmental influencer) to be an upstander and say something to the chair of the committee in the meeting or at least after. Bringing up the issue in the meeting has the benefit of holding a shared conversation and helping everyone in the meeting get on the same page. The drawback of talking in the meeting about the chair's actions is that the search chair might get defensive, stop listening, or even commit retribution later (more on retribution and bullying in Chapter 6). Speaking one-on-one after the meeting has the benefit of a private space but then the harm from the meeting is not addressed with everyone who was present. These are hard decisions and knowing your climate and the goals you have will help you decide the best venue for this conversation.

The same prompt as earlier can be used again.

If you need to chat with someone about the microaggression they have committed you can say: "When you say X, I hear Y, was that your intent?"

Note: It is important with this strategy to be patient and wait for their response.

Try this: "When you say you wonder if someone will take the job because you are concerned about their family arrangements, I hear that you think people don't want to work here because of their families. We all made the choice to work here and many of us have family obligations. It feels like you are saying we made bad choices to work here. Was that your intent?" Then indicate to them that you want searches to be places where the committee chooses the best person. Period. The person gets to decide if they want to come and work here. Their family life is off limits in every search. Remember there are legal obligations to not commit gender discrimination in hiring.

2. Systemic-Proactive: Next Steps to Develop and Implement

This story demonstrates the connection of implicit bias to microaggressions to discrimination. Gender, economic bias and the relation-ship to microaggressions is at the forefront in this story. First, engaging in speculation about how someone would feel about a position offer goes against fundamental hiring policies. The person who has the best skills and abilities that align with the job duties should be offered the position, and they should decide if they want to accept it.

Why you personally chose to work somewhere does not give you the ability to know what is best for another potential faculty hire. The amount that the position pays is the amount it pays. Bringing the person's potential wife into the conversation has no place in a hiring decision. He might have a wife, may have a partner, or might be single – none of this matters in the hiring decision. People take jobs for many reasons: location, time in their career, family, etc. Again, there are many variables that are in play and it is not your job to guess on those.

Offering the position to the female candidate to reduce costs in the first story does not make sense either. The best candidate should receive the offer of the position. However, if you offer the position to the female candidate as a strategy to preempt another person declining the offer, this is out of line as well. The female candidate may be the breadwinner for the family, you do not know. The female candidate may or may not be married, have a partner, etc. And again, her reasoning for taking the position can be because of location, time in her career, family, etc. as well. She gets to decide, not you. The committee's only decision is to offer the position to a candidate based on merit.

Discussions like these as they relate to hiring processes should be identified, because they can easily become institutionalized as a norm for a department and are illegal, which will have a systemic effect on the workforce hired. If you look at the workforce within a department, sometimes you may be able to see trends in the personnel that may alert you of this or a similar possibility.

Making searches work better

Have a departmental process for deciding who is on the search committee.

Make sure everyone on the search committee is knowledgeable about the role of implicit biases in hiring.

Set ground rules for confidentiality during the search process. Set rules for when it is OK to break confidentiality, like where there are legal reporting reasons.

Set ground rules for deliberation of candidates. Be careful about looking for a "good fit" as this has been linked to implicit biases.

Set ground rules for decision-making at each stage so that more powerful voices do not overtake the search process.

Think about the composition of the search committee to send an inclusive message to people who visit the campus.

The next story highlights how much students value faculty and what happens when students find out faculty do not value them back.

WHO CAN SPEAK FREELY AND OPENLY?

Another aspect of microaggressions comes from who feels like they can speak and when they can speak, who feels like they can't and who notices. Frequently people from

261

marginalized backgrounds are the ones who must speak up about diversity and equity issues. People from dominant backgrounds often do not notice the inequity or are afraid to hurt another person from the dominant background's feelings. (There is a whole literature on this called "emotionality of whiteness" and, similarly, "white fragility.")

Exclusion through inclusion: Why am I the only one?

In a small group meeting the other day, the Art Department was asked to revise the diversity statement for a department with one Native-American person out of 50 faculty. He was in the small group meeting. The team dived in to revise the statement as requested. Then the Native-American man stated, "I cannot believe I am the only Native-American, and I have to be the one to note how frustrated I am. Why are we revising the diversity statement to make a better one, when the last one has not resulted in us hiring any more people of color since I have been here? And why am I the only one bringing this up? I just wish for once someone else would bring up these issues." Then the meeting went silent. A few people came up after the meeting, in private, to apologize.

WHAT IS THE MICROAGGRESSION?

This faculty member feels like he is the only one to ever speak on diversity issues. He is also frustrated that prior statements have made no changes, so making new statements feels like emotionally-laden busy work. He feels singled out on the issue as no one else speaks up publicly. This is a racial microaggression towards him.

WHAT MIGHT BE THE MICROAGGRESSOR'S INTENT?

The intent is to promote positive change in the diversity of the institution.

WHAT MIGHT BE THE IMPACT ON THE MICROAGGRESSEE?

The impact on this faculty is isolation and demoralization about solving the issue. He also feels like others' silence communicates tacit approval of continuing on with the status quo and not really caring about creating a more diverse faculty, just creating a better statement. When people come up to privately talk to him, this actually makes the situation worse. Why aren't people brave enough to speak up in the meeting? Why don't people have his back in public?

WHAT WOULD YOU DO IN A SIMILAR SITUATION?

A. Tell him that you have to update the diversity statement – the dean said so.

B. Show him the small improvements since last time a diversity statement was written.

C. Publicly apologize and commit to spending time on being better allies in the next meeting and beyond. Make a list of actionable items.

Which option is best?

A. Tell him that you have to update the diversity statement – the dean said so.

   No. Perhaps you do have to update the diversity statement for some bureaucratic reason. Right now, that is not what your colleague is asking for. He wants to work in a department where he feels psychologically safe to speak up, and safety might come from not being the only one to speak up. He is asking to be heard, to be heard for the pain of seemingly being the only person to really speak up about hypocrisy in the department. Right now, he needs to hear that others have heard his pain, taken it seriously, and want to make meaningful departmental changes in the future.

B. Show him the small improvements since last time a diversity statement was written.

   No. Showing him the small improvements tokenizes his pain. He is not asking for more of the same with tweaks to the edges. He is asking that the diversity statement match the diversity actions in the department. Right now, he sees lots of words and few actions. Pointing out the few actions just digs the hole further to show how much there is left to do.

C. Publicly apologize and commit to spending time on creating structures and processes to be better allies in the next meeting and beyond. Make a list of actionable items.

   Yes. Read the more detailed response that follows about why this was the best option in this case.

How can the microaggression be more effectively addressed?

Use the Microaggression Reduction-Removal Instrument (MRRI).

1. Individual-Reactive:
Acknowledge, Understand, Empathize.

Whoever is the head of the small group can say publicly:

1. You are sorry no one has spoken up about diversity, too.

2. Thank him for bringing this to the group's attention.

3. Ask him if he would share more context about the microaggression to increase your understanding. Again, you must be non-defensive.

   In this case, he might say that he has said enough and is not interested in saying more. It is everyone else's turn to speak. That makes sense. He is tired of being the only one to speak up. Then continue on with Step 4.

4. Thank him again for sharing this experience with the group and trusting the group enough to even bother speaking up.

5. Indicate to him that you will work toward finding am institutional solution that will help him not feel so isolated and that you will work to speak up too in the future. You will also work to make meaningful changes that make the diversity

statement a statement that guides departmental actions, not just bureaucratic obligation.

2. Systemic-Proactive: Next Step to Develop and Implement.

The problem is that changing the statement itself will not create a more diverse faculty. This is a classic administrative misstep and often has an adverse effect on the organizational climate.

The resolution is to develop accountability touchpoints that link the diversity statement to the processes involving hiring. This will move the needle in the diversity of the department. The statement is probably fine, and diversity statements should be developed, implemented, and revised. However, they need to be a part of a larger project to promote diversity and inclusivity in the hiring process. All processes need to be reviewed and refreshed if diversity goals are not being met. See Chapter 3 for the University of Pittsburgh Diversity Recruitment Resource that might help, too.

BEING AN ALLY

People from marginalized identities should not be the only people to speak up about inequities in a department. In fact, it is often more dangerous for them to speak up due to the fact some people from dominant backgrounds do not "listen" as well to people seen as different from themselves and research shows that punitive forces are more often inflicted on people who do not "fit" in the first place. All this is to say that when you have privilege due to your race, class, role at the institution, etc., it is often less dangerous for you to speak up and use your privilege, even when you are scared, to address the inequity. You might experience some pain at the backlash or discomfort you feel speaking up, but your discomfort is not the point. The point is to make less discomfort for people who experience it more often than you do and at a higher personal cost.

Note: You must be careful in how you speak up so that you do not take space from someone who experiences marginalization who was intending to speak up first. And there is no need for you to speak for others. Speak for yourself about how the problem bothers and impacts you.

To Be An Ally

A - always center on the impacted

L - listen and learn from the impacted

L - leverage your privilege and position

Y - yield the floor

(From "Guide to Allyship," http://www.guidetoallyship.com/#the-work-of-allyship_)

The next story highlights how students experience their positionality and the lack of power associated with it.

When and how can students speak up?

Two students came into a faculty's office to mention that another faculty told the whole class that they'd "better give her all 5's" on faculty evaluations. The students were shocked as faculty are not supposed to influence evaluations. They came in to talk to Dr. Conner, because they did not know who to turn to. Dr. Conner said that she does not have power in this situation and feels uncomfortable hearing about someone else's class. She encouraged the students to speak with the chair. They then said that they were scared to talk to the chair, because if it got back to the faculty, then their grades might suffer. They felt powerless to make change.

WHAT IS THE MICROAGGRESSION?

These students are experiencing a hierarchical micro-aggression from their professor. They felt powerless from the professor's comments to mark her scores appropriately. They felt powerless to complain as they thought there might be retribution. They did not know who to turn to that could hear the problem and help them sort it out.

WHAT MIGHT BE THE MICROAGGRESSOR'S INTENT?

The faculty member might be trying to be funny. The faculty member might be trying to get all 5's and thinks that her comments are within the bounds of what to say to students before they evaluate faculty.

WHAT MIGHT BE THE IMPACT ON THE MICROAGGRESSEE?

The impact is that the students are scared of their professor and a possible impact on their grades. They know they have little power to change this situation but can also name the situation as unethical. This might make them worry about their overall education in this department and also worry if they have future concerns who will be there to listen to them and advocate for them?

WHAT WOULD YOU DO IN A SIMILAR SITUATION?

A. Send the students to the chair. That is what you would want another faculty member to do for you.

B. Offer to go with them to the chair to show the students solidarity.

C. Go tell the faculty member that students are about to complain about her.

Which option is best?

A. Send the students to the chair. That is what you would want another faculty member to do for you.

Yes, but.... As mentioned above, institutions often create reporting structures where those with the least amount of power are required to potentially academically harm themselves. So, although this way is the required way, it is often a monumental hurdle. The existing policies act as institutional hierarchical microaggressions.

B. Offer to go with them to the chair to show the students solidarity.

    Yes. Read the more detailed response that follows about why this was the best option in this case.

C. Go tell the faculty member that students are about to complain about her.

    No. If students come to you in confidence, please respect that confidence.

HOW CAN THE MICROAGGRESSION BE MORE EFFECTIVELY ADDRESSED?

Use the Microaggression Reduction-Removal Instrument (MRRI).

1. Individual-Reactive: Acknowledge, Understand, Empathize.

If the students are coming to you because you feel like a safe person to them, you can use your role as a departmental influencer to support them.

1. Acknowledge their discomfort with the faculty's actions.

2. Show understanding that it is hard to talk a faculty member when they are feeling unsafe about their grades.

3. Empathize with the complexity of the situation.

Advise them to go to the chair, and if they go together (or take even more people with them from the class), they might feel better. Offer to help set up the appointment or take them to the appointment if they think that would be helpful. Explain that there are structures in place where you cannot be in a meeting where they talk about another faculty member to the chair, but you are supporting their right to raise concerns with the chair. Often when they feel your support, it is enough to help them follow through with their concerns through the existing channels.

If you learn that they will not talk to the chair, go and ask the chair (or possibly the dean) yourself what the next steps would be if you learned about a situation like this, since it might be against the institution's Code of Conduct.

2. Systemic-Proactive: Next Steps to Develop and Implement.

Develop a Student Advocate Position. Ideally, this person is someone from outside the department, or even better, outside of the institution. Their outsider status helps them be a true advocate for students.

CHARACTERISTICS OF A GOOD STUDENT ADVOCATE

- A sincere concern for the students' well-being.
- Enough dedication to work on a student's issue, until the student feels like their needs have been met or the institutional process has been completed.
- The ability to be objective and non-judgmental.

- The ability to interact with people from many different backgrounds.
- Good verbal and written communication skills.

There are some drawbacks to hiring an outsider. Outsiders do not always know who the departmental influencers are. They do not always know the bureaucratic mechanisms or how to navigate them, especially initially. If those are concerns, you can choose an internal advocate. This person might also be a faculty who receives a course or two release to perform this task. If this route is chosen, it is even more important that the choice of this person reflects the students' needs, not the departmental needs.

The students' advocate undertakes the following activities:

1. The advocate meets with the student before attending a meeting they are concerned about to assist them to identify their ideas, views, and wishes.

2. The advocate discusses the meeting with the student, identifies any concerns that they may have, asks the student whether they would like the advocate to attend the meeting with them, and asks if they want the advocate to speak or just to be present.

3. The advocate records decisions and any timeframes agreed upon by participants at the meeting. This information is provided to the student and other significant people involved with the meeting.

4. The advocate will have at least one follow up session with the student to ensure that the decisions made at the meeting are being implemented.

The next story highlights the struggle between generalizing and stereotyping and the fine line between the two.

A welcoming environment: Who do you notice, and how do you notice them?

> You want to be an inclusive chair. You want to make sure everyone's voice is heard. You noticed that the two Asian faculty are not speaking at meetings. You decide to do something about it. You ask them three times during an hour-long meeting why they are so quiet and to please speak up if they have something to say. Finally, one of the faculty members says back, "Did you notice that there are two white faculty members who are not speaking up either? Why are you picking on us?" You are shocked. You were just trying to have an inclusive meeting.

WHAT IS THE MICROAGGRESSION?

This racial microaggression relates to bias and lack of cultural understanding. First, there may be bias in recognizing equal involvement. This example is similar to when white people wonder why all of the African Americans sit together at lunch and do not recognize that many white people sit together during lunch as well. Focusing on the Asian members of the group in this way draws attention to the chair's bias.

Also, there may be a cultural understanding element to this situation. In some Asian cultures, speaking over others is not as acceptable. In some Asian cultures, speaking openly in front of someone in leadership is not acceptable. This cultural identity may influence faculty from Asian decent to wait for an opening to speak rather than speaking over others in meetings, or they may prefer another way to share their thoughts. Understanding these cultures allows the chair to develop more inclusive strategies to draw out multiple perspectives and ideas from meetings continuously and not just rely on people speaking out during meetings. This will also work for other people who do not feel comfortable speaking in meetings.

WHAT MIGHT BE THE MICROAGGRESSOR'S INTENT?

The intent may be to be more inclusive and welcoming of ideas. However, the impact was isolation and may not have been respectful of a culture's practices.

WHAT MIGHT BE THE IMPACT ON THE MICROAGGRESSEES?

They felt that they were called out. They might have even felt reprimanded for their actions or lack of actions as they felt the need to defend themselves by comparing their actions to their white faculty counterparts.

WHAT WOULD YOU DO IN A SIMILAR SITUATION?

A. Tell them not to be so sensitive. You talk over everyone sometimes and ask everyone other times for their feedback.

B. Take a step back and think about who you asked for input when. Then apologize.

C. Say loudly, "That is not what I meant! Can we move on?"

Which option is best?

A. Tell them not to be so sensitive. You talk over everyone sometimes and ask everyone other times for their feedback.

   No. There are some catch phrases to never use if you want a conversation to progress. "You are too sensitive" is one of them. The phrase makes people angry and hurt that you do not understand where their feelings are coming from. At the end of this chapter, we offer a whole list of unhelpful phrases from *Resolving Conflicts at Work* (Cloke and Goldsmith, 2011).

B. Take a step back and think about who you asked for input when. Then apologize.

   Yes. Read the more detailed response that follows about why this was the best option in this case.

C. Say loudly, "That is not what I meant! Can we move on?"

   No. As explained in Chapter 3, the difference between Intent and Impact matters in conversations. We often explain our intent to deflect having to take responsibility for the fact our words or actions caused harm. Instead, seeking to understand the problem from the other person's point of view will go a long way for someone in a chair's role.

HOW CAN THE MICROAGGRESSION BE MORE EFFECTIVELY ADDRESSED?

1. Individual-Reactive:
Acknowledge, Understand, Empathize.

The chair needs to address this at the meeting:

1. You are sorry you called them out.

2. Thank the faculty member for bringing this to the group's attention.

3. Ask the faculty if they do not mind sharing more context about the microaggression to increase your understanding. Again, you must be non-defensive.

4. Thank them for sharing this experience with the group and increasing your understanding about the microaggression they received.

5. Indicate to them that you will work toward finding a solution that will make them feel less highlighted and that you will work to not commit this microaggression in the future.

2. Systemic-Proactive:
Next Steps to Develop and Implement.

People look to chairs to model departmental norms. You need to be aware that people watch you in this role and pay attention to the meanings (implicit or explicit) in your words and actions. Some statements the chair might want to stop using are found in Chapter 8. The tool below offers some suggestions about how to run a meeting more equitably.

TAKE FOR ACTION

When you are running a meeting:

- Make eye contact with everyone in the room who chooses to make eye contact.
- Make enough wait time for people who want to speak.
- Create multiple ways of sharing in meetings (e.g., writing, through email, out loud in small and large group, etc.).

THE DIFFERENCE BETWEEN STEREOTYPING AND GENERALIZING

Diversity issues are often complicated since people in leadership are told not to stereotype but then to acknowledge generalizations about groups. How are these two terms different?

Sociologist Joel Charon's lists six characteristics of stereotypes:

- Stereotypes pass judgment.

- Stereotypes leave little or no room for exceptions.

- Stereotypes create categories that often dominate all other features of a person, not allowing for other characteristics to be seen and appreciated.

- Stereotypes do not tend to change, even when proven wrong, which supports the idea that it is not backed by empirical evidence.

- Stereotypes are not formed by empirical evidence to begin with, but through anecdote and other socialization processes.

- Stereotypes do not help people understand their differences.

Generalizations basically reject all six.

- Generalizations are made with the primary intention of stating fact.

- Generalizations include and account for exceptions.

- Generalizations change with new empirical evidence.

- Generalizations are formed on the basis of empirical evidence.

Conclusion

This chapter focused on the role of chairs and departmental influencers to address microaggressions. Chairs are in a meaningful role as they interact so closely on a daily basis with other faculty, staff, administrators, and students. As much as senior leadership has a large effect on institution-wide climate, chairs have a large effect on the day-to-day climate of the department and interactions within the department.

Although chairs are rarely given the managerial training needed for such a position, chairs are still responsible for setting the tone of the department and encouraging other colleagues to abide by this tone. This is a big job.

Chairs also usually know their colleagues better given their daily interactions. Chairs can leverage these personal relationships to help colleagues work better together and to see each other's perspectives. Because of this deep level of contact, chairs need to be able to take concerns seriously and address microaggressions while they are still at the level of microaggressions.

Chairs are the first level of institutional defense against microaggressions evolving into microbullying and microbullying evolving into bullying. Chairs need to take this role seriously. This chapter offered many tools for chairs to use to examine their own practice as well as tools to use with their colleagues. We hope that this chapter and the tools provided empower chairs to create and maintain departments that feel safe and productive for all.

Think about it – Talk about it

This is an opportunity to think about and discuss some of the concepts in this chapter. On your own, with a few colleagues, or in a departmental or unit meeting, discuss one or more of the questions below.

1. What are some ways you have acted as an ally at work? What were the conditions that prompted you to feel it was OK to act?

2. What are some ways you wished you had acted as an ally? What kept you from acting? What could you do next time if you are faced with a similar situation?

3. Look back at the Emotion Specific Strategies in this chapter. How could these have helped you in a prior situation? Role play with a close colleague a situation where someone came to you with strong emotions. Use the tool to help you work out what you will say next time.

4. Talk through with a trusted staff member all the different activities and meetings that take place within your department. When are staff included? Do they want to be included in anything else? Learn why and see if there is a way you can use your position to help this conversation move into an action.

Cultural Shift Challenge

This is an opportunity to do something! On your own, with a few colleagues, or in a departmental or unit meeting, use one of the forms below that you (individually and/or collectively) can use as a tool to start to improve the culture in your sphere of influence.

1. Have your team take the Intercultural Conflict Style Inventory. It is a psychometric evaluation that describes your preferred approach to communicate and resolve conflicts. It helps you see if you prefer

to resolve conflict more direct or indirectly and if you are more emotionally restrained or emotionally expressive.

2. Look back at the Concerns, Strengths, Needs chart in this chapter. Find two areas of need that you want to work on. What is your first step to get started? Go do it.

3. Quickly list everyone you can think of in your department. Then compare that list to a list of everyone who works in the department in some capacity. Go say hi to people who were on the end of your list or who you left off your original list.

4. Spend a few months having someone act as a process observer in meetings. Their job is to track who talks to whom, for how long, and if possible, who interrupts who. Have them compile the data and then bring that data back to the group to discuss. Use this as a tool to discuss equity norms in future meetings.

Food for Thought

We work at colleges and universities, places of learning. Reducing and removing microaggressions and bullying is first and foremost an educational practice. Removing these actions from our organizations promotes a welcoming and inclusive climate thus allowing faculty, staff, and students to thrive. Below is a list of readings to continue your learning in these areas.

Cloke, Kenneth, and Joan Goldsmith. *Resolving Conflicts at Work: Ten Strategies for Everyone on the Job.* Jossey-Basse, 2011.

Ganote, Cynthia, et al. *Don't Remain Silent!: Strategies for Supporting Yourself and Your Colleagues via Microresistances and Ally Development.* Roy, P., et al (Eds). POD Diversity Committee White Paper at the 40th Annual POD Conference, pp. 3-4, 2015.

Trammel, Ming Shi, and Maria Gumpertz. "Maybe We're Not So Smart: Identifying Subconscious Bias and Microaggressions in Academia." *Diverse Issues in Higher Education.* 8 November 2012. diverseeducation.com/article/49342/

Winn, J. Emmett. *Communication and Conflict Management: A Handbook for the New Department Chair.* Academic Impressions, 2016.

Zehr, Howard. *The Little Book of Restorative Justice.* Good Books, 2002.

CHAPTER 5: MICROBULLYING

SUMMARY

The previous chapters explained how to spot and remove microaggressions and bullying; how to use the 4-Way Implementation Model to examine an institution's policies, practices, and programs; how deans, vice presidents and others in senior leadership can address microaggressions at an institutional level; and how chairs and departmental influencers can address microaggressions at the departmental level. This chapter moves the conversation from microaggression identification and removal to understanding the relationship between microaggressions, microbullying, and bullying. It also discusses how one behavior type can morph into the next if nothing is done to remove and reduce the negative behaviors. This chapter specifically focuses on the role of microbullying and what departments can do to address this problematic behavior.

Introduction

Microaggressions are often committed by well-intentioned people who are not trying to harm someone else, but through intent or lack of intent, they still cause harm related to that person's important identity characteristics. Microbullying is when microaggressions become targeted and repetitive. The microbullier might not yet realize the powerful effect their comments and actions are having on the receiver, or the microbullier is not engaging with the purpose of control, yet. If microbullying occurs (intentionally or unintentionally), the damage to the person receiving the microbullying actions is extremely painful. Moreover, because the microbullying act is often felt but is still difficult to name in observable characteristics by the person receiving it, or by a bystander, there are no specific policies developed to provide institutional enforcement to lessen these behaviors. This does not mean that departments should do nothing about the behavior. They should. Remember the microaggression-microbullying-bullying relationship model from Chapter 1. (See the following figure.) The model shows us how institutional leaders have opportunities to stop these negative actions at each step. And if not stopped, these actions tend to worsen over time until outside intervention is needed.

From microaggressions to microbullying

A department does not go from a climate in which everyone is working well together to a climate in which someone is bullied, overnight. There are many early signs and smaller situations that send the message to the bully that their behavior is acceptable in the department or unit. These signals come in many forms from lack of departmental accountability programs and leadership's disregard of complaints to gaps in institutional policies and procedures allowing for these behaviors to go essentially undetected.

Bullying behaviors often start as microaggressions. Microaggressions happen more and more until they turn into microbullying. When this behavior is not curtailed, the microbully receives the implicit message that their behavior is acceptable, perhaps even academically encouraged, and they continue harming others. Moreover, once the microbullying action moves to this stage, the element of control enters. At this point, the microbully will be able to see that they have an element of control over this person within the departmental dynamic. For example, the microbully will affect interactions in departmental meetings, attendance on departmental committees, selected departmental office hours, and even shape opinions and votes on important departmental business (i.e., curriculum, tenure and promotion, mission, and vision). The unmanaged negative behaviors turn into departmental bullying.

Microbullying is subtle to everyone except the person who is experiencing it. An excellent microbullier can bully someone in a room full of people and only that person will know they are being bullied. They might roll their eyes or make comments that suggest negative things but in a subtle way, where only the target will connect the dots. They might devalue research via a backhanded compliment like, "Your research is excellent for journal x." The first person considers the journal to be a second or third tier journal for the discipline, but others hear "excellent" and "journal" and do not notice the devaluing behavior.

Microbullying behaviors include, but are not limited to:

- Someone repeatedly interrupts the same person or group of people (like those who have the same research stance, same race, or have all been at the institution for a similar amount of time) in departmental discussions

- Someone repeatedly starts side conversations when a specific person or group of people speaks

- Someone repeatedly makes sarcastic comments when a specific person or group of people speaks

- Someone repeatedly ignores a specific person's or group of people's comments

- Someone repeatedly is argumentative with a specific person or group of people

- Someone repeatedly makes negative facial gestures towards a specific person or group of people

- Someone repeatedly down-plays a specific person's or group of people's contributions

- Someone repeatedly rejects feedback when it comes from a specific person or group of people

- Someone repeatedly disrespects a specific person's or group of people's comments nonverbally by checking their cell phone, sending texts, and emails.

Done even once, each of these items would hurt someone. It might hurt more if done to someone in relation to their salient identity categories. This is a microaggression. Each of these behaviors might not be noticed if they happen once or even occasionally. They might be noticed and cause pain but can often be explained away, even by the person experiencing them. Now, imagine working with a colleague who belittles you but only when you see each other at a bi-monthly meeting. This does not seem frequent – it only happens twice in the fall and twice in the spring, but the frequency starts to increase. The person continues their behavior and might even feel justified in belittling you given the implicit culture of critique in academia. This is microbullying—repetitive and targeted. The person who repeatedly sneakily rolls their eyes at you every time you speak, but no one else ever notices. This is microbullying. Sometimes the microbully targets a whole group of people. At that point, when the microbully harms someone, others in the group feel the harm as well. In many ways, the microbully kills two birds with one stone when the insult harms more broadly. Microbullies often fly under the radar.

A chair who spots the unspotable

These small, repetitive slights are only detected as systematically relevant by the target over time. Often the person committing these slights will use more than one strategy. Not only is each slight repeated, but there is also repetition in the very act of getting slighted. The microbully will hardly ever be detected by someone in senior leadership as these slights happen frequently but slyly, so they are very difficult to catch openly. If anyone beside the target is to catch this person's behaviors, they will have to be very purposeful. The chair or immediate supervisor may be in a role to notice these behaviors as they interact with colleagues more frequently than those in senior leadership.

If someone comes to you and tells you about multiple small slights that are affecting them, you might need to look further into the possibility of microbullying.

Here is one way: Ask the person being bullied to record the experiences they have been telling you about. Then take their documented recording and list the behaviors for yourself from their narrative. Then spend the next month actively looking and seeing if you can notice these same behaviors, now that you are paying attention to them. See an example below.

No hospitality from the hospitality department: Microbullying in action

One of the things I notice as I contemplate the departmental climate is the tendency of a particular long-time faculty member to engage in discourteous actions and behaviors toward a specific colleague of color, possibly counting on the victim's fear that they won't report to the Equal Opportunity Office (EOO). This fear comes from bad experiences with the former EO Officer years ago, and then the subsequent targeting of the same colleague of color by the initial microbully when the colleague finally responded with anger or frustration after too many incidents. This pattern of pushing people into responding with anger so that the microbully can then isolate/distort that response and end up claiming to be a victim is difficult to track.

Sometimes it's more like incivility, but it involves a range of things like repeatedly speaking loudly over the colleague of color to keep them from voicing their opinions at faculty meetings, muttering asides like "yeah, right" while the colleague of color talks at meetings, making faces and rolling eyes when the colleague of color speaks, and repeated rudeness that seems directed at this particular person. Although, looking back, everything independently looks so small, it all feels big when compounded over time. When the colleague of color has raised these issues as they happen, the senior faculty member who perpetuates the unprofessional behavior tends to say they didn't say/do anything, and that is just how they speak when passionate.

Sometimes they characterize the colleague of color as causing trouble over nothing. The microbullier asks the chair to look at one sole incident and asks if eye rolling one time, if saying "yeah right" one time, if speaking over someone one time is actually problematic, and the chair might feel that is is hard to argue back if these behaviors are "one-off's." This allows the microbully to state that the colleague is clearly being oversensitive, again. Sometimes the microbully claims to be the victim because of getting so many complaints against them but doing nothing wrong. They refuse to acknowledge any accountability for their own behavior.

Individual incidents can sometimes seem minor when in isolation but are actually part of a larger pattern that contributes to a negative climate. This person can continue to contribute to the negative climate in a micro-way, even when the leadership moves to find resolution. Oftentimes, the same faculty member will devalue the resolution process and make comments and actions throughout the department in an attempt to impede progress. For example, this faculty might communicate to others, "They're probably going to make us all go to cultural sensitivity training. They did that to us as a department years ago—what a waste of time."

How the chair needs to respond

First, by listing the behaviors in the story above:

1. Repeatedly speaking loudly over the colleague of color to keep them from voicing their opinions at faculty meetings.

2. Muttering asides like "yeah, right" while the colleague of color talk at meetings.

3. Making faces and rolling eyes when the colleague of color speaks.

4. Repeated rudeness that seems directed at this particular person.

5. Making negative comments when strides are made to possibly improve the climate, thus causing a chilling effect on the possibility of change.

Then, by looking for these behaviors in action and documenting each time you see them happen to this specific person or to anyone else. People are better able to spot specific behaviors when we know to look out for them. Is there a pattern to the behaviors? Are they targeted? If so, you probably have a microbully on your hands.

Unfortunately, the microbully will probably use the tactics listed in the preceding story to deflect blame from themselves. They will:

- Characterize the target as causing trouble over nothing.

- Ask the chair to look at each separate incident, since each incident is so small it is hard to argue back.

- Reiterate that the colleague is clearly being oversensitive.

- Claim to be the victim because of getting so many complaints against them but doing nothing wrong

- Refuse to acknowledge any accountability for their own behavior.

Below is a tool that might help you tease apart how to talk to the different sides in something as complicated as microbullying.

TAKE FOR ACTION

Document the behavior. Look for it yourself, too. Here are questions to ask yourself each time you see or hear of problematic behavior:

What can you do to manage this conflict before it escalates further, even if you do not see the evidence yourself?

What will your objective be? What and whose behavior must change to improve the situation? How would you approach the people who need to change their behavior?

Would you involve others in managing the situation? Who? And why?

Is there a way you can remain supportive of the people involved without harming departmental operations?

(Adapted from *Mending the Cracks in the Ivory Tower* by Susan Holton (Ed), 1998)

Microbullying through microactions

One faculty finds out that another faculty member, who is also the associate chair and in charge of course schedules and rooming in the department, opposes his tenure case. She moved his office and turned it into a break room, gave him classes at the beginning and end of the day, and brought the quality of his teaching and research into question with others in the department. She told him that she had heard through the grapevine that he might not get tenure.

How the chair needs to respond

First, by listing the problematic behaviors that are reported:

1. Opposes his tenure case.
2. Moved his office and turned it into a break room.

3. Gave him classes at the beginning and end of the day.

4. Brought the quality of his teaching and research into question with others in the department

5. Told him that she had heard through the grapevine that he might not get tenure

Look for a pattern. Does the microbullier target this one person? If so, seek to understand why. If they have reasons for doing what they are doing, ask how they came to their decision. Why did X have to move offices not someone else? Why did X's classes change but no one else? If these answers ring at all "funny," you might have a conversation like the following:

What You Can Say

"As chair, I have to think about the pattern of behavior. I don't know exactly what is going on, but I do know there is a list of behaviors that you are exhibiting which other people are not. You may have good reasons for all of these things, but when I put all of the information together it feels like you give X special attention in a negative way. I need this to stop. I need you to treat X as you treat everyone else in the department. If you plan to make changes that impact X in the future, run them by me first."

As with microaggressions, microbullying needs an individual reactive response like the one just presented and a systemic proactive response (like the one which follows) put in place, so more people do not have to go through these experiences. For people who experience troublesome behavior from colleagues, but the behavior does not meet the institutional definition of bullying, the department still needs to do something to address the problematic behavior in order to improve departmental experiences and climate (See Chapter 6 for more on this topic).

TAKE FOR ACTION

Improvement plans to address microbullying:

1. Have a specific plan in place that is used for everyone who acts unprofessional.

2. Identify problems with performance.

3. Develop a plan to improve the performance. Use observable characteristics so that the characteristics can be measured and tracked. Avoid using words like "respectful" and "professional" without defining what they mean.

4. Have the dean and chair meet with the person to design appropriate assessments, evaluations, and timeline for the faculty member. Indicate consequences for inaction.

5. Meet at agreed upon times to check progress.

If this is not enough:

6. Assign an experienced evaluator/mentor to work with the faculty member on the issue.

7. Have the evaluator design specific interventions to help the faculty member.

8. Have the evaluator submit a written report to the chair with recommended actions.

9. Evaluate and implement a specific plan with detailed schedule of compliance and consequences for inaction.

Out loud and under the radar all at once

Sumita was new to the Astronomy Department as an office manager. At first, the dean told her privately that she did not work fast enough, then told her privately that she did not do things the "right" way. Sumita decided to work harder and do better. The dean then started making fun of Sumita in front of others but only occasionally. In fact, it would only happen after Sumita had decided that she was overreacting, and the dean was actually a kind person. Then the dean would give her additional assignments and tell her what to do and how to do it. But when Sumita went to do the tasks, the dean would take them off of Sumita's desk and say, "Let me give it to Jorge. He does it right every time."

It is microbullying when the dean asked Sumita to complete a task and, after "the ask," made a comment suggesting incompetence: "On second thought, I will ask someone else as they do it better." This made Sumita feel devalued and not good enough at her job. This could be carried further with the dean not even finishing "the ask" because of the past pattern, and Sumita would feel the sting of the complete negative action as if it was delivered in its entirety. For example, the dean might eventually say, "Can you do this for ... never mind," and shakes her head. Sumita would know what exactly was going on, but no one else would.

This micro verbal and nonverbal communication may go unnoticed or seem like no big deal to others. However, because of the history and past repeated behavior, Sumita has just been microbullied, and she is the only one who knows it. You can see how subtle and quickly microbullying can happen and how microbullying seeps into the fabric of the department and eventually makes the climate toxic. Microbullying can be more toxic than microaggressions because of the possible intent to do harm, the stealth-like delivery, and the difficulty to address them. This is a new classification for adverse actions that are very hard to detect and do tremendous harm to individuals and to organizational climate.

If Sumita can keep detailed documentation, then she can report the repetitive behavior to HR (See how to document in Chapter 6). HR can work to capture data in other ways that identify a poor climate (due to the dean's repetitive behaviors) and then engage a climate intervention team to take a deeper dive on the issue and develop strategies to resolve it systemically.

TAKE FOR ACTION

Develop a Climate Intervention Team

What a Climate Intervention Team does:

Prevention: Recommends initiatives that support a positive campus climate.

Communication: Communicates to the campus the institution's commitment to diversity, tolerance, and civility.

Anticipation: Identifies issues that may give rise to microaggressions, microbullying, bullying, and other unprofessional conduct.

Response: Immediately implements specific procedures to ease tension and assist those subjected to microaggressions, microbullying, bullying, and other unprofessional conduct.

Management: Recommends steps to be taken after each incident to restore and maintains a professional environment.

Who you want on the team:

Usually, the team includes: the Chief Diversity and Inclusion Officer, someone from the counseling center, Directors from various centers on campus that relate to diversity and inclusion (e.g., Women's Studies, LGBTQIA, Disability Services, etc.), other faculty who have expertise in these areas, other people who fill this role at your institution, and the dean of the department or unit. Depending on your institution, you may decide to include different people.

What triggers you?

Sometimes people microbully and bully when they feel triggered by an event or by a person. When you are triggered, you have a strong emotional/physical response to a person or an event. When we are stressed, angry, tired, scared, or confronted (or some other heightened emotions) then we are more likely to lash out at others in unprofessional ways.

What triggers you at work? Here is a list of common negative, emotion-producing activities at work. Check off which ones affect you.

- If someone strongly disagrees with you

- If you do not agree with someone else's idea

- If you think someone is wasting time

- If you see someone flip flop on their own ideas from one meeting to the next

- If you see someone who does not act like they have to follow the rules everyone else follows

- If you believe someone said something inappropriate or offensive

HOW PEOPLE ACT WHEN TRIGGERED

The following is a list of common behaviors that are reactions to triggers and the precursors to microaggressions, microbullying, and bullying.

TAKE FOR ACTION

What are my behaviors when triggered? What are someone else's?

1. Check-off any of the following that you have experienced or witnessed from others during difficult situations.
2. Then, star (*) any that you have done when you felt triggered in difficult work situations.

- Aggressively attack and berate
- Dismiss or minimize the comments of others
- Explode and direct feelings onto others

- Be sarcastic or make comments under your breath
- Belittle through comment
- Intentionally try to embarrass others
- Criticize or accuse with the intent to humiliate and shame
- Make other people be quiet through voice or actions
- Turn their words against them
- Interrupt
- Think, act, and speak as if you know best
- Control or manipulate behavior
- Intimidate, threaten others

Use this guide to watch for behaviors you can address or mitigate before things escalate. There are tools throughout this book that help you address these behaviors in others around you and help you notice them in yourself so that you can self-correct.

(List adapted from https://drkathyobear.com/)

If you can recognize triggers in yourself or in a colleague, you can move quickly to correct them.

TAKE FOR ACTION

Sharing triggers to reduce triggers

Share the previous list in a departmental meeting and, if it is a safe space, ask people to share one item that triggers them and how they act when triggered.

This way, colleagues can know each other's hot spots and either intentionally avoid those hot spots or find an acceptable way to remind the person when they are acting triggered.

Ask each person what prompts might help them refocus to more professional actions. Here are some ideas:

- Have the list of behaviors up and point to the behavior as a reminder.
- Say, "Do you need a breath?"
- Say, "Can you rephrase that?"
- Say, "Redo, please."
- Touch the person gently on the arm.
- Add your own suggestions.

WHAT DO I DO ONCE TRIGGERED?

Although it sounds corny to take a deep breath when triggered, research shows that a deep breath actually does calm you down. There is a group of nerves in the brain that regulate breathing and have a direct connection to the arousal center of the brain. These nerves alert the brain to an emergency and set off the body's alarms (how you are about to act because you were triggered) or tell the brain to stay calm (not acting on your triggered responses). So, breathe.

Once you are calm you can change from attack mode to questioning and diplomacy mode—and questioning with diplomacy is more likely to get your needs met in the situation. As you read through the list of questions that follows, notice how each question makes you feel. Could you say that? Would you say that? How might you get the same point across but say something different? Try to choose one question from each area to practice and add to your repertoire.

TAKE FOR ACTION

Ask questions rather than attack

If someone is strongly disagreeing with you, you could ask:

- Can you give me some background on this situation?
- Can you help me understand how you came to that conclusion?
- Can you talk about the reasons you feel so strongly?

If you do not agree with someone's idea or opinion, you could ask:

- What are your intended outcomes for that idea?
- How does that idea advance our goals?
- How might it play out if we go in this direction?

If you believe someone said something inappropriate or offensive, you could ask:

- Here is what I heard you say. How well did I understand you?
- Can you repeat that?
- Can you help me understand what you mean by that?
- What did you want to communicate with your comment?
- What message do you think that comment could send?
- I trust you didn't intend to _____. Is that correct?

If you want to interrupt and shift unproductive conversational dynamics, you could say:

- I'd like to try a different approach to this conversation.
- I'm going to interrupt and shift us to refocus on….
- I don't feel we are engaging according to our group norms.
- Let's take a breath and slow down for a moment.
- Let's table this discussion for now. Why don't you and I talk after this meeting?
- I think we'll be more productive if we talk directly about the issues and not make assumptions or negative comments about the people involved.

(List adapted from https://drkathyobear.com/)

Constructive criticism versus microbullying

Constructive criticism is the process of offering job-focused and well-reasoned opinions about the work of others. It usually involves both positive and negative comments in a friendly or direct manner, rather than an oppositional one, with the goal of improving job performance. It does not include attacks on the person or on their personality.

Can a negative evaluation be misconstrued as bullying?

Yes. People who have not experienced supportive criticism in the past might take any and all attempts to improve their job performance as negative critique. People who seek to be negative to others often take all feedback as negative themselves.

You decide. Is Dr. Johanssen picked on?

Dr. Johanssen does not have tenure. Colleagues complain that Dr. Johanssen will not collaborate and does not listen to feedback well. He shouts down other colleagues in staff meetings when they disagree with what he is saying. When students come to his office for academic advising, he often gets heated when speaking and starts to use profanity if they question his suggestions. The chair asks Dr. Johanssen to come in and talk about communicating with colleagues and with students in a more professional way. Dr. Johanssen says that he is always being picked on. He says he has good enough evaluations and does not understand why he is even in the chair's office in the first place.

How the chair needs to respond

First, by listing the problematic behaviors that are reported:

1. Dr. Johanssen will not collaborate.

2. He does not listen to feedback well.

3. He shouts down other colleagues in staff meetings when they disagree with what he is saying.

4. When students come to his office for academic advising, he often gets heated and starts to use profanity if they question his suggestions.

MYRON R. ANDERSON AND KATHRYN S. YOUNG

The chair can ask Dr. Johanssen to do some work before coming to the meeting in order to help the two of them get on the same page—to calibrate the conversation.

TAKE FOR ACTION

Calibrating Conversations

1. Ask someone, before meeting with them, to look at the stated objectives of their position (or the stated policy of professional conduct according to AAUP, etc.). Ask them to evaluate themselves and give specific examples that support their self-rating.
2. You also complete the same task before the meeting.
3. When they come in to talk with you, go over the results.
4. If the results are very different, move the conversation to "How can you help me and others see you how you see yourself?" "What can you do differently at work so I, your colleagues, and the students see all these skills and competences that we cannot currently see but that you can see in yourself?"
5. Make a plan for when to check back in and re-evaluate.
6. Actually meet again to review progress.

Address microbullying before it becomes bullying

This chapter demonstrates how microbullying, if left unaddressed, lays the foundation for bullying. The institution, departments, and units can stop this progression to bullying by focusing on creating supportive systems that let people know the behavioral expectations at the institution and the consequences for not following them. As we have mentioned throughout this book, it is always better to spend institutional resources on proactive and systemic strategies to maintain a warm campus climate.

Here is a list of general good practices that keep bullying at bay from *Stop Bullying at Work* by Teresa Daniel and Gary Metcaff (2016):

- Expand orientation programs (at the institutional and departmental or unit level)

- Hire people with high emotional quotients

- Conduct extensive background checks, not just from higher ups, ask for references from people lateral in their last institution/organization and below them as well.

- Provide leadership training specific to conflict management skills

- Provide soft skills training for leaders

- Modify performance evaluations and reward systems to highlight efforts to build climate

- Use 360-degree performance reviews

- Provide early intervention for abrasive administrators, staff, and faculty

- Offer coaching and feedback for staff, faculty and administrators

- Enact post-project reviews to check on actions and behaviors taken in the project that moved the project forward and those that hindered the project

When institutions make things worse

There is so much data and anecdotal evidence that shows colleges and universities are really good at not wanting to address problematic behaviors. We let behavior get so bad that people leave or that legal action is required. Here are some of the ways that we justify not addressing problematic behavior:

- Dismiss conflict as a personality clash.

- Sense a problem is developing and not deal with it early.

- Take sides with the bully.

- Ignore the problem because the bully is a friend or a strong performer.

- Refuse to conduct an objective investigation because the target is perceived as a problem employee.

- Do not address the problem because the faculty member is tenured.

- Do not address the problem because the faculty member has a large grant.

- Do nothing and hope the situation goes away.

Conclusion

If you nodded your head to any bullets on the preceding list and you tend to try to ignore problems away, you will really need the next chapter on bullying.

We developed this new term microbullying, because we found that there is a great grey area between micro-aggressions and bullying where people repetitively harm each other, but that harm would not usually be enough to open a bullying investigation. We needed the term microbullying. When people are experiencing micro-bullying, they know it is more severe than microaggressions (and the microbully might use repetitive microaggressions to do their dirty work). But when they try to explain what is going on, it often sounds not big enough to complain about. That is why on-going documentation is helpful. Documentation shows a pattern, that the behavior is not just a one-off or that someone is being too sensitive. Departments have an opportunity to address problematic behavior through a variety of improvement plans, but none of these will work if there is not follow-up by the chair, dean, or unit leader. In addition, it is important to be able to align your institution's accountability policies (i.e., code of conduct policies, AAUP guidelines, etc.) with these behaviors to provide an avenue to hold faculty and staff accountable. Microbullies need to learn the bounds of professional conduct in the department and follow those. If these initial forays into working with colleagues is not enough, HR needs to be involved. Microbullying, if left unaddressed, will turn into bullying. A bully is bad for the target and bad for the department.

Think about it – Talk about it

This is an opportunity to think about and discuss some of the concepts in this chapter. On your own, with a few colleagues, or in a departmental or unit meeting, discuss one or more of the questions below.

1. Can you think of any examples of microbullying—now that you have a word for the experience?

2. If so, have there been institutional responses to the microbullying? What were they? If there was no institutional response, why do you think that is?

3. Do you think your department or unit would be willing to talk about their workplace triggers? If not, what would have to change to make it a space where people would share?

Cultural Shift Challenge

This is an opportunity to do something! On your own, with a few colleagues, or in a departmental or unit meeting, select one of the following forms that you (individually and/or collectively) can use as a tool to start to improve the culture in your sphere of influence.

1. Does your institution have a climate intervention team? If you do, how it is functioning? How could it function better? If you have a concrete idea for the team, send an email with a suggestions. If not, list

who you think would be good members of one. Go talk with them about getting one started.

2. Make a list of triggers in your department or unit. Share it with others and expand the list. Ask people in your sphere of influence if they would like to be alerted if they do not notice how they are triggered and how they would like to be alerted. Make copies for everyone.

3. How are people on-boarded in your department? Is it formalized? Is there a binder or some other document to share with new people? If not, get a team of people together and make one. Then have a process of sharing it with new people that allows for their questions and for follow-up as they become more acclimatized. Have the team re-evaluate yearly so that the document stays up-to-date.

4. Look at the questions you usually use for interviews. Rework the questions based on how people have resolved conflict with colleagues in the past. Use the new document for your next hire.

Food for Thought

We work at colleges and universities, places of learning. Reducing and removing microaggressions and bullying is first and foremost an educational practice. Removing these actions from our organizations promotes a welcoming and inclusive climate thus allowing faculty, staff, and students to thrive. Below is a list of readings to continue your learning in these areas.

There are no articles for this chapter as microbullying is a new term. At the time of this book's publication, microbullying has not yet been written about elsewhere. We encourage you to read through the list of resources at the end of the next chapter.

CHAPTER 6: BULLYING

SUMMARY

Chapters 1-4 explained how to spot and remove microaggressions and bullying, how to use the 4-Way Implementation Model, how senior leadership can address microaggressions, and how chairs and departmental influencers can address microaggressions. The previous chapter introduced microbullying and its deleterious, yet pervasive, impact on climate as many are unwilling to address microbullying in units and departments. This chapter explains how institutions often foster bullying through socialization and institutional processes and offers ways to combat bullying through departments, units, and the institution.

Introduction

As mentioned in Chapter 1, bullying is a real problem in the academic workplace. Institutions of higher education are beginning to confront bullying as something that must be addressed in order to improve campus climate. Institutions usually have policies related to Code of Conduct for students, staff, and faculty. They also have policies that address sexual harassment, harassment, and discrimination. These are important and necessary; however, they leave a gap. These policies leave a grey area around toxic employees who attack others in ways that are not related to someone's protected class. Thus, people do not have laws protecting them against many forms of aggressive behavior. Often, even if there are policies, many employees don't know about them and/or the policies are not enforced, so they are not part of the socialized fabric of the institution. Harvard Business Review (2015) found that avoiding toxic employees cost organizations $12,500 a year in turnover. Even if you do think hiring the toxic person is worth it because they are a superstar, apparently they only add about $5,300 to the bottom line at the organization. They contend that these costs might be even higher if you add in potential litigation fees, lower morale, and upset students and colleagues. How much are toxic employees costing your institution? When institutions have reports of bullying, this needs to act as a wake-up call—campus-wide cultural change is needed.

> *Bullying is an individual problem*
> *that can morph into an*
> *organizational problem. When*
> *rising to an organizational level, it*
> *needs organizational solutions.*

The following chart shows how behaviors span the climate of an institution. The chart also shows why it is so important to address microaggressions and microbullying systemically. Because if you don't address these things institutionally, you pave the path for bullying, harassment, or worse.

Definitions are context dependent, but bullying usually has to be persistent, repetitive, intentional, and enacting a power differential in some way—although not always through traditional power relationships. Strategies to address bullying go from subtle to severe, from more general to more specific, and from more verbal to more written and formal in order to respond with increasing intensity if initial forays into solving bullying do not work.

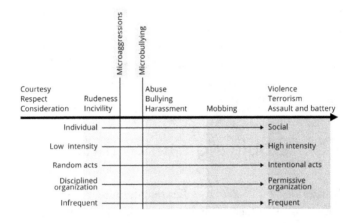

Adapted from Twale and Deluca, 2008.

College and universities should be places where learning comes first. When there are problems chairs, deans, and Human Resources need to intervene to make things better. However, the research shows that:

- Women experience 65+% of the bullying in workplaces.

- 40% of targets are believed to suffer adverse health consequences from bullying.

- Bullying only stopped when the target lost their job in 54% of cases.

- In only 10% of cases did people feel the employer did something positive like enact a new policy or investigate the bullying meaningfully.

(WBI, 2017)

Bullying impacts those who experience it deeply, and often, they are the ones to leave. The bully often remains at work, teaching, researching, and performing administrative duties; they remain to bully someone else another day. Bullying also impacts people who witness the behavior. They experience anxiety, stress, depression, and sleep disruption, too. When an environment becomes toxic due to bullying, we must remember that it can be toxic for everyone, not just the people targeted.

Where bullying cannot thrive

Institutions that have an educational strategy and a clear code of conduct policy that establish bullying as unacceptable that *all* employees know about (even faculty) have lower rates of bullying. If there is an environment where people are taken to task the first time they act negatively towards someone else, they are more likely not to bully again. Leadership that actually enforces anti-bullying and other code of conduct policies sends a clear message to the rest of the institution what behaviors will and will not be tolerated. And leadership that has policies but does not enforce them sends a clear message too: bullies are welcome here. As with microaggressions, systemic responses and modeling from senior leadership (and on down) win the day to reduce bullying from an institution.

Who is bullied

Bullying often looks different for faculty and staff on campus, but what they do have in common is that 72% of bullies have a higher status (not always their actual job, sometimes their contextual status in the institution) than those being bullied. Faculty are often bullied by other faculty, usually senior faculty—though not always. Staff are usually bullied by their supervisors, but not always. People from marginalized backgrounds experience bullying more often than people from dominant backgrounds, because they can be singled out for somehow differing from expectations, but not always. Given these differences, institutions need to be mindful of the different institutional dynamics for tenured faculty who bully versus staff or administrators who typically work on an annual contract renewal process.

There are now many studies with differing prevalence data about who gets bullied and how much resulting in wide ranges of percentages of these behaviors exhibited and experienced on campuses. The studies differ due to the measures researchers use, the specific definition of bullying behavior used, etc. A good read of the complexity of tracking down the data meaningfully can be found in *Workplace Bullying in Higher Education* edited by Jaime Lester (2012). Regardless of the specific data from specific studies, bullying is a problem and an increasingly recognized problem in higher education.

3 types of bullies

If you can figure out the type of bully, you can probably create a supportive intervention. If a faculty member's problematic behavior reflects struggles with managing relationships, managing their emotions, or a lack of awareness of the impact of behavior on others, coaching to increase interpersonal skills may help. If someone just wants to make someone else quit for reasons related to personal gain, then interpersonal skills training will not work. Intervention by leadership will be necessary.

1. They can have the inclination to treat others badly.

2. They can read cues in a competitive and political workplace and see that bullying actions do help them get ahead.

3. They can become bullies accidentally. They see others acting in this way and internalize the message that bullying actions are not actually bullying; they are just how their colleagues act. So, they will start to act the same way through the socialization process (Namie and Namie, 2011).

The problem is that is it often difficult to tease out the reasoning behind people's bullying. However, it is important not to get so wrapped up in identifying intent but to stay focused on the impact and then employ the appropriate strategies for removal. If you can sort it out, provide supportive interventions like:

1. Education and professional development that incorporates both on-line and face-to-face training on what bullying is and the actions and behaviors associated with bullying.

2. Skills development around how to negotiate difficult conversations.

3. Specific development opportunities with an executive coach to better understand when their own behavior could be categorized as bullying by others and then work to change those specific behaviors.

4. Letting someone go because their ways of being clash with institutional expectations of treating people with respect.

These levels of intervention depend on the characteristic of the bully and can be implemented as a system of increasing attention on the person's behaviors or, depending on the offense and the characteristics of the bully, leadership might jump to a specific level of intervention.

The institutional seeds of bullying

Large and hierarchical institutions are at greater risk of workplace bullying because they are more decentralized, rely on chain of command, and often have fragmented and/or poor communication and messaging about institutional norms. Institutions undergoing instability also are ripe for bullying since the instability means that people are receiving mixed messages about acceptable behavior norms. Mixed messages or no messages about professional norms deeply impact the culture. This is impacted further when the institutional leadership feels helpless to enact their own changes, when the institution and its departments and units are poorly organized, and when people experience role conflict, not knowing exactly what is expected of them in their job.

The socialized seeds of bullying

Bullying does not happen in a vacuum. The seeds for faculty bullying happen even before they become faculty. When going through doctoral programs, students are taught that discussion, critique, and debate are part of what it means to be an academic. What is often missing in these learnings is HOW to discuss, critique, and debate. These terms do not have to mean tearing someone down, but they often do mean that in academia. Therefore, many faculty have already learned lessons in harmful forms of discussion, debate, and critique that set the stage for bullying behaviors later on.

Then they enter academia as professors—a space that is often competitive, short on resources (e.g., time, space, equipment, and money), and often politicized. These characteristics are also those of environments where bullying can proliferate. The biggest types of bullying in academia are indirect in nature: 1.) threats to professional status and 2.) obstructive behaviors. Both of these are types of behaviors that are designed to keep someone else from achieving their goals. People self-select into doctoral programs, and institutions of higher education socialize faculty into having "big egos, an individualistic ethic, and tolerance for behaviors not accepted elsewhere" (Stallworth cited in Schmidt, 2010)—all determinants of bullying by faculty.

Although faculty may not like to admit it, tenure is part of the problem (though it does not have to be). The longer and more interactive people's relationships are, the greater the opportunity for conflict and potential aggression. While tenure is mostly a "job for life," it also restricts mobility since, once you have tenure, the desire to move on to a new institution where you may not have tenure makes many people want to stay and try to weather the bullying storms. If faculty believe that having tenure will protect them, then they are also more likely to bully since they think they can act without professional consequences. And if there are no consequences, then new faculty and graduate students will learn to perpetuate a bullying culture.

To make matters worse, higher education is getting more competitive. Working with less resources increases the likelihood of bullying as higher education budgets continue to get squeezed. Institutions are employing more and more part-time labor and offering fewer tenure track positions. Therefore, the drive to attain those positions and then achieve tenure is all part of a system that makes the hierarchy stricter between those on the tenure track and non-tenure track faculty and the resources even scarcer. This is why it is so important to put systems (like tenure and promotion review and resource allocation systems) in place to ensure fair and transparent campus policies (See Chapter 2).

A long list of possible bullying behaviors

Gossip or malicious rumors spread about you/someone.

Belittling remarks made about you/someone.

Belittling and/or humiliating remarks made to you/someone in front of others.

Not taking your/someone's concerns seriously, especially when contrasted with the concerns of others.

Ignoring, or overlooking your/someone's work contributions.

Ignoring your/someone's legitimate requests, i.e. insubordination.

Stopping conversation when you/someone enter(s) the room (e.g., to emphasize exclusion).

Unwarranted and unprofessional remarks.

Punishing trivial errors you/someone may have made.

Verbal harassment including abusive or offensive telephone messages.

Written harassment including abusive or offensive emails, letters, or memos.

Teasing or name calling when it is obviously causing you/someone distress.

Isolating or ostracizing you/someone from others.

Overriding your/someone's decisions without justification.

Bypassing hierarchy for complaints.

Questioning your/someone's decision(s) excessively and/or aggressively.

Challenging your/someone's authority.

Intentionally not being given information or equipment to do a job.

Unwarranted criticism of your/someone's performance.

Purposely interrupting class to distract the class.

Purposely interrupting class to communicate lack of respect.

Removing areas of responsibility without prior notice or reason.

Alienating you/someone from colleagues.

Shouting, swearing, or sarcasm directed at you/someone.

Setting you/someone up to fail.

Blocking promotion.

Being assigned tasks/responsibilities inappropriately or punitively.

Made the subject of lies or accusations.

Given an unreasonable workload or deadline.

Excessive monitoring.

Excluded from relevant meetings.

Excluded from social events.

Taking credit for your/someone's work or ideas.

Being the subject of eye rolling, sighs, and/or dirty looks.

Being lied to.

Having your/someone's property maliciously damaged or stolen.

Incivility and rudeness.

Being treated unfairly or differently than others.

Unfairly refused time off or leave.

Criticized for taking time off due to illness.

Implied threats of personal/professional harm.

Being talked down to.

Excessive pressure or coercion to change your/someone's stance (e.g., change a grade).

The following list might also fall under discrimination/ harassment and, if found to be discrimination or harassment, then this form of bullying follows a different set of policies and procedures:

Uninvited comments about your/someone's body or appearance.

Uninvited comments about your/someone's gender or sexual orientation.

Myron R. Anderson and Kathryn S. Young

Uninvited comments about your/someone's age (young or old).

Uninvited comments about your/someone's personal life or beliefs (e.g., religion).

Uninvited comments about a (dis)ability you/someone may have.

Threats regarding your/someone's gender or sexual orientation.

Threats regarding your/someone's personal beliefs (e.g., religion).

Threats regarding a (dis)ability you/someone may have.

Threats of personal/professional harm.

Racist comments or jokes.

Sexist comments or jokes.

Inappropriate physical contact like patting, hugging, or stroking.

Intrusion into your/someone's home life (e.g., unwarranted phone calls to you at home outside work hours).

Inappropriate visits at your/someone's office.

Physical violence directed towards you/someone.

Sexual assault.

Other.

Adapted from McKay, R., et al.
"Workplace Bullying in Academia: A Canadian Study," 2008.

Academic freedom ≠ Say anything you want

It is not always easy to tease apart a lack of collegiality in the form of bullying from heated academic debate. But even the American Association of University Professors (AAUP), the association who fights most strongly for academic freedom for professors, suggests weaving expectations of collegiality throughout performance measures for teaching, research, and service (American Association of University Professors, 2016). Their statement indicates that "malfeasance," "professional misconduct," or "efforts to obstruct the ability of colleagues to carry out their normal functions, to engage in personal attacks, or to violate ethical standards" (40) are issues worthy of investigation and evaluation. They acknowledge that behaviors related to "name calling, belittling, false accusations, rumor spreading, ignoring memos or messages, deliberate exclusion, assigning work overload or taking away meaningful work, turning others against the target, public criticism, interrupting, silent treatment, withholding information or resources, and imposing unreasonable deadlines" are problematic (Lester, 2013). In this book, we argue that when criticism crosses the line into personal and pervasive attacks, it has gone too far. The question is how do you create a climate where people can have passionate differences professionally?

The definition of professional responsibility is not even agreed upon in many departments and units. When a definition is not agreed upon, it is easier for people to interpret it however they want. Their personal interpretations are often the foundation for misalignment of departmental values. Spend time with your sphere of influence creating a shared understanding of professional responsibility.

TAKE FOR ACTION

Whose responsibility is professional responsibility?

1. Ask people in your department to each list five observable characteristics of professional conduct.
2. If they write down things like "respect" ask them to clarify—What does respect look like, sound like, or feel like?
3. Compile their lists and share the collated list with everyone. Ask them to find the overlaps.
4. Create a list of the themes that the department or unit agree are important for professionals to adhere to at work.
5. Develop a list of behavioral norms using observable characteristics together.
6. Hold each member of the team to those norms and let them know that you will be having yearly check-in conversations about each norm with each person.

In the previous chapter on microbullying, we shared a story of a colleague who belittles you but only when you see each other at a bi-monthly meeting.

Fast forward to you being on a committee with this person that meets monthly. This person now belittles you in department meetings and committee meetings, over and over, and just made a comment like, "I am happy you are finally learning to hold your tongue. My advice must be helping." The microbullying has now become bullying—persistent, targeted, repetitive, and purposeful—the bully is gaining control and is seeing results from their efforts. You no longer speak, and no one has told the bully to stop the belittling behavior.

As in prior chapters, in the pages ahead we will provide you with stories from real institutions to inspire you to think about how you might make the same or different choices. Interspersed throughout this chapter are conceptual and practical tools to use in your own practice. Think through what aspects of the 4-Way Implementation Model will help you respond to the microbullying and bullying in the stories that follow.

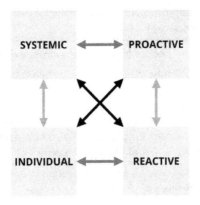

Conduct a behavioral inventory of your institution

The research on workplace and university bullying shows that many places have policies implemented, but either many constituents do not know about the policies, the policies are not enforced, or that the policies are enforced inconsistently. You can take a close look at your institution

to see how much alignment and integration you have
between your policies and your practices.

BEHAVIORAL INVENTORY
1. Does everyone know the behavioral expectations at the institution and at the departmental level? • What documents exist to teach people about behavioral norms at each level? • What is the on-boarding process that shares these norms aloud? • Where do people go if they need to refresh themselves on these norms?
2. How do new people learn of behavioral expectations? • Do you have a mentoring system? • Do you have written documentation of departmental behaviors norms?
3. How do current employees (i.e., staff, faculty, and administrators) learn of changes to policies? • Do you have an electronic system to quickly update employees of changes? • Do you have a system to ensure that they have read through the changes? • When is hard copy better than electronic for sharing changes?
4. Are people (even faculty) recruited, promoted, or fired based on ethical principles grounded in the institutional mission? Is interpersonal and intercultural communication taken into account? • How are hiring, promotion, demotion, and firing aligned with the institutional mission?

- What criteria are written that people can refer to about interpersonal and intercultural communication?

5. What structures and policies help people know what bullying is and what to do if they see it happening?

- Do you have a document that is shared with employees at least yearly about institutional expectations related to bullying and how to report it?

- Do you have spaces where leaders can reiterate this information?

6. What structures and policies help people know what happens once they report bullying?

- Do you have a flow chart that shows each step in the bullying reporting structure?

- Do you have expected timelines for each step?

- Do you have the right person/ office to contact for follow up at each step?

7. How does leadership model anti-bullying behavior?

- Do you include a question on a campus climate survey about if leaders model anti-bullying behavior?

- Do you have an anonymous "drop box" where people can share "catching a leader doing good" or "asking a leader to do better" comments?

This inventory will help you think through what systemic policies you have in place and which you need to add. It will help you look deeply at your policies to determine how effective they are, even if they are in place. A good policy is only a good policy if it goes hand-in-hand with good practice of that policy.

Bully archetypes

It is helpful to have mental models of the ways people often bully others. It helps you see the behavior in the light of your knowledge on bullying. These archetypes come from the work of Drs. Namie and are adapted here for the higher education audience. Notice the relationship between these bully archetypes and the AAUP guidelines and Lester's 2013 research discussed earlier. You can give bullying types different names, but the actions replicate in a variety of settings.

The Screaming Mimi

The Screaming Mimi is a bullying type that prefers a public setting. Their goal is to control the emotional climate of the workplace. They want to inject fear in the target in order to better control situations that relate to the target. The fear forces the target to begin to question their own decision-making and even become immobilized from making new decisions. They are going to curse, yell, and might even throw things. Yelling at someone in front of others impacts the rest of the team, too. They do not want the wrath of the screaming mimi to focus on them. They will do everything possible to stay out of the bully's gaze. Later, they might become allies of the bully and might even be involved in mobbing with the screaming mimi. This is the stereotype of the bully prototype. But in reality, we know from academic research, it's statistically the rarest form, especially on a university campus where most bullying is subtle but does still happen.

Constant Critic

This type of bully gets the target behind closed doors to tell them everything that is wrong with them and the work they do so that the bully has possible deniability. No one else hears or sees it. The targeted person is seldom believed and has no documentation or proof. Since the majority of these bullies are in leadership (e.g., chairs, deans, and directors), the leader will usually be believed. Constant critics misuse performance appraisal systems to do their dirty work. Often a constant critic is a new leader with a long-time competent employee. They see the long-time employee as everyone's go-to expert, the one who's skilled, knowledgeable, and really well liked. For those reasons, the constant critic chooses that person as the target, and they tear into them privately. The bully is trying to control the person's workplace identity. They try to redefine the competent person as incompetent, even in that person's own eyes.

The Two-Headed Snake

This bully is kind to the target's face and awful behind the target's back. They will take credit for the target's work or tell others how terrible the target's work is while praising it to their face. They will assign the target work, tell them that they can do the work how they see fit, and then admonish the target severely for doing the work wrong. The two-headed snake may also start negative rumors about the target in the workplace. The goal is to damage the target's character and create an environment where coworkers look at the target negatively.

The Gatekeeper

This bully is excellent at withholding resources. This person can get in the way of other people doing their work. Typically, departmental forms and confirming of processes (like travel authorizations) pass through their area, and they only let through that which they want to let through in the timeline that they see fit. By not sending along documents and confirming processes in a timely manner and not sharing important departmental information to key people, they can make life hard for others in the department. They sometimes set unrealistic deadlines or purposely miss deadlines that then impact the target and their work. They are not uniformly bad at their job. They may use selective poor performance to hinder the target at their job. Sometimes, if they are in a leadership position, they will assign somebody a job out of their knowledge base and then deny them professional development to go learn how to do that work, and then critique the work.

Bullies can carry several of the above archetypes at once. The following is an example.

Best friends – Not behind closed doors

Monroe was the president of the student senate. Everyone loved her. That is how she was chosen as student body president. Kamil was the vice president. They were best friends before the election. Several months later people could see that Kamil no longer spent time with Monroe unless it was required. Finally, he went to Student Affairs and asked to speak to someone. He told them that every time he and Monroe met to plan the next senate meeting, she would close the door and start berating him. Why didn't he have any good ideas? Did she have to think of everything? She told him he looked much smarter than he was. She told him she was getting exhausted having to do everything herself. She told him she felt like she was running senate on her own. She even started to poke him in the chest and shout at him in the small conference room they used for meetings. He couldn't take it anymore and felt like he was starting to believe he was stupid. Meanwhile, she was still outwardly kind to him and to others when they were together in public.

Monroe was acting as a screaming mimi, a constant critic, and a two-headed snake. Lucky for Kamil, their institution had a bullying policy embedded in their student code of conduct, and someone listened to Kamil and took his concerns seriously. Monroe's actions were persistent, repetitive, intentional, and enacted a power differential between her and Kamil.

Speaking up for yourself or for others

Since we already know that silence sends a message of tacit approval to someone exhibiting negative behaviors, we need to change our reticence to confront someone in the moment and do something. Like in the chapters on microaggressions, we need to begin to prioritize the experiences of someone who is experiencing pain, rather than the person causing it.

What does a bully usually say when confronted?

It is important to know the reasons why people who are deemed bullies say they were bullying. If you know these ahead of time, you can work to craft your response – before they come in with their excuse.

1. I was doing what I thought I was expected to do.

2. This is nothing more than a misunderstanding.

3. I'm being misperceived. I'm the victim here.

What to say to a bully

Many of us dislike confrontation and speaking directly to someone when we do not like what they are saying or doing. Others of us are more direct but then are chastised for our directness. When bullying is concerned, someone needs tell a person exhibiting negative behavior to STOP so that they have a chance to correct themselves, in case the behavior is accidental (at least in the beginning, before we would call it bullying).

TAKE FOR ACTION

What to say and what to do

1. Start by talking to the person about their negative behavior. Maintain a professional tone, while informing them that their behavior is harmful. Reinforce your words with strong body language. You can even raise your hand to gesture STOP. Say something like "Stop raising your voice at me" or "Stop raising your voice at him."

2. Avoid getting into an argument. If they argue back, "I was not raising my voice," just reiterate that it sounded raised to you. If they try to argue again, you can always say, "maybe we can talk about this later with someone in a more senior level (e.g., chair, associate dean, dean, director, or coordinator) to try to work this out.

3. Document. (See how later in this chapter).

4. If the person changes their behavior, reinforce the positive changes by actively mentioning it to the person, "Thanks for keeping your voice calm in the meeting today," but keep documenting in case things worsen again.

5. If the person continues to negatively engage with you or with someone else, enlist the help of someone in a senior position. (If your boss is the bully go up one level from their position.) Bring your documentation. Explain the situation, show your documentation, explain why the behavior is unacceptable, and detail the effect it is having on you and on others.

Tough Leader versus Bully Leader

It is sometimes difficult to be perceived as being mean at work—especially when you self-identify as a kind person. But being tough at work so that the job gets done is not being mean, it is doing your job. This does not mean that you cannot be kind *and* tough—you can. In K-12 education, Dr. Lisa Delpit found that being a "warm-demander" in the classroom is correlated with high achievement. A warm-demander "expects a great deal of their students, convinces them of their own brilliance, and helps them to reach their potential in a disciplined and structured environment." The same is true of people in leadership in higher education. You need to be firm about the things that matter and then flexible with the rest. Firm does not equal mean.

A vice president, dean, chair, director, or coordinator who accepts responsibility, makes clear and decisive decisions, provides detailed constructive criticism, resolves conflict quickly, engages in difficult conversations with faculty and staff, and addresses poor work performance is just doing their job. If they do those things in a personalizing and belittling way, then they are a bully.

TOUGH LEADER VS. BULLY LEADER

Some other signs of a tough leader:

- Is decisive
- Has an appreciation of short-, medium- and long-term needs, goals, and strategy
- Accepts responsibility
- Shares credit
- Acknowledges failings

- Learns from experience and applies knowledge gained from experience
- Is always working to improve education, communication, language, and interpersonal skills
- Is consistent
- Is fair, treats all equitably
- Is respectful and considerate
- Includes everyone

Some signs of a bully leader:

- Is random and impulsive in interactions and in decision-making
- Is rigidly short-term
- Abdicates responsibility
- Plagiarizes, takes all the credit
- Denies failings, always blames others
- Cannot apply knowledge gained from experience
- Uses knowledge gained to be manipulative
- Acts inconsistently, always critical, singles people out, shows favoritism
- Name calls
- Is disrespectful and inconsiderate
- Constantly devalues others
- Includes and excludes people selectively
- Enacts retribution

Clearly you can also be a bully and *not* exhibit the signs above. The idea is that as a leader, you have a responsibility to lead. *How* you lead has a lot to do with whether you act as a bully or not.

How to know if you are the bully

It is rare that someone actually wants to bully others out of malice; although, it does happen. Because people in leadership are not often as good at seeing the workplace from other's perspective and think people agree with them much more than they do, it is important to turn the gaze of who might be a bully onto yourself once in a while.

Here is a list adapted from *The Bully at Work: What you can do to stop the hurt and reclaim your dignity on the job* (Namie and Namie, 2009) to give yourself some warning signs that you or another senior colleague might be the problem in the department, unit, or institution. And although this might feel awkward, imagine learning that you have tendencies towards bullying behaviors. It is always easier to change yourself than it is to change everyone else.

BULLYING SELF-CHECK

1. Check off any of the following that you think others in leadership believe at your institution. Do the form once for each person rather than for leadership as a whole.
2. Then star any that you believe.

- Your job is to be the visionary leader of the institution. All managing of people and operations are done by others.
- In meetings, your positions are rarely, if ever, challenged as inappropriate or wrong.
- You feel that no one has the same high-performance standards you have.

- You understand people like collaborative decision-making, but you really prefer to make all work decisions on your own.

- People you personally appointed/promoted experience the highest rates of turnover or transfer requests compared to the rest of the institution.

- Others often misunderstand or do not appreciate your "style." They find you abrasive – you see yourself as honest.

- If a decision you've made fails, it was based on incomplete or inaccurate information provided to you from someone else.

- Your staff changes often. You know you only need the best of the best working with you.

- When you are told that people at work are experiencing high levels of stress, you think they better learn how to deal with their stress or get a new job.

- You believe that fear is a great motivator. You like staff knowing they could be fired at any time. They will work harder.

- You value loyalty within the leadership team above all other values. If we stick together, we can weather any institutional crisis.

Most everyone will check a few of these. If you checked more than a few, it is time to think about what sort of leader you are and what sort of institution, unit, or department you want to lead. Remember, you model the culture. Everyone takes their cues from you. So, if you want less bullying, microbullying, and microaggressions, think about small steps you can take to shape the environment for people who work around you. If you really cannot think of any, this might be time to gain more knowledge on how to create a welcoming environment as a leader, or to enlist the help of an Executive Coach.

When is it bullying, and when is it just bad behavior?

General bad behavior is not considered bullying. Remember, bullying needs to be persistent, repetitive, intentional, and enacting a power differential in some way. Look at the following situations.

Ask yourself, is this bullying? (And remember, the answer could change depending on your institution's specific definition of bullying.)

1. A chair or supervisor who shouts at or criticizes everyone in the department.

    _____ Yes, this is bullying.
    _____ No, this is not bullying.

    No. This is not usually bullying. This is a bad chair or supervisor and makes the department unpleasant, but it is not bullying unless only one or a few individuals are repeatedly being unjustifiably singled out.

2. A colleague who is critical of everything and blames everyone else for mistakes.

    _____ Yes, this is bullying.
    _____ No, this is not bullying.

    No, this is not bullying. Unless the critique and blame is directed at one individual, they represent poor social skills but not a departmental bully.

3. A staff member repeatedly makes negative comments that are based on a person's gender

_____ Yes, this is bullying.
_____ No, this is not bullying.

Trick question. This is a form of bullying but is also harassment due to the gender element, and federal law supports the complaint procedure. It is illegal. Contact your EO office immediately.

When bullying becomes mobbing

Bullying becomes mobbing when more and more people are involved in the bullying of one individual or a small group of individuals. Mobbing occurs most in workplaces where workers have high job security, where there are few objective measures of performance, and where there is tension between loyalty to the institution and loyalty to some higher purpose. Higher education ticks all of these boxes. (See works by Kenneth Westhues for more on this topic.) Mobbing is more likely to happen the longer a situation continues because it becomes harder for bystanders to remain impartial and out of the bullying sphere as bullying intensifies. Since many faculty stay once they arrive at an institution especially if they have tenure, once bullying begins and the longer the department and the dean let it continue, the more likely it is that other colleagues will be drawn into the bullying, too. Bystanders take sides willingly or through convincing or coercion and worsen the situation. If mobbing remains unaddressed, the situation can turn into a dysfunctional department of which many, if not all, of us know about.

The target can be almost anyone at the institution and can start out as emotionally strong. Individually they project strength and have all of the "traditional" skills and abilities to perform at a high level. The target is often considered as different from the majority of the group. They may have other elements that may identify them as different, such as their gender, race, age, sexual orientation, academic discipline, or their association with another marginalized group.

When mobbing takes place, the target receives negative behaviors and/or actions from multiple people (the Mob), which leads the target to feeling devalued, embarrassed, isolated, and a host of negative slights that often drive them from the institution. Mobbing is like getting hit from all angles with multiple negative forces, big and small, leaving the target with the feeling that there is no way out of the situation. It leaves the target doubting their skills, abilities, and self-worth, and it destroys their sense of belonging to the department or to the institution.

Mobbing is a growing element of bullying and usually appears in high stress work environments. Because of the group nature of this bullying action, it can quickly turn a department or unit toxic if not addressed swiftly and systematically.

Mobbing Carlos – What to do when no one believes you

Microbullying

Remember this scenario from the previous chapter. One faculty member, Carlos, finds out that another faculty member, Karen, who is also the associate chair and in charge of course schedules and rooming in the department, opposes his tenure case. She moved his office and turned it into a break room, gave him classes at the beginning and end of the day, and brought the quality of his teaching and research into question with others in the department. She told him that she had heard through the grapevine that he might not get tenure.

And it goes on...

Karen continues to make his life harder by sitting down with other faculty members to tell them of all the things she thinks is wrong with Carlos. She is lying to them about how much he publishes, but since she is an associate chair and has always been kind to them, everyone believes her without checking into the information. Karen keeps talking about Carlos until the rest of the department starts to shun him, too. They tell students not to take his classes. They sit far from him at meetings and ignore him or roll their eyes when he speaks. They look for confirming evidence of what Karen is saying. Carlos knows he is one of the top researchers in his field and knows that he teaches students well, but he is being torn down comment by comment, action by action.

He went to the chair and shared his concerns. The chair said that it is sometimes hard to work with so many strong personalities and is sure Karen is not doing those things on purpose. The chair told Carlos he was probably over-reacting to the eye rolls as she has not seen any of it. Carlos is so dispirited by his departmental functioning and is now looking for work elsewhere.

Karen is acting as a gate keeper when she schedules Carlos into the most undesirable teaching time-bands and also when she uses her role to change his office. She acts like a two-headed snake, because she has maintained a collegial attitude with others in the departmenwhile focusing her negative energy on Carlos. Now, she has the rest of the department believing Carlos is terrible at teaching and subpar at research. Karen's actions are persistent, repetitive, intentional, and enacting a power differential by using her role as associate chair to make Carlos' work life difficult. Additionally, there could be racial biases directed toward Carlos in these interactions. This case of microbullying has becoming bullying, and the bullying has become mobbing.

Inaction is action

The bully often takes other's inaction (especially from chairs and deans) as permission to act the way they are acting. In the preceding case, Carlos went to the chair; however, since the chair decided to do nothing about his concerns, Carlos felt lost as to next steps. Chairs and faculty often feel that due to the autonomous nature of being faculty, they do not have the right to comment on another's behavior. Commenting sometimes feels like it might infringe on someone else's academic freedom. It doesn't. And unfortunately, those who are supposed to step in, like chairs and deans, have often come from the rank of faculty and have not learned managerial skills about how to deal with bullies. Chairs are often in those positions for only a few years, so they have little incentive to deal with problematic colleagues (especially as they will return to the role of colleague and might feel the wrath of the person themselves). They often leave the problem for the next chair. Departmental and institutional leaders can begin to address their actions and these situations earlier in order to change a culture that allows bullying to surface, grow, and continue.

Actions a university can take to address a case of bullying

In the early stages of negative behavior, before it has been deemed bullying according to policy, chairs, directors, and deans can take action. At each stage, the person who is bullying can, and should, receive an official letter of reprimand from someone in leadership. (See the sample letter that follows.)

Early stages

- Informal conversation with the person about their negative behavior. State the behavior. State that it is not acceptable. State what behavior you need to see going forward. Document.

- Same as above but include a person senior to you as well in the conversation.

- Use a system of restorative justice if you have a trained facilitator.

- Use mediation if you have a trained facilitator.

Note: *This is prior to the behavior being classified as bullying.* Once the behavior becomes bullying, these strategies are no longer valid. A mistake that organizations make is to try and incorporate these early strategies after bullying is established. These will not work. You do not want to mediate between a bully and a person being bullied. Mediation implies that there is a responsibility for the negative interaction from both parties. With bullying, this is not the case. Once the interaction moves to bullying, the responsibility is one-sided, and the bully is responsible for the negative exchange. The bully needs to be the sole person that undergoes intervention.

Mid stage

- Deans can request the person attend some sort of professional development (e.g., conflict management PD, courageous conversations PD, etc.).

- Deans can highly encourage the person to talk with someone about individual counseling from the state employee assistance program or elsewhere.

Once the conversation reaches the stage where the person needs to talk to the dean, more measures can be taken.

Late stage

- Involve HR and share that your in-house interventions have not been successful, and you need more institutional support.

[Subject: Normally bold, summarizes the intention of the letter] -Optional-

Dear [Name],

I would like to commend you for [state things the person is good at or doing well], I also want to remind you that our department and the institution have (departmental norms, an ethics policy, a bullying policy) we all have to uphold.

I have received several reports of your negative attitude towards the people in your suite. Complaints have also been filed stating that you have a habit of [using your role to make people's lives easier or harder depending on if you like them or not]. Because I have not heard your side of the story yet, I do not want to pass any judgment at this point.

I would like to invite you to visit me in my office before the week is over. I want us to discuss what has been going on, and I welcome hearing what you have to say about the complaints being filed against you. Let me know a possible time we can meet in the next week.

Sincerely,

MYRON R. ANDERSON AND KATHRYN S. YOUNG

How do you stop constant devaluing of colleagues?

Scenario: The evolution of bullying

Read the story below and see if you have ever experienced or witnessed something like it at your institution.

Be quiet. You are an assistant professor.

After working as an affiliate faculty member, I earned a tenure-line position at a post-secondary institution. My chair interfered with how I ran my own grants. My chair took courses away from me at the last minute and gave me new preps with only a few days to prepare. She made frequent negative comments regarding my research and teaching. She scheduled meetings at times I could not attend and then asked why I did not participate more. When I went to colleagues to ask what to do, I was told to put my head down as I was an assistant professor and, if I wanted a chance at tenure, to be quiet.

After two years of this, I decided I needed to do something or else I had to leave the institution. I contacted the dean, then the Ombuds person, and then Human Resources. Each person told me that there was nothing that was actually illegal going on, so they could do nothing. The dean even mentioned that if it came down to the senior faculty versus me, I would lose as the chair was a senior faculty member who brought in large grants, had been at the institution a long time, and could make the dean's life hard. The message was to back down and be quiet.

This story is an example of power bullying—where the bully is showing off their power to the person being bullied and/or to others. This person is experiencing persistent, repetitive, and intentional negativity from the chair. Although this situation is painful to read, we know it is a common experience. Junior faculty are told to be quiet and put their heads down until tenure. People in positions of leadership mention that bullying is generally not illegal. So even though the chair is insulting, intimidating, and generally making this person's life hard, the law is not being broken; therefore, there is nothing to do – or so we are led to believe.

Every person who works with someone else can treat others with respect. The dean can step in and state that belittling people is not acceptable in the department. The dean can model treating others with respect and asking the chair to model those behaviors as well. The dean can remind and enforce the established institutional accountability policies and processes that are in place to promote equity, collegiality, and a healthy work environment. The dean can engage in systems thinking and spend time each semester examining the departmental politics and working with a team to think through what to do about them. This ongoing self-reflection helps a department function better.

TAKE FOR ACTION

Systems thinking

Work on these questions with a team/with a colleague. Make sure to return to this once each semester.

- Does the current system contribute to a healthy community or to an unhealthy community? How do we know? What evidence do we have? Does that evidence show similar patterns across diverse groups?"

- Do I know of alternatives? What are they? Could they work here? How would they need to be adapted?

- If not, how can we learn about alternatives that do contribute to a healthy system? (Good places to start: The work being completed under the leadership of Dr. Donald Pope-Davis at The Ohio State University, and the *Higher Education Today* blog.)

People in relative positions of power can also devalue colleagues. Read the following story and think how you might handle this situation, knowing that, if you don't, the situation will probably worsen with time.

Scenario: Repeated put downs

In the past six months, I have counted at least 10 instances where a full faculty member has acted in ways that put me down, intimidated me, and made me feel like I was too stupid to be a faculty member.

He undermined my authority with students by hearing about complaints about my course and taking those complaints to the chair himself. He told students how to act in my classes to make my life more difficult, gave them arguments to use against me, and encouraged them to question the relevance of the course. He told them to even question the validity of assessment questions.

> In meetings, anytime I spoke he spoke over me until he had the floor. If I did get a sentence in, he would remind everyone that he had gone to an Ivy League school while I went to a state school. Then he would dress down my idea point by point until no one else felt free to talk.
>
> Eventually he was right, I did not talk anymore in meetings.

In this story, the junior colleague felt devalued in terms of teaching and research. The junior faculty experienced actions by the senior faculty that were persistent, repetitive, and intentional. The junior colleague did not receive any support from colleagues who wanted to avoid the faculty member and not upset him themselves—this can leave someone relatively new to the institution feeling alone and possibly cause them to start looking elsewhere for a job.

As a chair, you might feel powerless to address objectionable conduct by one of your peers, or you might feel like it is not your job to "police" your colleagues' conduct, but you are in a position of leadership and have a responsibility to set the tone for the meetings and for the department. This is a case when a bullying policy would be helpful, so the chair feels like there is some recourse and institutional support. Short of a formal bullying policy, norms can be developed and referred to using a Communication Protocol (pioneered by UC Davis in the 1990s).

Having an agreement of "how we work here" can be a good tool for managing difficult interpersonal behaviors and for establishing a more constructive departmental environment. The communication protocol makes it more difficult for bullying to be the preferred mode of behavior change on others.

TAKE FOR ACTION

Communication Protocol

Ask people in the department to name an individual in your institution who "causes problems." After a brief reflection, the participants are asked, "Who has thought of their own name?" Typically, no one has. Most often people define problems as outside of themselves.

Next, ask people to write down the answers to these questions. After everyone has written their responses, ask them to share aloud. Write responses on a board.

1. If someone is having a problem with you, how would you like them to handle it?
2. If a coworker comes to you to complain about someone else in the department, what should you do?
3. If you have made a "good faith" effort to follow what was developed in #1 above, but you can't successfully address the issue, what is your next step?
4. Agree on a protocol to be followed and revised as needed.

(This is a short version of the communication protocol created by UC Davis. To read the whole document with many more steps, please see Hoover, H. "Developing departmental communication protocols." *Conflict Management in Higher Education Report*, 2003.)

Why does leadership ignore bullying?

We are sure you have heard stories, or might have your own, of bullies getting to keep their jobs and perhaps even get promoted within the institution. Sometimes the chair, director, or dean are also afraid of the bully. Sometimes the bully is so sneaky that they are only a bully in private, so most people will think they're a wonderful colleague. Sometimes the bully is seen as someone who has such a long institutional history that institutional leaders are just waiting for the person to retire rather than start a battle they don't feel they will win. Sometimes the bully is assumed to be indispensable in some way (brings in big grants, students love them, works closely with the president of the institution on a big initiative, etc.).

Whatever the reason, you, as a leader, need to think about the harm being caused to the person being bullied and need to think about the larger climate issues that will worsen over time if a bully is allowed to bully others.

Mismatched expectations: staff vs faculty

Sometime staff feel bullied from faculty because of misaligned expectations. The following story offers an example of this.

John Collins works in the nursing department. He asks all faculty for textbook orders six weeks into the semester for the following semester. Dr. Sirhan wants to debate the necessity to submit orders so far in advance as he is not even sure if he likes the book he is using yet. He debates John by sending 20 emails in one day, pointing out all of John's inconsistencies in his argument to get the book order in on time. Dr. Sirhan feels like he is pointing out a logical inconsistency and expect to have a back and forth about this topic. John feels like he cannot contradict a faculty member, because he is staff.

This is not the first time Dr. Sirhan has treated John this way. John feels increasing uncomfortable around Dr. Sirhan and lets him do what he wants about book orders and anything else for fear of getting electronically yelled at. John, meanwhile, is hounded by the bookstore clerk when orders come in late. John is focused on deadlines set by the bookstore and is trying to live up to them. John feels lost and does not know of any policy to help him show Dr. Sirhan the importance of these deadlines. He doesn't know how to tell Dr. Sirhan that receiving 20+ emails a day that point out argument inconsistencies feels like he's being badgered.

Dr. Sirhan is bullying John. Email is like having a conversation, and conversational bullying takes place all the time in all bully types. Dr. Sirhan's actions are repetitive put downs towards John that go on for an extended period of time. They are intentional and enact a power differential between the two. It is unlikely Dr. Sirhan sends this many emails to everyone else in a single day.

Ideally, John will find out if there is a policy about standard operating procedures for textbook adoption and then reach out to Dr. Sirhan by email and state the process in writing. He also needs to indicate that receiving this many emails is counterproductive. Then he needs to request a stoppage of excessive emails. This might sound frightening, but often times stating what you are willing to do and not to do according to institutional procedures goes a long way in helping people learn their boundaries. If Dr. Sirhan is annoyed, then what? If Dr. Sirhan goes to someone to complain, John can show the trail of emails which will clearly show Dr. Sirhan is out of line.

If emailing Dr. Sirhan with clear boundaries does not help, then John needs to contact his next level supervisor within the department. And if that does not help, then he should contact HR.

Issues like faculty wanting to deal with institutional bureaucracy their own way can be addressed by developing and then communicating standard operating procedures for on-going tasks that support the functioning of the department. These standards can be sent out yearly and referred to as necessary. This way the policy is the problem, not John.

Why does the bully so often claim bullying happened to them?

Cameron went to HR to file a formal bullying complaint. She cannot figure out why people will not sit by her in meetings or will pull off of committees if she is on them. She thinks the chair is picking on her by always calling her in to talk about her "behavior" after faculty meetings.

Is she being bullied?

Or did her behavior precipitate these problems because of her outburst of anger at colleagues?

Cameron explains she was always trying to help her colleagues see the deleterious changes going on at the institution. When she would shout down Raquel and call her stupid in faculty meetings for not seeing how the provost was killing the institution one policy at a time, she was just trying to help Raquel see that she was being duped by the institution. When she would talk over Raquel in meetings when Raquel offered solutions to policy changes, she just didn't want the department to have to waste time on a solution that would not work. Her passion is what was speaking, not her anger.

What should the chair do knowing that Cameron has filed a bullying complaint against her and Raquel?

In this case, similar to intent vs impact with microaggressions, when bullying behavior is taking place and you are seeking resolutions, don't get derailed by intent and reduce your chances of resolution.

It is important to note that bullies sometimes also feel bullied. They do not associate behaviors like people pulling away emotionally, not wanting to be on committees with them, or physically steering clear of them as having anything to do with their own toxic behavior toward others. This is often because no one tells the bully, "Stop. Do not treat me like that." Everyone else is trying to be collegial or non-confrontational. Eventually, people remove themselves from the bully's sphere of influence and the bully starts to think people are actively excluding them as a bullying tactic, not as a response to their own behaviors.

This tension becomes more complex as chairs, deans, directors, and ultimately Human Resources have to step in to decide what is going on. Although difficult and confusing, often a formal inquiry will show that people have been emotionally and physically pulling away from the bully due to the bully's behaviors, not the other way around.

> HR conducted an inquiry by first talking to Cameron about her experiences, then talking to the dean, the associate dean, the chair, and people in the department – all confidential conversations. HR found that Cameron had been shouting at people, especially at Raquel. HR also found that the chair did not document any of her many conversations with Cameron, because the chair felt like it was "awkward" to "write notes on a colleague." The dean did not document conversations she had with concerned faculty. Raquel never wrote anything down either. She felt that would be "weird to do that to a colleague," "like policing departmental conversations," and "can things like that even be documented?" She didn't know. She just though Cameron was "like that," and she had to get used to it.

The moral to this story is that people who hold a leadership position have to document potentially contentious conversations with colleagues EVERY time. Do not let your good will get the better of you. Do not let your lack of knowing how to document get in the way of you documenting these interactions. If you document the conversation and you never have to address the issue again, fine. Then you have a file you will never have to look in again. However, if this does become repetitive action, you will wish you had documented the contentious conversations from the start.

TAKE FOR ACTION

How to document workplace bullying

1. Create a file.
2. For each instance of bullying include the date, time, who was there, and details of the incident. Be very specific. Use describing words as much as possible rather than: "He was mean to me on this date." How was he mean? What did he do or say that felt mean? What did you do or say back? How did the experience end?
3. Email the file to yourself to show the date stamp from the email so you have evidence of documenting the occasion close to when it happened.
4. If you are ready to share it with the next level of supervisor (e.g., director, dean, etc.), email documentation to them so you have evidence of reaching out through appropriate channels.

INCIDENT REPORTING FORM

Date _____

Time _____

Details of the incident:

Who is involved in the incident?

Who else was present?

What was going on?

What did the person say?

What did the person do?

What did others say to respond to person #1?

What did others do to respond to person #1?

Can you document bullying instances later?

The short answer is yes. People often do not think of documenting bullying right away. In fact, they think of it only after several incidents have happened or incidents continue to happen over a long period of time. You can still recreate a log of the instances and try to include as much information as you can in as much chronological detail as possible. Go back through emails to see if you have any written documentation that might help too. It is never too late to get the process started, but it does help HR if you document closer to the event so they can build a stronger case against the bully.

How much micromanagement is OK?

Sometimes bullies see their actions as part of their job descriptions. They think they need to keep tight control over a department or unit so that it functions well. What begins as small slights can turn into full-fledged bullying. Management turns into micromanagement turns into hostility from management. This can happen from anyone in leadership, a chair, an associate dean, a dean, or a director of a center or program on campus.

Scenario: Are you talking about me?

In our office we sometimes meet behind closed doors. In the past this was not an issue. It helped keep the noise down for the rest of the office. We have a new supervisor. He comes in repeatedly to ask if he is being talked about when we are meeting with the door closed. Finally, I started turning the computer screen around, so he could check on the actual content of the meeting each time he came in.

Then it got worse. He started to tell people that they could not sit next to each other in programmatic meetings, because he thought they would be talking about him. Now no one is allowed to walk down the hall together or even have lunch together. And if you do, he tells you that he will "give you a hard time on your next performance evaluation."

Now, many of us are looking for other jobs.

In this story, office staff used to be able to do their jobs and meet where and how they thought was useful to getting work done. The new supervisor is always worried someone is talking about him. Perhaps, initially, he really wanted to check that work was being accomplished as he was new and did not understand the internal culture. But quickly, his micromanaging behavior went from overbearing to outright controlling. His behaviors became persistent, repetitive, and intentional. He used his position of power to change departmental interactions. Staff in the department could not go to him to report the bullying as he was the bully. Instead, they all started looking for new jobs. They did not think to go to his supervisor, because they were always told in personnel matters to go to their immediate supervisor, and this was not an option.

At the institutional level, someone needs to be tracking when many staff leave from a department or a program or when there are more formal complaints from that department or unit than from the rest of the institution. This is often a sign of a hostile culture in that space. The person to monitor this data might be in the Equal Opportunity Office or someone in Human Resources. If regular institutional attrition is 10% per year per office and you have an office with 30% attrition (either leaving the institution or going elsewhere on campus), this is something to look into more deeply even if there are no formal complaints.

Often, bully leaders work under the radar for years in institutions without bullying policies. They do not get noticed, because employees leave their positions rather than file complaints. The bad behavior is problematic but not against policy in many institutions. So, bad leaders stay, and many good employees leave.

TAKE FOR ACTION

Engage in quarterly data analysis.

Have someone in HR (or elsewhere) track staff and administrators who leave an office or program. Also track complaints from all parts of the institution. This person needs assurance that their position is protected from retaliation.

- What is the average percentage of people who leave the institution or transfer within?

- How many people left _____ program? How many people formally complained about _____ program?

- Is it more than the average?

- If so, examine the pattern. Wait at least four weeks after someone has left their position, then:

- Send out a confidential exit survey.

- Ask to conduct exit phone calls.

- Look for patterns in behaviors.

- If there is a pattern, contact the problematic person's supervisor with the data in hand.

In the next story, a director looks like a wonderful supervisor on the surface, but she sends mixed messages to staff and creates an environment that they do not feel is safe.

Scenario: Is it safe to speak up?

Staff are told meetings are a "safe space" to offer suggestions and air grievances. So, they do. Shortly after, each staff member who aired a departmental concern is written up by their director for "not being a good team player." Staff quickly learn if they share any negative aspects of the job, are critical of a professional development opportunity or of the lack of PD, question the resources, etc., they will be written up. If they speak about how the department is starting to have low morale, they will be written up again for insubordination. Recently, a staff member was told that they were bullying the director by asking out loud in a meeting why so many people were leaving.

In this case, staff are told they should speak up, and then are disciplined when they do so. They thought they were going to have space to talk about what is not working, so it could be fixed. Instead, they learned to be quiet about any and all work-related issues. The director is persistent, repetitive, and intentional in using their position of power to write up staff. This makes for a dysfunctional department that cannot grow as the employees cannot talk about what is needed to be more successful. Unfortunately, this person's bad behavior probably is not bullying as defined by most institutions since it is not directed at specific people. This does not mean that nothing can be done to help this person grow and change their behavior, or to remove them from the environment.

Even if an institution does not have a bullying policy yet, there are a set of skills that help supervisors to be good supervisors and to keep the workplace free from bullying, from themselves, or from others.

TAKE FOR ACTION

12 things a chair, dean, or any supervisor can do to create an environment free from bullying:

1. Practice good supervisory skills.
2. Be available.
3. Be open to suggestions.
4. Notice when staff and faculty go above and beyond.
5. Address interpersonal conflicts in a constructive manner.
6. Be fair in evaluations.
7. Encourage staff to get more PD.
8. Encourage staff to go to institutional events, be involved.
9. Create an environment where people can raise concerns.
10. Treat people with respect.
11. Ensure co-workers treat people with respect.
12. Ask staff to do things within their job description.

Conclusion

Unfortunately bullying is rampant on college and university campuses and is probably rampant due in part to our socializing processes and our increasing scarcity of resources. It is also likely because so many people do spend so many years together that behaviors worsen over time and become difficult to ferret out. And tenure does not help.

Colleges and universities are so concerned about taking firing action against tenured faculty that they often do not adequately sanction faculty who engage in unprofessional and bullying behavior. As a result, the bullying continues. Institutions of higher education must find ways to protect tenure while also requiring productive behaviors from faculty and staff.

So many of us in positions of leadership at colleges and universities have adopted the attitude that we cannot do anything to change the behavior of our problematic peers—and that is problematic, too. People do follow norms if norms are created, expected, and reinforced. People do lessen bullying behaviors after you educate an institution about them. Sometimes people just don't know they are bullying others. Other times, bullies decide that negative outcomes toward them are not worth the pain they are putting another through.

In this chapter, we have pointed to many resources to help you on your way to systematically address bullying. Try them out. Remember, we no longer have to prioritize the pain of the person who is harming others. We can work to prioritize the pain of the people being bullied. Additionally, if you do not yet have a bullying policy at your institution, read the next chapter to see how one university underwent a systematic transformation to develop a university bullying policy for staff and faculty at the university and then educated the whole university about bullying and about the policy. The next chapter also has a template for a university bullying policy that might be helpful.

Think about it – Talk about it

This is an opportunity to think about and discuss some of the concepts in this chapter. On your own, with a few colleagues, or in a departmental or unit meeting, discuss one or more of the questions below.

1. Do you have a bully in your department? If so, what archetype does the bully represent? How long has it been going on? What is being done about it? Are those strategies working? What would you like to see done about the bullying?

2. How do you balance academic freedom and critique that comes across as bullying? What is more important to you? Why?

3. Have you seen instances of mobbing? If so, at what points could the behaviors have been addressed before they turned into mobbing?

4. What behaviors do faculty think are OK that staff think are demeaning? If you don't know of any, how can you find out?

5. What norms are or could be in place in your department to stop bullying even before it starts?

Cultural Shift Challenge

This is an opportunity to do something! On your own, with a few colleagues, or in a departmental or unit meeting, select one of the following forms that you (individually and/or collectively) can use as a tool to start to improve the culture in your sphere of influence.

1. Use the 4-Way Implementation Model to conduct a behavioral inventory of your department.

2. Take the **Take for Action** activity entitled "Whose responsibility is professional responsibility?" to your next departmental meeting. Use it. Then talk about it.

3. Complete the bullying self-check.

4. In your own words, write a script to stand up to a bully. Memorize it. Use it next time.

5. Bring the communication protocol to your next meeting. Use it. Then talk about it.

Food for Thought

We work at colleges and universities, places of learning. Reducing and removing microaggressions and bullying is first and foremost an educational practice. Removing these actions from our organizations promotes a welcoming and inclusive climate thus allowing faculty, staff and students to thrive. Following is a list of readings to continue your learning in these areas.

Berryman-Fink, C. "Can we agree to disagree? Faculty-faculty conflict." Susan A. Holton (Ed.), *Mending the Cracks in the Ivory Tower: Strategies for conflict management in higher education.* Anker Publishing, 1998, pp. 141– 163.

Cipriano, Robert. *Facilitating a Collegial Department in Higher Education: Strategies for success.* Jossey-Bass, 2011.

Daniel, Teresa and Gary Metcalf. *Stop Bullying at Work: Strategies and Tools for HR, Legal, and Risk Management*

Professionals. Second Edition. Society for Human Resources Management, 2016.

Ensuring Academic Freedom in Politically Controversial Academic Personnel Decisions. American Association of University Professors, 2011.
www.aaup.org/AAUP/comm/rep/A/ensuring.htm

Fogg, Piper. "Academic Bullies: The web provides new outlets for combating workplace aggression." *Chronicle of Higher Education*, B10, 2008.

Gill, Raj, et al. *NVC Toolkit.* BookSurge Publishing, 2009.

Hornstein, Harvey A. *The Brutal Boss Questionnaire in Brutal Bosses and Their Prey: How to Identify and Overcome Abuse in the Workplace.* Riverhead Books, 1996.

Journal of Academic Freedom, Volume 9. American Association of University Professors, 2018. Note: This volume is all about the debate between academic freedom and collegiality.

Lester, Jaime. *Workplace Bullying in Higher Education*, Routledge, 2012

Namie, Gary and Ruth F. Namie. *The Bully-Free Workplace: Stop Jerks, Weasels, and Snakes from Killing Your Organization.* Wiley Hoboken, 2011.

On Collegiality as a Criterion for Faculty Evaluation. American Association of University Professors, 2016.
www.aaup.org/file/AAUP%20Collegiality%20report.pdf

Rosenberg, Marshall. *Nonviolent Communication: A language of life.* PuddleDancer Press, 2005.

Twale, Darla J. and Barbara M. De Luca. *Faculty Incivility: The rise of the academic bully culture and what to do about it.* Jossey-Bass, 2008.

Westhues, K. "The Unkindly Art of Mobbing." *Academic Matters: The Journal of Higher Education*, Fall 2006, pp. 18– 19. www.ocufa.on.ca/Academic%20Mat ters%20Fall2006/Unkindly_art_of_mobbing.pdf

CHAPTER 7: CREATING A BULLYING POLICY (CASE STUDY)

SUMMARY

This chapter offers a case study of how one university developed a bullying policy, including the steps needed and challenges faced in this endeavor. The chapter provides a template of a bullying policy and flow charts of the process from complaint to resolution for different constituent groups.

Introduction

You have now read this whole book and, if you made it to this chapter, that probably means your institution does not yet have a bullying policy, and you are thinking about investing some time to learn if a bullying policy makes sense at your institution. The short answer: yes, it does. This chapter leads you through how one university, Metropolitan State University of Denver, went about understanding the need for a bullying policy, developing one, implementing one, and educating the campus community about the whole process. If this sounds interesting to you, we welcome your interest. But you have some internal work to do first.

The work before the work:
What is your reasoning for needing a policy?

Answer these questions now. You need to make sure you know why you are doing what you are doing.

1. Who can you enlist as a thinking partner right now as you think about creating a bullying policy?

2. Why do you think you need a bullying policy?

3. What gaps in policy do you hope it will fill?

4. How do you think such a policy will be received?

5. Where do you anticipate stumbling blocks at your institution?

What makes a good bullying policy?

1. **An introduction.** State the purpose of the policy and how it relates to the institution's mission, vision, and strategic plan.

2. **Definitions.** Define what counts as bullying. Make sure to include the statement "including, but not limited to" and write your list.

3. **Consequences.** Detail the consequences for the bully, the complainant, the bystander(s), and the organizational unit. These are not always negative, but people need to know what they are getting into.

4. **Process.** Clearly explain how and where to file a bullying complaint. Clearly explain how to appeal if someone accuses you of bullying and you disagree with the results of the decision. Clearly explain the whole process, how long each step of the process takes, who to contact at each step in the process if needed, and how people are notified of the outcomes of each step. Explain differences in the policy for faculty, staff, and administrators.

5. **Workarounds.** Clearly explain if there are workarounds to the process. Can the bully accept responsibility for the behaviors and end the process, accepting the consequences? Are mediation, negotiated agreements, or restorative justice possible resolutions? If so, at what step in the process can these take place? Is there a formal process with a board of colleagues for faculty if a more systematic resolution must be reached?

The appendix to this chapter has MSU Denver's full policy, complaint procedure, and flowcharts for the complaint procedure for different constituent groups (e.g., staff, faculty, administrators, and non-tenure track employees).

Terminology

You will see the terms Anti-Bullying Policy and Bullying Policy used by different institutions. MSU Denver chose the term Bullying Policy to denote the fact that the policy was put in place to address bullying. Other institutions are using Anti-Bullying Policy to denote the fact that they are trying to make a policy that deters bullying.

Myron R. Anderson and Kathryn S. Young

Case Study: Developing a University Bullying Policy at Metropolitan State University of Denver (MSU Denver)

Climate issues are not like fine wine, they do not get better with time.

Why a university bullying policy

Our university was starting to receive more reports around civility through Equal Opportunity Office complaints, HR Office complaints, Code of Ethic complaints, and Ombuds Office trend data. MSU Denver needed more comprehensive data to better understand how widespread this problem was.

MSU Denver conducts a climate study every two years. Before introducing a bullying policy, we decided to include six questions that were designed to identify if bullying was taking place and provide a measure of how much bullying occurred at our university:

1. I believe that MSU Denver's policies and practices are effective at preventing bullying.

2. I have experienced university bullying (i.e., the persistent use of aggressive, overbearing, or unreasonable behaviors) directed toward me by a member of the MSU Denver community.

3. I am aware of other employees at MSU Denver who have experienced university bullying.

4. Faculty, administration, and staff understand that university bullying is not tolerated in MSU Denver.

5. Instances of alleged university bullying are taken seriously by my supervisor/department chair.

6. MSU Denver has clear and effective procedures for dealing with university bullying.

The climate survey results revealed that there was a significant amount of bullying taking place at MSU Denver. This data was used in collaboration with national data on university bullying as well as some other data points within the university (Equal Opportunity Office complaints, HR Office complaints, Code of Ethic complaints, and Ombuds Office trend data) in regard to lack of civility incidents. These data points revealed that there was bullying activity taking place that was unidentified or was unable to be captured and then corrected.

Looking at all these data points confirmed that there was a gap in being able to identify and being able to remove these types of offenses systemically. Without a policy being able to reduce and remove this activity from the community would be left up to individuals. This gap was significant and prevented the campus from being a welcoming, inclusive, and healthy environment for all. All this unwanted and unhealthy activity promoted negative engagement amongst the faculty and staff. This unhealthy activity further demonstrated the need for a policy to close this gap within existing policies and remove bullying activity that had an adverse effect on the institution's climate. The administration had to act.

In our work, we found that the campus community embraced and even wanted a university bullying policy. The campus community knew that they had colleagues who fell through institutional loopholes and whose bad behavior persisted. It was our understanding that the community wanted a policy in place that would deter negative behavior throughout the institution.

What we did and how we did it

WHERE WE LOOKED FOR MODELS

Using Canada as a model, since they were far ahead of the curve in regards to university bullying, we researched their university-based policies and programs and used them as a benchmark to develop and generate the draft policy for our university. We also conducted research of national standards, averages, and non-university policies around workplace bullying. We researched the work of Drs. Gary and Ruth Namie (Dr. Gary Namie in particular, as he was the president of the National University Bullying Institute) and looked into multiple publications in regard to bullying and the psychological behavior that may be related to it.

We also were careful in confirming the relationship between unlawful discrimination in regards to bullying to ensure that our university's bullying policy and unlawful discrimination policy would work in concert with each other—as bullying can also take the form of unlawful discrimination when the bullying is related to a protected class. Finally, we researched the work within United States' colleges and universities to see what work was being done on bullying policies here; although, there was not much in this regard.

We put together draft policies and university bullying examples to begin educating the campus community about what our policies might look like and what behaviors our policies would address.

Getting the legal team involved

As we moved closer to developing the policy, we met with our legal team and received concerns about developing this policy since there was no legal statute for one at the time. Most legal teams would like a policy to be backed by law as this is ideal for enforcement. Many institutions adhere to this philosophy, as they believe it is difficult for a college or university to develop and enforce a policy that is not linked to law. This sparked many challenging conversations in which we communicated that there was something missing in their understanding. We needed to develop this policy since it could be enforced through the direct link to the mission and core values of the institution. These core values would serve as the backbone for the policy and demonstrate to the community that it was important. Having many of these conversations also served as an additional way to get buy-in from constituent groups. In reflecting on the process, it was very important to get buy-in from the legal team as this policy could have ended before it got started without legal support.

KEY TAKEAWAYS

- Involve people from the legal department as soon as you decide you need a bullying policy. They know the state and federal law. They are there to help you develop the policy.
- Be ready to "make a case" to Legal. They need to understand why this policy is important and does not currently exist within your existing policies.
  - Know your institutional data about bullying when you make the case.
  - Know national data about bullying when you make the case.

375

> ## QUESTIONS TO GET YOU STARTED – INVOLVING LEGAL
>
> If you are undertaking your own bullying policy, think about at what steps you will need to involve the legal team.
>
> 1. Have you worked with Legal before? (If not, who do you know who can guide you through this process?)
> 2. How did it go?
> 3. How could it go better?
> 4. Does your legal team like to be involved at every step along the way or only when a finished product is getting ready to be shared with the campus community?
> 5. What do they like you to bring to them?

Avoiding overlapping institutional policies

Another big conversation point centered on people feeling like there was no need for an additional policy, because we have the Code of Ethics policy. We examined this policy. Since actions in regard to bullying behavior were up for interpretation, it further confirmed the existing gap and the need for an additional policy. There were many conversations and point and counter points between constituent groups and myself (Dr. Myron Anderson) to communicate the need for the policy.

Key takeaways

- Make sure people from legal and HR are there. Legal helps with the policy development. HR helps with the process development.
- Note what is covered by AAUP and what is not covered by AAUP.
- Check Student Affairs. Some student code of conduct policies contain language about bullying; others do not.

Questions to get you started – Checking policy

If you are undertaking your own bullying policy, think about at what policies might actually overlap and how to make sure you have done your due diligence around this matter.

1. Who do you need at the table to answer this question?
2. How long do you expect it will take to answer this question?
3. What will be your system to double check you did not miss any policy overlaps?

Educating the campus community

We also needed to educate the campus community as there was little to no education regarding university bullying for the campus. Having a stand-alone policy opened an educational route to train and develop the university community's understanding on what bullying was, what were the core bullying types, and why university bullying was detrimental to an institution.

More than we knew at the time, this buy-in process and the opportunity to educate the campus community on university bullying provided more support for developing the policy and implementing a process. We also knew that this knowledge acquisition had to be ongoing and in multiple formats. This graphic helped us with our education strategy:

BULLYING EDUCATION STRATEGY

Face to Face
Workshops
and Seminars

**Continuous
Knowledge
Acquisition**

Online
Training

Learning
Communities

If you are undertaking your own bullying policy, think about
who needs to learn what and how.

1. Who do you need at the table to answer this question?
2. What different modalities will work to educate your
   campus community?
3. Where will you find resources to support the education
   component?

Recap: The Plan to Develop
a University Bullying Policy:

1. Research university bullying definitions.
2. Review national data.
3. Gather Equal Opportunity Office data.
4. Gather Ombuds Office data.
5. Gather Human Resource Office data.
6. Gather data from the Office of the President Code of
   Ethics.
7. Show the needs of the campus through a campus climate
   survey.
8. Review the standard set by Canada and elsewhere.
9. Enlist the desire of the university community once the
   topic is broached.

We knew implementing a policy like this would have a huge benefit to our campus. The university bullying policy provided an additional avenue for the university to be responsive on issues related to campus climate. Being responsive and thorough would lead to the creation of a more welcoming environment where people enjoyed working and they would thrive at our institution.

A champion

Even after all this work has been done - the research, the data collection, and the communication of the need for a policy—there also needs to be a champion of this project. The champion is important for connecting all the dots, all the people, and all the policies. This person is the hub of information, the energy and face of the policy, and the key to moving a policy like this forward.

How do you develop an institutional bullying policy and get buy-in from your institution?

STEP ONE

The first thing you need to do is to present the information to the senior leadership and administration with the goal of getting buy-in. This might take a little bit of time, so do not rush this process as this will serve as a foundation for developing further buy-in for the policy.

This part of the process took approximately one year—one year to convince the senior leadership and the administration of the need. See the appendix for a short document we shared with senior leadership. We were at the forefront of this number of years ago, and we were the second policy in the state of Colorado to be developed. So, this might not take as long by today's standards where bullying in higher education is more a part of the national conversation.

STEP TWO

Second, create a comprehensive committee or a cross-functional team. The goal is to get membership from multiple elements of the institution, so they can weigh-in on the creation of the policy and be able to bring perspective from their respective constituent groups to the development of the policy.

Educate this cross-functional team. Provide them with the background information. Organize the information and present it to them in a way that they will be able to receive it quickly and be able to understand the need for the policy as an essential goal of the institution. You need buy-in from the cross-functional team that this is an issue that needs to be addressed. Once they are involved with the process, they will go back to their constituent groups and be able to help educate others about what is taking place regarding the policy, so they too can act as internal champions.

The education process at our university took the development and dissemination of multiple presentations: defining the bullying leader vs the tough leader, identifying the bullying types, drawing the link between bully and negative campus climate, and identifying that there was a gap in our policies that allowed bullying to continue. We were intentional in communicating these points because we did not want people to be just calling everybody a bully if that wasn't warranted. This element of the education process was key to understanding that tough leaders are not necessarily bullies and there are also bullies out there. We needed to be able to understand the difference.

Step Three

Third, we expanded the education process campus-wide. We held forums and town halls, went to department meetings, constituent group committees (e.g., counselors, admin-istrators, classified staff council, faculty senate, council of chairs, senior leadership, vice president cabinet, presidential cabinet, and student government association), and organizations that wanted to hear this information. Eventually, once the policy was passed, we implemented a cycle where the whole campus community must be (re)trained on bullying behaviors and policies through online modules every two years.

The education process really had two stages: Stage one was to educate the campus community about bullying and the differences between tough leader and bully leader. Stage two was to educate people on what the bullying policy and procedures were and how they would be implemented.

It is important to note that you need to be intentional in discussing issues in this intended order. If people are exposed to the wrong order, these policies are sometimes difficult to digest in a college or university setting where people prize autonomy. You need a clear message to help with maximum understanding.

One policy, four routes

This policy is clearly defined, and the four routes appear in the Appendix to this chapter.

For our university bullying policy, we needed the procedures and policy to align with other institutional policies and to work for each constituent group. The mistake that many institutions make is they will implement an institutional bullying policy as a blanket policy for the entire institution but not clearly outline the procedures to adhere to the policy. They might not take into consideration the multiple job groups that may have different procedures to allow for the enforcement of the policy.

Many institutions have multiple employee types (i.e. tenured faculty, tenure-track faculty, classified staff, exempt administrators, and non-tenure-track faculty). These different employee types have different procedures when it comes to corrective action. It is important to understand each classifications system and align them with the policy for enforcement. Not taking this into consideration will create a policy that will not be able to be enforced and therefore the policy will be ineffective and can cause more harm than good. When a policy can't be enforced, confidence declines and trust gets lost. Then the issue of removing or reducing bullying at your institution fails, and the climate deteriorates even more.

We took a year to develop one policy with four different processes that aligned with each employee classification so that we could create a clear process to implement our bullying policy. See the Appendix of this chapter to view different flow charts for the different reporting processes at MSU Denver.

This is often a difficult policy to pass. It takes buy-in and time but to really make it happen you need to bring the proper people to the table for the development process to make sure it meets the needs for all work groups at your institution.

A shortcut to this work may be to look at your current complaint processes for each employee classification and model the processes for the institutional bullying policy after those complaint processes already in place. There may need to be some adjustments but using the existing complaint process will give you a foundation that has already been developed for different employee class-ifications. This will actually make it easier for the institutional bullying policy to be enforced. It is paramount that your processes are detailed, transparent, and in sync with the institutional structure, leadership, and constituent groups prior to launching the policy.

KEY TAKEAWAYS

Step one. Establish institutional buy-in for the need of a policy, starting with senior leadership.

Step two. Develop sample policies with a cross-campus and cross-functional team.

Step three. Develop sample procedures to support the policy.

Step four. Educate the campus by enacting the policy and having everyone participate in the learning modules.

Step five. Conduct policy and process revisions as needed.

Should mediation be a part of the bullying policy?

Colleges and universities sometimes make a mistake to include mediation in the bullying process. Mediation should not be a part of the bullying process because mediation suggests that there are issues or concerns from both parties. Oftentimes in bullying, the issue is one-dimensional, and that issue is coming from one party directed to another. Mediation sends a message that the person that is being bullied may be the problem and this is often not the case. This slows down the possible corrective action that could take place regarding removing bullying from the institution. Mediation is counterproductive to enforcing an institutional bullying policy and gives the bully more time to bully and maintain a negative climate for a longer period of time.

To this end, we elected not to place a mediation component into our policy.

QUESTIONS TO GET YOU STARTED – MEDIATION?

If you are undertaking your own bullying policy, think about if and when you think mediation will help or will hurt in your process.

1. Who do you need at the table to answer this question?
2. What research do you need to answer this question?
3. If you decide on mediation, at what steps in the process will mediation be a solution and at what steps will it no longer be a solution?
4. How will you let the campus community know about their options in this process?

Is anonymous reporting worth it?

At the beginning of the bullying reporting process, there is an allowance for anonymity. This is important as it protects the accuser and the person being accused. In addition, the complaint must be filed by the person experiencing the bullying action at many institutions. This is filed through HR, and it also has to be determined that the complaint is a case of bullying according to institutional policy before the complaint can move forward, and this is handled through legal affairs. Determining that it is bullying according to institutional policy is sometimes call receiving jurisdiction. This confirms that the action meets the threshold of bullying. If the action does not meet that requirement, then the complaint officially goes away, the accused is not notified, and the accuser's identity is not revealed.

If the complaint is deemed to bullying, then it is classified as such, and the complaint process continues. The accused will receive the complaint and will provide a response to the claim and the process will then take its course.

In short, anonymity is important as it will allow complaints to come forward. Anonymity will also allow for complaints that do not rise to the level of defined bullying to be addressed through other mechanisms within the organization (like those mentioned in the microaggression and microbullying chapters). Often an institution will use the legal office to chime in on reviewing and deeming if a complaint rises to the level of defined bullying, as institutions do not want to start the formal process if the case is not strong enough to follow through on the concerns.

Ensure the investigator has the proper training

Persons investigating institutional bullying complaints should be trained investigators, not just members of HR. This training can be from varied areas, such as a legal background, American Association for Access, Equity and Diversity (AAAED), Equal Opportunity (EO), Human Resources (HR), Society for Human Resource Management (SHRM), Title 9, or specific investigative training. The important thing is that the investigator understands the investigation principles, administers fair and objective questions and lets the facts lead them throughout the investigation process.

What if someone is accused of bullying but did not bully?

Being accused of bullying can be scary and disheartening. People may feel confused, angry, sad, defensive, and even unsupported by the institution. However, it's important to reassure the person to remain calm and cooperative. Let the person know that, even if accused wrongly, they are to take the complaint seriously. They need to:

1. Cooperate with the investigation and report what they know.

2. Tell the truth. Giving false information during an investigation is grounds for internal discipline.

3. Avoid repeating any behavior related to the complaint.

4. Do not retaliate against the complainant or anyone else involved in the process.

5. Keep a record of all communications, even retro-active communication that you can document of interactions with the complainant.

People who investigate bullying claims know that not all claims are what they seem. Sometimes even bullies file complaints against the person they are bullying in order to deflect further inquiry into their own behaviors. Other times bullies file a complaint because they are starting to feel the bullied person avoid them at work and are confused by the change in interaction patterns. They do not equate their own behavior with why the bullied person is shying away. The investigators work hard to be thorough and confidential. Usually, the behaviors of the bully will be called into question when enough people have remarked on how the bully treats others.

How is our policy working?

As we implemented a campus climate survey every two years, we were able to see that after we developed the policy and educated the campus as to what bullying was, we saw a 20% reduction of bullying activity—even before the policy went into effect. Educating the community about bullying allowed for many people to change their behaviors before enforcement of the policy started. Most people try to do what is right once they know the boundaries for acceptable behavior, and additional knowledge will help them do that. The fact that there was a policy with clear enforcement procedures on the way may have sparked institutional behavior change on this issue as well. Having our university see a 20% reduction in bullying activity did so much to promote a welcoming and healthy campus climate.

Additional thoughts and recommendations when you go on this journey

1. It is a long road.

2. You will deal with resistance.

3. Make sure to align the bullying policy with other policies.

4. Do not rush the buy-in process.

5. Educate your campus.

6. Change is slow.

1. IT IS A LONG ROAD.

This is an institutional culture shift, and oftentimes there are bullies who, because of their institutional positions, are involved in the policy and process development and may try to derail the development and implementation process to reduce possible self-exposure. If you run into this, it is important to have transparency, data, and significant support to dilute them and move the process forward. Another strategy is to intentionally bring some of the nay-sayers to the policy and process development table to hopefully develop early buy-in and promote them as being a part of the resolution.

2. EXPECT AND DEAL WITH RESISTANCE.

There will also be some nay-sayers who are not bullies, such as faculty, staff, legal practitioners, etc. It is critical for the champions of the policy to know the national data and know your institutional data as champions will be challenged every step of the way in this process.

3. ALIGN YOUR POLICY.

Develop a policy and process that is co-created by those in your institution and align the goals and objectives of this policy with the core values and mission of the institution to allow for the sustainability of the development and implementation of this policy. These connections will allow for the policy to hold up through the long process.

4. DON'T RUSH THE PROCESS.

Do not rush the process as buy-in needs to be achieved at all levels. If you do not achieve buy-in at every level of this journey, the policy will be ineffective. For example, if you have buy-in at the policy level but not with the process, the policy will be ineffective. If you have buy-in at the implementation level but not at senior leadership, the policy will be ineffective. Institutional buy-in is the key to success, and if you need more time to confirm buy-in, then we recommend that you take more time.

5. EDUCATE YOUR CAMPUS.

Education is such a big element in developing and implementing an institutional bullying policy, that the education component alone can significantly reduce bullying at your institution. Further, when you implement the bullying policy to complement the education component you create an accountability touchpoint that will assist those for whom education is not enough to reduce their bullying actions.

6. CHANGE IS SLOW.

This process may not be as difficult today as there were only four higher education institutions in the country that had an institutional bullying policy in place at the time that we developed ours. In addition, there is more national data, conversations taking place on a national stage, and documentation of the link between bullying and organizational climate now.

The implementation of an institutional bullying policy will hold people accountable, promote a healthy climate, and promote positive engagement between the human capital of an institution.

Your institution's constituencies would like to have an institutional bullying policy—they just might not know it yet.

Conclusion

As much as we hope bullying will not happen at your institution, we know it probably will. This chapter shared the process at one university to create a bullying policy, to fill in the institutional gap between code of conduct, discrimination, and harassment policies. It shared about the need to build faculty, staff, and administrators' understanding of the need for a bullying policy, how to create buy-in, and how to educate the campus community.

It is very important to put a bullying policy in place in your institution because it is a key component in the overall quest to promote a welcoming and inclusive climate that happens partly through institutional policies. The implementation of a bullying policy sets the systemic foundation to expect a healthy climate, ultimately allowing for your institution's workforce to thrive.

Reflect back to the 4-Way Implementation Model. Institutional bullying policies can serve as both a proactive and a reactive action advancing your institution's actions toward reducing bullying from your institution. Proactively it can serve as a reminder in the promotion of non-aggressive interaction between colleagues. Reactively it can be an enforcement mechanism.

An analogy that comes to mind relates to our traffic laws. You may travel down a street and you know the speed limit is 45 miles per hour. Your intent is to honor this speed limit as you drive down the road. Taking this analogy further, one morning when you are driving you happen to see a police officer monitoring traffic on this street. Again, your intent is to follow the speed limit and, for all intents and purposes, you are. However, after seeing the police officer, you might look down at your speedometer to confirm your speed. You might even tap your breaks to slow down a little to ensure that you are not speeding. In this example, you are incorporating your understanding and the monitoring of a traffic law, a policy, into how you drive. This analogy aligns with the importance of developing and implementing a bullying policy at your institution. Many people want to do what is right in their engagement at work and do not want to engage in behavior that may cause harm. The policy helps them check their emotional speed with others.

A bullying policy serves as a proactive and reactive intentional step toward removing bullying actions from your institution. Simply put, having the policy in place may remove many bullying actions before they even take place.

As indicated earlier, we have seen a 20% reduction of bullying through implementing a bullying education strategy and policy at our institution.

Having a policy without a process is not enough. A policy without an implementation process will be detrimental to the long-term effectiveness of the policy. This initial success will disappear and possibly communicate an unintentional message that bullying is welcomed if there is no process in place to enforce the policy.

Having an institutional bullying policy in place sends a message to your community that bullying behavior is not acceptable. It communicates a clear line of behavior that the institution insists everyone follows, much like obeying the speed limit. Having an institutional bullying policy in place allows for people to take a closer look at their engagement with each other and possibly "tap their brakes" in regard to bullying, thus improving engagement with colleagues and being intentional in advancing a welcoming environment that supports the institution's mission.

Given the importance of cultivating a healthier workplace and a more positive culture where all employees feel safe and are able to use their fullest talents in service to the institution's mission, we hope your institution is not in need of a bullying policy, but it is a good idea to put one in place just in case you ever do.

Food for Thought

We work at colleges and universities, places of learning. Reducing and removing microaggressions and bullying is first and foremost an educational practice. Removing these actions from our organizations promotes a welcoming and inclusive climate thus allowing faculty, staff, and students to thrive. Following is a list of resources to continue your learning in these areas.

Suggested reading

Barratt-Pugh, L. G. B. and D. Krestelica. "Bullying in Higher Education: Culture change requires more than policy." *Perspectives: Policy and Practice in Higher Education,* vol. 23, no. 2-3, 2019, pp. 109-114.

Helpful resources

Colleges and universities in the UK and other commonwealth countries have had anti-bullying policies in place for years. Some institutions of higher education in the US finally have them as well. For examples of such policies, see:

- University of Wollongong
- University of Portsmouth
- Northumbria University
- Chicago State University
- University of Wisconsin-Madison
- Oregon State University
- Penn State University
- University of Birmingham

Appendix

The Appendix to this chapter includes three resources:

- University Bullying Policy Definitions and Descriptions

- Four flowcharts for process to follow for bullying claims:

    o Administrators

    o Classified employees

    o Tenured/tenure track faculty

    o Visiting, full time lectures, part-time lecturers, non-tenure track faculty

- MSU Denver policy and complaint procedure

University Bullying Policy Definitions and Descriptions

This document was shared with different constituent groups to disclose more about the policy in a bite-sized way while still creating buy-in.

DESCRIPTION

This document describes the MSU Denver university bullying policy, which addresses all employees, including student employees, applicants for employment, and others in the university environment, including members of the public.

POLICY STATEMENT

MSU Denver shall provide a secure work environment for all employees free from bullying and will not tolerate any behavior in the university that constitutes bullying activity as defined in this policy. Bullying may be directed toward an employee by a manager; co-worker, subordinate, appointing authority, vendor, contractor, or member of the public. Bullying conduct may be challenged even if the complaining party is not the intended target of the conduct.

This policy is not intended to, and will not be applied in a way that would, violate rights and responsibilities with regard to academic freedom and freedom of expression, nor will it be interpreted in a way that undermines a supervisor's authority to appropriately manage their work unit.

This policy prohibits retaliation against employees who report potential university bullying or participate in the investigation of the complaint.

Any employee violating this policy will be subject to corrective or disciplinary action, up to and including dismissal.

DEFINITION

Unwanted **repeated aggressive behavior** that manifests as verbal abuse, conduct that is threatening, humiliating, intimidating, or acts of sabotage that interfere with work, consequently creating a hostile, offensive and toxic university. For more detail, please see the University Bullying Complaint Procedures.

REPORTING

When an employee, including a student employee, believes that he or she is the target of behavior that they believe may satisfy the definition of university bullying, as defined in the University policy on bullying, the employee should report any and all incidents immediately to their supervisor, or the supervisor of the alleged bully.

Administrators and Classified employees have the right to report alleged bullying activity directly to Human Resources by submitting a written complaint with supporting documentation.

Tenured, Tenure Track, Category II, and Category III faculty have the right to report alleged bullying activity directly to their Dean's Office by submitting a written complaint with supporting documentation.

MANDATORY COOPERATION

All employees, supervisors, managers, appointing authorities, and agents of MSU Denver shall cooperate, unless there are extraordinary circumstances, (such as conflict of interest) with any investigative process or resolution, whether informal or formal, by the appropriate investigator. Any MSU Denver employee who fails to cooperate and/or attempts to impede participation in an investigation will be subject to disciplinary action, up to and including dismissal. To enable MSU Denver to achieve the goals of this policy, Human Resources and the Deans' Offices shall have access to all relevant and necessary information.

NON-RETALIATION

This policy prohibits retaliation against employees who report potential university bullying or participate in the investigation of the complaint. Any employee bringing a complaint under this policy, or assisting in the investigation of such a complaint, will not be adversely affected in terms and conditions of employment, nor dismissed because of the complaint. Anyone who engages in retaliatory action will be subject to disciplinary action, up to and including dismissal. Retaliation is defined as activity that may dissuade a reasonable person from exercising his or her rights under this policy.

Employees who report alleged bullying complaints that they know are false may be subject to disciplinary action within the University, and/or external legal action from those they have falsely accused.

CONFIDENTIALITY

To the extent feasible, information provided in the complaint and investigation process will be treated as confidential. However, MSU Denver will disclose information if deemed reasonably necessary to investigate and take appropriate corrective or disciplinary action, or to defend such corrective or disciplinary action, if required by law.

WITNESSES

When an employee has witnessed or been made aware of behavior that they believe may satisfy the definition of university bullying (as defined in the University policy on bullying), the employee should report any and all incidents to their supervisor, or the supervisor of the alleged bully, Human Resources or the appropriate Dean's Office if a faculty member is involved.

SUPERVISORS

When a supervisory level employee is notified about possible university bullying behavior, he or she must immediately notify Human Resources or the appropriate Dean's Office if a faculty member is involved.

Training

In order to prevent and reduce the number of incidences of bullying, the University Offices of Equal Opportunity, Human Resources, and Institutional Diversity will implement workshops for employees (including student employees) on what constitutes bullying, what the University's policies and procedures are, the employees' role in reporting incidents of bullying, and how to access the grievance process.

Policy Review

The Offices of Equal Opportunity, Human Resources, Institutional Diversity, and General Counsel shall review this policy on an annual basis and make updates as necessary.

See the following pages for bullying complaint flowcharts.

BULLYING COMPLAINT FLOWCHART
ADMINISTRATOR EMPLOYEES

Bullying complainant meets with Human Resources (HR) to review the complaint form. Human Resources explains the grievance process and the definitions of unlawful discrimination, bullying, and the code of ethics.

Bullying complaint filed within 90 working days of last incident

Once complaint is received, a letter of acknowledgment is sent to complainant

Upon receiving written complaint Human Resources (HR) in consultation with the Office of General Counsel will determine jurisdiction

No jurisdiction

Complaint is dismissed, and/or appropriate referrals are made, complainant is notified of the status and the respondent(s) is not notified of the complaint

Jurisdiction

Investigation Begins. Complainant is notified of the status, the respondent(s) is notified of the complaint and the University's zero tolerance policy against retaliation.

Copy of complaint is sent to
respondent(s) with timeline for
their response and complainant is
copied

Respondent(s) file written
response to complaint within 10
working days of notice. The
response is sent to complainant
with an opportunity for rebuttal
within 10 working days

Human Resources will
either investigate or
facilitate an
investigation by an
External Investigator
(EI)

No factual
basis for the
complaint

Complaint is dismissed and/or
appropriate referrals are made

HR or EI (within 60 working days)
sends findings, conclusion, and
recommendation(s) to the
appropriate Administrator to take
the appropriate corrective action

Factual
basis for
corrective
action

The complainant will
be given periodic
reports on the
investigator's progress

Within 10 working days the
appropriate Administrator issues
the appropriate corrective action

Factual
basis for
disciplinary
action

Within 60 working days HR or EI
refers to President for final
decision with recommendation(s)
from investigative report

Within 10 working days President
reviews disciplinary
recommendation(s)

President issues appropriate
non-appealable sanction

BULLYING COMPLAINT FLOWCHART
CLASSIFIED EMPLOYEES

Bullying complainant meets with Human Resources (HR) to review the complaint form. Human Resources explains the grievance process and the definitions of unlawful discrimination, bullying, and the code of ethics.

Bullying complaint filed within 90 working days of last incident

Once complaint is received, a letter of acknowledgment is sent to complainant

Upon receiving written complaint Human Resources (HR) in consultation with the Office of General Counsel will determine jurisdiction

No jurisdiction

Complaint is dismissed, and/or appropriate referrals are made, complainant is notified of the status and the respondent(s) is not notified of the complaint

Jurisdiction

Investigation Begins. Complainant is notified of the status, the respondent(s) is notified of the complaint and the University's zero tolerance policy against retaliation.

Human Resources will either investigate or facilitate an investigation by an External Investigator (EI)

The complainant will be given periodic reports on the investigator's progress

Copy of complaint is sent to respondent(s) with timeline for their response and complainant is copied

Respondent(s) file written response to complaint within 10 working days of notice. The response is sent to complainant with an opportunity for rebuttal within 10 working days

No factual basis for the complaint

Complaint is dismissed and/or appropriate referrals are made

Factual basis for complaint

HR or EI (within 60 working days) sends findings, conclusion, and recommendation(s) to the appropriate Administrator to take the appropriate corrective action

Within 10 working days the appropriate Administrator issues the appropriate corrective action

For actions for Classified Employees, see state personnel rules

If a Classified Employee disagrees with the supervisor's action then the Classified Employee needs to follow the MSU Denver Classified Grievance Procedure found on the HR Department website

BULLYING COMPLAINT FLOWCHART
CATEGORY I FACULTY
(TENURED & TENURE TRACK FACULTY)

Bullying complainant meets with Office of the Dean (OD) for explanation on how the grievance process works and the definition of unlawful discrimination, bullying, and the code of ethics.

Bullying complaint filed within 90 working days of last incident

Once complaint is received, a letter of acknowledgment is sent to complainant

Upon receiving written complaint Office of the Dean (OD) in consultation with the Office of General Counsel (OGC) will determine jurisdiction

No Jurisdiction

Complaint is dismissed. Complainant is notified of the status and the respondent(s) is not notified of the complaint

Jurisdiction

Investigation Begins. Complainant is notified of the status, the respondent(s) is notified of the complaint and the University's zero tolerance policy against retaliation.

FIX YOUR CLIMATE

Office of the Dean or
External Investigator
(EI) investigates
complaint

Copy of complaint is sent to
respondent(s) with timeline for
their response and complainant is
copied

Respondent(s) file written
response to complaint within 10
working days of notice. The
response is sent to complainant
with an opportunity for rebuttal
within 10 working days

The complainant will
be given periodic
reports on the
investigator's progress

No factual
basis for the
complaint

Complaint is dismissed and/or
appropriate referrals are made

Factual
basis for
complaint

OD or EI submits a report with
findings and recommendation(s)
for resolution

Factual basis for
disciplinary action

OD or EI (within 60 working days)
sends findings, conclusion, and
recommendation(s) to the Provost
to take the appropriate corrective
action

Yes

Within 60 working
days OD or EI refers to
President for final
decision with
recommendation(s)

Within 10 working days the
appropriate Administrator issues
the appropriate corrective action

Within 10 working
days President reviews
disciplinary
recommendation(s)

 No

President issues appropriate
corrective action for resolution

Yes

President issues their
appealable or
non-appealable
sanction

 No

See MSU Denver Faculty
Handbook Section XVII

BULLYING COMPLAINT FLOWCHART
CATEGORY II AND III FACULTY

Bullying complainant meets with Office of the Dean (OD) for explanation on how the grievance process works and the definition of unlawful discrimination, bullying, and the code of ethics.

Bullying complaint filed within 90 working days of last incident

Once complaint is received, a letter of acknowledgment is sent to complainant

Upon receiving written complaint Office of the Dean (OD) in consultation with the Office of General Counsel (OGC) will determine jurisdiction

No jurisdiction

Complaint is dismissed. Complainant is notified of the status and the respondent(s) is not notified of the complaint

Jurisdiction

Investigation Begins. Complainant is notified of the status, the respondent(s) is notified of the complaint and the University's zero tolerance policy against retaliation.

Office of the Dean or External Investigator (EI) investigates complaint

Copy of complaint is sent to respondent(s) with timeline for their response and complainant is copied

Respondent(s) file written response to complaint within 10 working days of notice. The response is sent to complainant with an opportunity for rebuttal within 10 working days

The complainant will be given periodic reports on the investigator's progress

No factual basis for the complaint

Complaint is dismissed and/or appropriate referrals are made

Factual basis for complaint

OD or EI submits a report with findings and recommendation(s) for resolution

Corrective action

OD or EI (within 60 working days) sends findings, conclusion, and recommendation(s) to the Provost to take the appropriate corrective action

Within 10 working days the appropriate Administrator issues the appropriate corrective action

MYRON R. ANDERSON AND KATHRYN S. YOUNG

University Bullying Complaint Procedures

This is the MSU Denver policy and complaint procedure document from Fall 2017. It has since been slightly revised.

I. UNIVERSITY BULLYING DEFINITION

A. Description

This policy addresses all employees, including student employees, applicants for employment, and others in the university environment, including members of the public.

This policy is not intended to, and will not be, applied in a way that would violate rights and responsibilities with regard to academic freedom and freedom of expression, nor will it be interpreted in a way that undermines a supervisor's authority to appropriately manage their work unit.

Bullying is a form of aggression; the actions can be both obvious and subtle, **forming a pattern of behavior** where more than one incident takes place. University bullying can involve supervisor to subordinate, peer-to-peer, mobbing (group bullying) and situations when a subordinate subjects a supervisory-level employee to bullying.

B. Definition

Unwanted **repeated aggressive behavior** that manifests as verbal abuse, conduct that is threatening, humiliating, intimidating, or acts of sabotage that interfere with work,

410

consequently creating a hostile, offensive, and toxic university.

C. Examples

Below are examples of bullying; however, it is important to note that **the following is not a checklist, nor a complete and absolute indicator of all forms of bullying.**

Examples include:

Bullying by Supervisor

- Intimidating a person
- Purposely excluding an employee from an essential meeting
- Threatening physical abuse
- Invasion of another person's personal space
- Removing areas of responsibility without cause
- Unreasonably changing work guidelines
- Assigning unreasonable duties or workload which are unfavorable to one person (in a way that creates unnecessary pressure)
- Underwork - creating a feeling of uselessness
- Unwarranted (or undeserved) punishment
- Unreasonably blocking applications for training, leave or promotion
- Excluding employees from matters in which they would be expected to be included as part of their job

- Denying training to a specific employee that is related to their job and not others
- Criticizing a person persistently or constantly
- Belittling a person's opinions
- Personal attacks (angry outbursts, excessive profanity, name calling)

Bullying by Co-Worker

- Staring, glaring, or other nonverbal demonstrations of hostility
- Spreading malicious rumors, gossip, or innuendo
- Excluding or isolating someone socially
- Encouragement of others to turn against the targeted employee
- Undermining or deliberately impeding a person's work
- Making jokes that are offensive by spoken word or email
- Sabotage of co-worker's work product or undermining of an employee's work performance
- Intruding on a person's privacy by pestering, spying, or stalking
- Tampering with a person's personal belongings or work equipment
- Using confidential information to humiliate a co-worker privately or publicly
- Withholding necessary information or purposefully giving the wrong information
- Continuously taking credit for someone else's work

- Ensuring failure of an employee's project by not performing required tasks, such as sign-offs, taking calls, working with collaborators, etc.

- Undermining or deliberately impeding an employee's work

- Withholding key information from a specific employee and not others

- Conduct that a reasonable person would find hostile, offensive, unacceptable, and unrelated to the employer's legitimate business interests

D. Not Bullying

A supervisor who accepts responsibility, makes clear and decisive decisions, provides detailed constructive criticism, resolves conflict quickly, is truthful, and values others is not a bully. A coworker who provides honest first-hand information to their supervisor, reports criminal and harmful activity, and reports institutional policy violations is not a bully.

Below are examples of non-bullying actions; however, it is important to note that **the following is not a checklist, nor a complete and absolute indicator of all forms of non-bullying.** This list is included as a way to show some of the actions that may take place in a university that are not bullying.

Examples include:

- A supervisor making clear and decisive decisions

- A supervisor engaging in difficult conversations with employees

- A supervisor addressing poor work performance

- While participating in a 360 evaluation process a co-worker gives a poor performance rating

- A supervisor or co-worker reports a perceived violation of a policy or procedure

- A supervisor or co-worker reports criminal activity

II. REPORTING

When an employee believes that he or she is the target of behavior that may satisfy the definition of university bullying, as defined in the University policy on bullying, the employee should report any and all incidents immediately to HR if the employee is an Administrator or Classified Employee, or to their Dean if the employee is a faculty member. The person who is alleging being bullied must file the complaint.

Administrators and Classified employees have the right to report alleged bullying activity directly to Human Resources by submitting a written complaint with supporting documentation.

Category I (Tenured, Tenure Track), Category II, and Category III faculty have the right to report alleged bullying activity directly to their Dean's Office by submitting a written complaint with supporting documentation.

A. Mandatory Cooperation

All employees, supervisors, managers, appointing authorities and agents of MSU Denver shall cooperate, unless there are extraordinary circumstances, (such as conflict of interest) with any investigative process or resolution, whether informal or formal, by the appropriate investigator. Any MSU Denver employee who fails to cooperate and/or attempts to impede participation in an investigation will be subject to disciplinary action, up to and including dismissal. To enable MSU Denver to achieve the goals of this policy, Human Resources and the Deans' Offices shall have access to all relevant and necessary information.

B. Non-retaliation

This policy prohibits retaliation against employees who report potential university bullying or participate in the investigation of the complaint. Any employee bringing a complaint under this policy, or assisting in the investigation of such a complaint, will not be adversely affected in terms and conditions of employment, nor dismissed because of the complaint. Anyone who engages in retaliatory action will be subject to disciplinary action, up to and including dismissal. Retaliation is defined as activity that may dissuade a reasonable person from exercising his or her rights under this policy.

Employees who report alleged bullying complaints that they know are false may be subject to disciplinary action within the University, and/or external legal action from those they have falsely accused.

C. Confidentiality

To the extent feasible, information provided in the complaint and investigation process will be treated as confidential. However, MSU Denver will disclose information if deemed reasonably necessary to investigate and take appropriate corrective or disciplinary action, or to defend such corrective or disciplinary action, if required by law.

D. Witnesses

When an employee has witnessed or been made aware of behavior that they believe may satisfy the definition of university bullying (as defined in the University policy on bullying), the employee is obliged to report any and all incidents to Human Resources or the appropriate Dean's Office if a faculty member is involved.

E. Supervisors

When a supervisory level employee is notified about possible university bullying behavior, he or she must immediately notify Human Resources or the appropriate Dean's Office if a faculty member is involved.

III. PROCEDURES

A. Filing

1. Complaints that are related to unlawful discrimination (e.g., retaliation or harassment) take precedence over the university bullying policy's internal process and must be filed in accordance with the appropriate procedures provided in the Office of Equal Opportunity Bullying Policy Complaint Procedures Rev. 9-14-17.

2. All bullying complaints shall be filed using the Bullying Complaint Form in Section IX of this document and shall be filed in Human Resources or the appropriate Dean's Office if a faculty member is involved.

B. The complaint form shall:

1. be signed by the complainant;

2. describe in detail the specific incident(s), occurrence(s), decision(s), and other factual matters believed to constitute bullying;

3. name as the respondent(s) the individual(s) whom the complainant believes to have engaged in prohibited behavior; and

4. include a brief statement describing the resolution, relief or action requested by the complainant.

C. Jurisdiction under these procedures is met when:

1. the allegations of the complaint meet the definition of a complaint as defined in the University Bullying Complaint Procedure; and

2. the complainant has complied with Section B above.

IV. REPORTING DEFINITIONS AND TIME PERIOD

A. Working day means:

A day on which the University holds regular class sessions or exams, and excludes Saturdays, Sundays and University holidays.

B. Complaint means:

1. a dispute which is filed by a complainant on the form set forth in this University Bullying Complaint Procedures document; and

2. alleges that a respondent engaged in bullying prohibited by University policy.

C. Complainant means:

1. any employee of the University and any applicant for employment or admission who alleges bullying by an employee of the University; or

2. any person who has been threatened with or subjected to retaliation by an employee of the University as a result of:

   a. opposing any bullying;

   b. filing a complaint or charge under this procedure;

   c. representing a complainant under this procedure; or

    d.   testifying, assisting, or participating in any manner in an investigation, proceeding, hearing, or lawsuit alleging bullying; and who has filed a complaint under these procedures.

D. Party means:

a complainant or respondent.

E. Respondent means:

any employee who is alleged to have engaged in bullying.

F. In computing any period of time:

The day of the act or event from which the designated period begins shall not be included in the period. The last day of the period shall be included, unless it is a Saturday, Sunday, University holiday, vacation day, or other non-working day, in which event the period shall run until the next day which is a working day.

G. When an act must be done by a certain day:

it shall be done by 5:00 p.m. on that day.

H. Extending time periods:

Human Resources or the Office of the Dean, as appropriate, may extend or shorten the time periods prescribed herein except that provided for the initial filing of a complaint.

I. Timeline

Complaints of bullying should be reported as soon as possible after the events which give rise to the complaint, but no later than 90 working days on which the complainant knew, or reasonably should have known, of the last incident of bullying behavior.

V. Investigation Process for Complaints Involving Administrators and Classified Staff

A. Human Resources

Administrators and Classified Staff have the right to report potential bullying activity directly to Human Resources by submitting a written complaint with supporting documentation.

1. Upon receiving a written complaint, in consultation with the Office of General Counsel (OGC), Human Resources (HR) will determine if a proper complaint of bullying was stated per the bullying definition and guidelines. If it is determined that a proper complaint is not stated, the complaint shall be dismissed. If a proper complaint of bullying is stated, the investigation by a trained investigator will proceed.

2. In consultation with the OGC, HR will determine whether the behavior may be more appropriately

addressed as university violence, university harassment, or sexual harassment and refer the complaint to the Office of Equal Opportunity.

3. HR, or an External Investigator (EI), will conduct a thorough and impartial investigation of the reported university bullying behavior and apply the "reasonable person" standard to the investigative record

4. For Administrators: HR, or an EI, will prepare a report, within 60 working days, of its findings and make recommendations to the appropriate MSU Denver administrator to dismiss the complaint or take either corrective action (e.g., verbal/written warning, letter of reprimand, etc.) or disciplinary action, if appropriate.

    For Administrators: The appropriate MSU Denver administrator shall issue, within 10 working days, the appropriate corrective action. If there is a factual basis for disciplinary action, HR or the EI will, within 60 days, refer the complaint to the President for final decision with recommendations from the investigative report. The President will review, and within 10 working days, issue the appropriate and non-appealable sanction.

5. For Classified Employees: HR, or an EI, will prepare a report, within 60 working days, of its findings and make recommendations to the appropriate MSU Denver administrator to dismiss the complaint or take corrective action (e.g., verbal/written warning, letter of reprimand, etc.) Within 10 working days, the appropriate Administrator issues the appropriate corrective action. (For actions for Classified employees, see state personnel rules.) If Classified employees

disagree with the supervisor's action, they may follow the MSU Denver Classified Grievance Procedure found on the HR Department website.

VI. Investigation Process for Complaints Involving Faculty

A. Academic Deans

Faculty have the right to report potential bullying behavior directly to their respective Dean's Office by submitting a written complaint with supporting documentation.

1. Upon receiving a written complaint, the Office of General Counsel (OGC) will determine if a proper complaint of bullying was stated per the bullying definition and guidelines. If it is determined that a proper complaint is not stated, the complaint shall be dismissed. If a proper complaint of bullying is stated, the investigation by a trained investigator will proceed.

2. The OGC will determine whether the behavior may be more appropriately addressed as university violence, university harassment, or sexual harassment and refer the complaint to the Office of Equal Opportunity.

3. The Dean's Office or an External Investigator (EI) shall conduct a thorough and impartial investigation of the reported university bullying activity and apply the "reasonable person" standard to the investigative record.

4. For Tenured and Tenure Track Faculty: The Dean's Office or the EI will prepare a report,

within 60 working days, of its investigative findings and make recommendations to the MSU Denver Provost to dismiss the complaint or take corrective action (e.g., verbal/written warning, letter of reprimand, etc.)

If there is a factual basis for disciplinary action (e.g., suspension, etc. or termination), the Dean's Office or EI will, within 60 working days, refer the complaint and recommendations from the investigative report to the President for review. Within 10 working days, the President will issue an appealable or non-appealable sanction. Only tenured faculty members are eligible to appeal disciplinary actions.

5. For Category II and III Faculty: The Dean's Office or the EI will prepare a report, within 60 working days, of its investigative findings and make recommendations to the MSU Denver Provost to dismiss the complaint or take corrective action (e.g., verbal/written warning, letter of reprimand, etc.). Within 10 working days, the appropriate Administrator will issue the appropriate corrective action.

VII. CORRECTIVE ACTION FOR EMPLOYEE(S) FOUND IN VIOLATION OF THE UNIVERSITY BULLYING POLICY

A. Respondent

The appropriate MSU Denver administrator will direct the department to refer the known perpetrator(s) to a professional organization/agency, (e.g., Colorado State

Employees Assistance Program (CSEAP) or to the Human Resources training program for coaching in regard to bullying. Other forms of corrective action may include a verbal/written warning, letter of reprimand, disciplinary action (e.g., suspension or termination), if appropriate.

VIII. Education and Assessment

A. Training

The University Offices of Equal Opportunity and General Counsel will be responsible for Bullying Policy Complaint Procedures Rev. 9-14-17 acquiring and implementing investigative training for the appropriate University personnel that will conduct investigations for complaints of bullying behavior.

B. Complaint Data Collection

Prior to September 1 each year, the Human Resources and Deans' Offices shall prepare a report of the dispositions of complaints initiated during the prior academic year. This report shall be prepared without names of the concerned parties and shall be submitted to the President.

Metropolitan State University of Denver

University Bullying Complaint Form

Date: _____

Name: _____

Work ID# (if applicable): _____

Mailing Address: _____

City/State/Zip Code: _____

Email: _____

Phone: _____

Alternate Phone: _____

Metropolitan State University of Denver

University Bullying Complaint Form

Name: _____

Date: _____

___Faculty ___Administrator ___Classified ___Other:

_____ (Fill in)

Type of Bullying Alleged

___Bullying by Co-Worker

___Bullying by Supervisor

___Other

Summary of Alleged Complaint

1. Date on which alleged conduct first occurred:

_____

2. Date on which alleged conduct most recently occurred:

_____

3. Names of witnesses (please specify whether employee, student, or other):

_____

_____

_____

4. Name of person(s) who engaged in bullying (respondent):

_____

5. Describe in detail the specific incidents, occurrences, decisions, and other factual matters believed to constitute bullying (if more space is needed, please attach additional sheets):

_____

_____

_____

6. Harm caused:

_____

_____

7. I request that the following action be taken: _

_____

_____

Metropolitan State University of Denver

University Bullying Complaint Form

Acknowledgements

I understand the following:

1. I have the right to be free of retaliation for filing this complaint. I agree to report any conduct, which I believe is motivated by retaliation for filing this complaint. I understand, however, that if this statement contains accusations which I know are false, I may be subject to disciplinary action within the University and/or external legal action from those I have falsely accused.

2. The Investigator will try to protect my identity from public exposure. The respondent, however, will be given a copy of this grievance in order to have an opportunity to respond to it.

3. I have received a copy of the Bullying Policy of Metropolitan State University of Denver.

4. I understand that the Investigator is an advocate for neither the grievant nor the respondent. The role of the Investigator is to investigate complaints from a neutral position to determine whether violations of the University's Bullying Policy have occurred.

CERTIFICATION

I CERTIFY THAT THE STATEMENTS MADE IN THIS COMPLAINT ARE TRUE AND ACCURATE AND THAT I HAVE READ AND UNDERSTAND THE STATEMENTS MADE IN THE ACKNOWLEDGMENTS SECTION OF THIS COMPLAINT

_____

Signature   Date

CHAPTER 8: ADDITIONAL TIPS, SCRIPTS, AND WORKSHEETS

1. List all the put downs you can come up with.
2. Categorize them related to identity categories.
3. Who is represented? Who is not?

Put downs are often taken from language used to harm marginalized groups.

Examples: "That's so gay." "You are lame." "You throw like a girl." "That idea is so crazy," "Hey guys" to refer to a multi-gendered group. "I am so ADHD today." "I totally have OCD about my desk."

4. If you, or people around you, say any of the ones on the list you created, stop.

THINGS NOT TO SAY

As a chair, dean, or director, people are going to come to you with concerns. They, first and foremost, want to be heard. They do not want you to sound dismissive of their concerns. The following list of sentences often comes across as dismissive and just makes the situation worse for the person coming to you (adapted from drkathyobear.com).

1. Yeah, but....
2. That happens to me/my group, too....
3. I know someone who... and they don't agree with you....
4. I don't see it that way; therefore, it doesn't really happen...
5. That doesn't happen to me... (so it doesn't exist)
6. Don't you think that...You're over-reacting
7. Don't you think that... You're too sensitive...
8. He/she's good person...They never meant to do that....
9. That was not my intent! You misunderstood me!

PHRASES THAT LEAD TO MISCOMMUNICATION

Order

You must...
You have to....
You will....

Threaten

If you don't....
You'd better or else....
You'll pay a big price if....

Interfere

What you should do is…
Here's how it should go….
It would be best if you…

Judge

You are lazy, stubborn…
You'll never change.
I know just how you are….

Blame

It's your fault….
If you only had….

Accuse

You lied to me.
You started this mess.
You won't listen.

Categorize

You always…
Every time this happen you do the same thing…
You never…

Excuse someone else's behavior

It's not so bad if…
It isn't your problem.
You'll feel better when…

Personalize

You are mean.
This is your personality.
You are the problem here.

Assume

If you really respected me, you would…
I know exactly why this happened.

Diagnose

You're just trying to get attention.
Your personal history is what caused this to happen.
What you need is…

Label

You are being unrealistic (emotional, angry, hysterical…).
This is typical of you.

Manipulate

Don't you think you should…
To really help, you should…

Deny

You did not…
I am completely blameless.

Double bind

I want you to do it my way, but do it however you want.

Distract

That is nothing. Listen to what happened to me.

Taken from *Resolving Conflicts at Work: Ten Strategies for Everyone on the Job* by Kenneth Cloke and Joan Goldsmith (2011), pages 47-49.

THINGS YOU CAN SAY TO TRY TO IMPROVE A DIFFICULT CONVERSATION

(Remember your tone and body language are just as important as your words.)

I understand that is how you feel / what you think. Would you like to know how I feel / what I think?

Would you tell me one thing I can do right now to improve our communication? Then can I tell you one thing, too?

It would help me listen to you and perhaps do what you are asking if you would lower your voice when speaking to me. What can I do to make that possible?

Is the reason you are yelling is that you want me to know how strongly you feel about this or because you feel I have not been listening to you? What can I do to change that?

This issue presents us with a real challenge.

What would you like to see happen instead?

We now have a chance to make things better.

You have a good point. What could we do together to address it?

Reframe issues so they cannot be answered with a simple yes or no.

Reframe to depersonalize the problem.

I'm sorry, but this conversation is not working for me. Can we discuss this without yelling at each other?

Taken from *Resolving Conflicts at Work: Ten Strategies for Everyone on the Job* by Kenneth Cloke and Joan Goldsmith (2011), pages 47-49.

SCRIPTS: IN CASE YOU NEED HELP KNOWING WHAT TO SAY

Something you can say: "I know you probably don't mean anything by it, but I find it hard to listen to those kinds of anti-gay jokes."

Something you can say: "I know I may not understand exactly what is happening right now, but I am feeling more and more uncomfortable with the tone of this conversation."

Something you can say: "I am sure you did not intend this. I hope you can also realize the impact was very different on _____ than what you consciously intended."

Something you can say: "I know you are a good person. Most of us are, and we can still make hurtful comments that have a negative impact and come across as (racist, sexist, etc.). The fact that you are a well-intended colleague has me hopeful that you will care about the unintended impact of your comment and that you will want to stay in the conversation to better understand what happened, why it was hurtful, and what to do about it."

Something you can say: "When someone tells me that I have microaggressed against them, I have the opportunity to see how I need to shift my actions to better align with my core values."

Something you can say: "You tell me you are (generous, not a racist, very understanding, etc.). Right now, your actions are sending a message of (racism, sexist, not being a good colleague, talking down to people, etc.). I want to make sure we can find a way for others to be able to see you how you see you. What can we do to make sure your actions speak loudly enough people can see that you are (generous, not a racist, very understanding, etc.)?"

WAYS TO REDUCE YOUR OWN IMPLICIT BIAS:

- Look for counterexamples.

- Imagine a positive contact with the group with whom you may have a bias.

- Pay particular attention to your choices when you're feeling tired rushed or stressed as the situations tend to activate our biases.

- Write down your reasoning behind a particular choice and see if that same reasoning works for other genders, races, language groups, etc.

(adapted from Implicit Bias Video Series from BruinX, the R&D unit within UCLA's Office of Equity, Diversity, and Inclusion)

MYRON R. ANDERSON AND KATHRYN S. YOUNG

Work through microaggression scenarios in your own institution

Here are scenarios you can use to role play and troubleshoot common microaggressions. Following the list of micro-aggressions is a worksheet you can use to stimulate the conversation.

A new faculty of color comes in, is given her key, and told where to find her office. She goes into the office, opens the door, and there are still boxes and papers to be dealt with in the existing office. The floor needs vacuuming, and there is not even a desk.

The Director of Student Affairs walks through an office with a guest from another institution. He tells the guest the ethnic origin of ever worker they pass in the hallway without greeting anyone. One person walks to another person's office and says, "Does he think we are animals in a zoo?"

The Director of the LGBTQ+ program comes to the Vice President. She mentions that she needs $3,000 for workshops and $5,000 for a guest speaker. This should be a formality as the Director has a budget, and she just needs approval to use it. The VP tells her that he does not think this is a good use for the funds and "to go back to the drawing board."

An older, female administrator walks by a younger, female administrator, who she knows interacts with people through her role in Financial Aid, and says, "Smile. If you don't want to smile, please fake it. Because girls look more approachable with smiles on their faces." The older woman walks away.

My chair constantly makes fun of my age. "Bob, what a good idea. I didn't know they taught about that topic these days." "Bob, you probably don't even know what life was like without internet. We actually had to do research." I know I am young, but it does not limit my ability to work in a professional environment.

The new Dean of Aerospace has a meeting to meet the staff. As she lays out her vision, she states, "You are here to support faculty. Faculty are the life blood of the institution. You can be replaced so make sure you focus your role on how you can best help faculty do their roles."

An administrative assistant is greeted by a faculty member who asks the assistant to: "Please, drop what you are doing and prepare these copies for me now." He did not ask if she had time or was already busy.

A faculty comes into the office and greets other faculty but does not say hello to the staff or to the work study students. Then the faculty member turns to one work study student and says, "Can you get three chairs for my office" and walks away.

WORKSHEET FOR MICROAGGRESSION SCENARIOS
1. What is the microaggression?
2. What might be the microaggressor's intent?
3. What might be the impact on the microaggressee?

4. Address the microaggression:
 	
  a. Individual-Reactive: acknowledge, understand, empathize
 	
  b. Systemic-Proactive: Next steps

> **GENERAL PROMPTS TO ADDRESS MICROAGGRESSIONS**

- If someone microaggresses against you, you can say: "When you say X, I hear Y, was that your intent?"

- If someone brings a microaggression to you that you are not involved in, but you are in a formal or informal leadership role, you can say: "Thank you for telling me about this. It sounds like when (s/he/they said X, you heard Y message), is that right? How does that make you feel? (What) would you like me to do about it?

Work through microbullying and bullying scenarios at your own institution

Here are scenarios you can use to role play and troubleshoot common microbullying and bullying scenarios. Following the list of microbullying and bullying examples is a worksheet you can use to stimulate the conversation.

> A staff member calls Human Resources to complain about and seek information on her rights when a new supervisor consistently and publicly humiliates her. The supervisor comments on the staff member's clothing and lack of productivity in meetings.

A new faculty member is distraught when a student consistently, openly, and aggressively challenges her in the classroom every single class period.

Mika described a VP who was excellent at her job while treating lower-ranked staff members horribly but, due to the turn-over in administration, was never held accountable. The fact that she never had that horrible personality with the provost, and there were four provosts while Mika was there, they never saw the VP's behaviors towards everyone else. Higher ups stay for a few years and then move on, so they never see the real institutional workings of this VP.

**WORKSHEET FOR MICROBULLYING
AND BULLYING SCENARIOS**

---

1. Does this scenario fit the definition of microbullying? Of bullying?

---

2. At what points could this situation have been addressed before it got to this point?

---

3. What would be a chair's response to this situation? A dean's response? A director's response?

---

4. What systems can be put in place so a situation like this is less likely in the future?

FIX YOUR CLIMATE

ACKNOWLEDGMENTS

We would like to thank Ms. Julie Sharer-Price and Mr. Jeremy VanHooser for their diligent work behind the scenes and Dr. Percy Morehouse, Jr. for mentorship and leadership in crafting and implementing the MSU Denver workplace bullying policy. We would also like to thank the countless people at colleges and universities and in communities, around the world, who have shared their experiences of microaggressions, microbullying, and bullying with us.

ABOUT THE AUTHORS

DR. MYRON R. ANDERSON

Myron Anderson is the founding Vice President for Inclusive Excellence at The University of Texas at San Antonio (UTSA) as of January 2, 2019.

Anderson comes to UTSA from Metropolitan State University of Denver (MSU Denver) where he served as the Associate to the President for Diversity and Professor in the School of Education. As a member of the president's cabinet, Anderson was the University's chief diversity officer, responsible for developing an inclusive campus, and articulating and resolving current and future issues related to campus climate, diversity and inclusion. In addition, Anderson identified campus climate trends and was responsible for developing a strategic vision across all academic and administrative units to establish strategies for resolution of campus climate issues. As the Associate to the President for Diversity, Anderson consistently worked with executive officers (President, Provost, Vice Presidents, Deans) to lead institution-wide efforts to promote equity, inclusivity and to advance the University mission.

Anderson's leadership promoting a systemic focus on Inclusive Excellence led to MSU Denver being a five-time recipient of the Higher Education Excellence in Diversity (HEED) award, a national award that recognizes Colleges

447

and Universities that demonstrate an outstanding commitment to diversity and inclusion across their campus. Recently, MSU Denver has received its third Diversity Champion award that recognizes the top 15 Colleges and Universities in the United States, that exemplify an unyielding commitment to diversity and inclusion throughout their campus communities, across academic programs, and at the highest administrative levels.

MSU Denver's goal is for the faculty to reflect the students. Since 2007, student of color enrollment has increased by more than a third, making up approximately 42% of the student body. Anderson's leadership has led to the increase of faculty of color by more than 50% since 2005 with a university workforce greater than 30% of color. Anderson has led the development of innovative recruitment and retention programs, i.e. the Tenure Track Mentorship Program, the Stealth Recruitment Portal, and the systemic implementation of the University-wide Campus Climate Survey, thus contributing to improving the campus climate and a 35% increase in the retention of faculty of color.

Anderson raised and managed millions of dollars in an effort to align the University's mission with regional and national constituent goals and objectives. He led the development of two self-sustaining Institutes, designed to connect MSU Denver's intellectual capital to address educational, social justice and leadership needs of the Denver community and beyond. Anderson served as the Principal Investigator (PI) for the $8.6 million-dollar Western Educational Equity Assistance Center grant and was a contributing writer and Co-Principal Investigator of the previous 4.9 million-dollar Equity Assistance Center grant ending in 2016. Anderson has worked in higher education for more than 25 years, in both administrative and academic positions. He also earned the rank of full professor of education technology in the School of

Education. Prior to his current position, he served as Associate Chair of the Teacher Education Department at MSU Denver, Program Leader in Continuing Education and Director of Student Services at Virginia Tech and Winston-Salem State University, respectively. His areas of expertise are instructional delivery in virtual environments, organizational climate and strategic planning.

Anderson has performed research in the areas of instructional technology, distance education, campus climate, diversity, and microaggressions in higher education. His research has led to the creation of a new term "hierarchal microaggressions" identifying new territory where these actions take place. He has developed interactive professional development programs to enhance student and professional leaders' programming, leadership and life skills. He has published, designed and presented regional, national and international workshops, in the areas of student development, education technology, equity pedagogy, microaggressions, diversity and campus climate.

Anderson led the University's implementation of the Inclusive Excellence framework, focused on campus climate, recruitment and retention, diversity development, diversity initiatives, civic engagement and the quest to become a Hispanic Serving Institution. He developed the University's diversity strategic plan and has led three successful university-wide campus climate surveys each yielding a 63% (or greater) full-time workforce response rate. Survey results have led to the creation of 25 new policies and processes designed to promote a more inclusive environment.

Anderson earned a Ph.D. in instructional technology, and a bachelor of arts in political science from Virginia Tech, and a master of science in curriculum and instruction from Radford University.

DR. KATHRYN S. YOUNG

Kathryn Young is a full Professor of Secondary Education at Metropolitan State University of Denver and served as the Faculty Fellow with the Office of Institutional Diversity at the university for 3 years. Dr. Young has worked as an educator for 20+ years with the past 12 years in higher education in the School of Education.

Dr. Young has 20+ published papers and numerous present-ations across her research interests of Disability Studies in Education, Inclusive Education, Cultural Competence, Multicultural Education, Diversity in Higher Education, and Microaggressions in Education and in the Workplace. Dr. Young's publications include a chapter in Micro-aggression Theory: Influence and Implications (co-edited by the leader in microaggression research, Dr. Derald Wing Sue) titled *Microaggressions in Higher Education: Embracing Educative Spaces*, an article in the Journal Diversity in Higher Education titled *Hierarchical Microaggressions in Higher Education*.

She has presented numerous times on the topic of microaggressions and workplace bullying and consults for non-profit, governmental, private and university entities on campus climate, implicit bias, microaggressions and work place bullying. This work includes consulting nationally on campus climate, developing personalized assessments, and and analyzing qualitative and quantitative bullying assessment data to assist institutions in developing healthy and welcoming climates. She works to help institutions develop individual positive reactions to reducing microaggressions and bullying and build systemic solutions to these issues. Her research has led to the creation of a new term "hierarchical microaggressions" identifying new territory where these actions take place. She has developed interactive professional development programs to enhance student and professional leaders' programming, leadership and life skills. Dr. Young is a trained facilitator of the Intercultural Developmental Inventory (IDI) and helped lead an initiative to bring IDI to the whole campus. She is also a leader in embedding Trauma Informed Practices (TIP) into higher education curriculum.

Dr. Young earned a Bachelor of Arts in French Education from University of North Carolina, Chapel Hill, a Masters of Arts in Teaching from North Carolina Central University, and a Ph.D. in Educational Policy from University of California, Berkeley.

CPSIA information can be obtained
at www.ICGtesting.com
Printed in the USA
LVHW050903271222
735906LV00008B/520

9 781948 658164